CW00820660

Glamorgan Seascape Pathways

~ 52 Walks in the Southern Vale of Glamorgan ~

Terry Breverton

Photographs by Cathy Crompton and Martin Green

Wales Books
Glyndŵr Publishing
2003

ISBN 1-903529-115

Terry Breverton is a Fellow of the Chartered Institute of Marketing, and a Fellow of the Institute of Management Consultants. He studied in the universities of Manchester, Birmingham and Lancaster, has had a career in international management consultancy, and has been a board level director of multinational companies. Returning with his family to live in Wales, he is a Senior Lecturer in Marketing and International Business Management at UWIC Business School, Cardiff. He founded Wales Books (Glyndŵr Publishing), to counter-balance existing material upon Wales, and to promote Welsh heritage and culture to the Welsh people and potential tourists. Glyndŵr Publishing's website, www.walesbooks.com is developing a unique listing of Welsh societies across the globe, to encourage further research and publications upon 'forgotten' Welshmen such as Dr Richard Price and Owain Llawgoch. It is hoped that such work will also rehabilitate Iolo Morganwg in the eyes of academics and force them to reassess history from original sources, rather than from the opinion of their teachers' teachers.

Breverton has in the past published research papers upon multinational tax avoidance, children's books and is the author of the acclaimed 'An A-Z of Wales and the Welsh', 'The Secret Vale of Glamorgan', 'The Book of Welsh Saints', '100 Great Welsh Men' , 'The Path to Inexperience','100 Great Welsh Women', 'The Welsh Almanac' and 'The Book of Welsh Pirates and Buccaneers'. In the 30 months that the Welsh Books Council has been running the award, three of Terry Breverton's books have been chosen as **'The Book of the Month'** in the English language category. No other author has received the award more than once. This book has, like all other Wales Books publications, been priced to break even and to cover the costs of publishing more books upon Wales. Forthcoming publications are detailed in the back of this book. We welcome submissions of manuscripts, by which method we will soon be publishing a rational reassessment of Prince Madoc, a life of the great warrior Owain Llawgoch, Princesses of Wales and Glamorganshire Castles (Volume I of Castles of Wales).

Also by Terry Breverton:

An A-Z of Wales and the Welsh (Christopher Davies 2000)
300pp ISBN 0 715407 341

The Secret Vale of Glamorgan (publisher Wales Books 2000)
228pp, illustrated 1 903529 00X

The Book of Welsh Saints (Wales Books 2000)
614pp hardback, illustrated ISBN 1 903529 018

100 Great Welshmen (Wales Books 2001)
366pp, illustrated ISBN 1 903529 034
Welsh Books Council **'Book of the Month'**

100 Great Welsh Women (Wales Books 2001)
304pp, illustrated ISBN 1 903529 042

'The Path to Inexperience' (Wales Books 2002)
160pp, illustrated ISBN 1903529077

'The Welsh Almanac' (Wales Books 2002)
320pp hardback, illustrated ISBN 1903529107
Welsh Books Council **'Book of the Month'**

'The Book of Welsh Pirates and Buccaneers' (Wales Books 2003)
340pp, illustrated ISBN 1903520093
Welsh Books Council **'Book of the Month'**

Also published by Wales Books (Glyndŵr Publishing):

The Dragon Entertains - 100 Welsh Stars, by Alan Roderick 2000 220pp
ISBN 1 903529 026

A Rhondda Boy, by Ivor Howells 144pp, illustrated, ISBN 1 903529050

David Thomas - From Wales to Pennsylvania, by Dr Peter Williams 2002
112pp illus. ISBN 1903529085

Glyn Dwr's War - The Campaigns of the Last Prince of Wales, by G.J. Brough 2002
240pp illus. ISBN 1903529069

For my family,
Jane, Sophie and Alexander

Cover picture by Cathy Crompton
Wild Leeks on Flat Holm, Steep Holm in the distance.

Copyright 2003 Terry Breverton

Published in 2003 by Wales Books (Glyndŵr Publishing),
Porth Glyndŵr, Sain Tathan, Bro Morgannwg CF62 4LW
www.walesbooks.com

Printed and bound in Wales by
J&P Davison, 3 James Place,
Trefforest, Pontypridd

INTRODUCTION

The original purpose of this book was to extend the protection extended by *Heritage Coastline* status, which exists from Porthcawl to Gileston. My intention was to lobby for similar status to be granted from Gileston to Cardiff Bay. The official guidance for 'Heritage Status' is that *'Like National parks and Areas of Outstanding Natural Beauty, **Heritage Coasts exist to protect these remaining unspoilt stretches of coastline of England and Wales from development and to make them available to the public for recreation and enjoyment.*'* As a native of the Vale of Glamorgan, who left the area for thirty years to find work in England and overseas, on my return I was dismayed to see what had happened to the area of my youth. The 'progress' of these years seemed to take the form of additional concrete blocks (called 'buildings') which must be halted, to preserve this wonderful resource. The existing Glamorgan Heritage Coast Project's Objectives are:

Conservation: Maintaining the ecological diversity and protecting the area from undue pressure;

Enjoyment: Providing public access and recreational use, sympathetic to the environment;

Community: Managing the coastal resource in the interests of farmers, landowners and other local community groups; and

Quality: Helping to ensure the quality of the coastline is maintained, all these objectives supported by a professional Ranger Service, based at Dunraven Park, Southerndown.

Unfortunately, I discovered that 'Heritage' status will be impossible to grant to the area of coastline in question. It is a pity, for that would have protected these walkways, paths and sites for ever. As one who remembers the 'Leys' and Pleasant Harbour before their further despoliation, the views across the Vale before the ugliest building in Britain was erected (the BAE hangar at Rhoose Airport) and Nell's Point before Butlin's was built over it, I feel that we owe it to future generations not to allow any more building along the fragile areas of unspoilt coastline which remain. People do not seem to realise what an asset they have along this tidal coastline. I have walked with my family from Penarth to Bendricks Rock and back, on a fine Sunday afternoon, and not seen another walker except some people taking their dog for their 'exercise' on Sully playing-fields. If we do not appreciate what we have, it will be taken away from us. I also discovered that the idea for a path along this particular piece of coastline was not a new one. I left Barry to attend university in 1965 and worked outside the country until returning to the Vale in 1996. During this time, the 'old' South Glamorgan Council proposed and agreed a **Seascape Trail,** continuing the Glamorgan Heritage Coast eastwards. This explains the title of the book.

The book is made up of a series of inter-linking walks along the coast from Cardiff Bay to Gileston, from where one can take the Heritage Coastal Path to Porthcawl. There are also walks inland from the coast, so one can make up any combination of walks. All the walks in the book were carried out by the author in the months of December and January, to check on their ease of use in poor conditions. There are also some inland walks of real merit, with lovely views of the Bristol Channel. All walks are inside the 'Southern' Vale of Glamorgan, south of the A48 Cardiff to Bridgend road, as I intend to write further books on walks in the 'Northern' Vale, and west along the existing Heritage Coastal path to Porthcawl, in the following years. The Vale of Glamorgan contains a population of over 120,000, and includes the towns of Barry (46,800), Penarth (21,000), Dinas Powys (8800), Cowbridge (4300) and Rhoose (3800). The population of St Athan is unknown until the next census - the former housing for the RAF was bought by a Japanese company and sold to civilians. The remaining villages of the vale are particularly attractive - Flemingstone, Bonvilston, St Nicholas, St Hilary, Llancarfan, Llanbethery, Llanbleddian, Llanbethery, Llantrithyd, Penmark and Fonmon all have a 'picture postcard' quality.

The book was made possible by an ARWAIN grant from the Wales Council for Voluntary Action, which helped with photographers' expenses and part-subsidised the printing costs. The book is published on a not-for-profit basis. One-hundred and fifty copies have been given away free to libraries, Assembly Members, politicians and the media, with the intention of making more people concerned with protecting and preserving the paths in question. Once a public amenity is destroyed, it can rarely be recreated, and with the growing pressure of population in this area, we must ensure that the mistakes of the past are not repeated. The walks include flora, fauna, historical sites and viewpoints. I would recommend that anyone interested in Cardiff and the Vale buys the Ordnance Survey 'Explorer' 151 map. It is double-sided, covers Cardiff to Bridgend, and costs £6.99 from any bookshop or branch of W.H. Smith. The Stationery Office (TSO) in High Street, Cardiff, is a terrific resource for any maps of Wales, and also offers 'custom-made' colour maps of your area of interest.

One of the reasons that ARWAIN part-funded this book was that it has been printed for a community benefit. The Welsh are amongst the most unhealthy people in Europe - we are generally over-weight, unfit, and with a life expectation lower than most other Europeans. (The author includes himself in this description). Much has been written about diet. Unfortunately, the mantra, *'eat less, eat better, exercise more'* is not enough to sell a book. Every slimming and health book that has ever been written comes with special 'revolutionary' diets and exercise regimes. My book on diet and health would consist of the above six-word phrase, which is all we need to know, and would thus not be a runaway best-seller. The best form of exercise for most of us is walking - humans are made for it, and it causes little abnormal stress. The benefits of walking, injury-free, three times a week are demonstrable. The *Walking Health Initiative* is trying to encourage us to leave the couch and TV 'blabber' behind and also try and shed our excess 'blubber'. There is even a *'Walking Your Way to Health'* scheme, backed by the British heart Foundation and Countryside Commission, which will give grants for setting up a 'walking for health' scheme (01242 533258).

In a recent survey of 21 European nations, British women were the most overweight, and our men the third most overweight. (Welsh women are the second most likely to develop cancer in Europe, after the Danes). Following the American pattern, we are also breeding a nation of semi-sedentary children, whose health and weight problems will be even greater. Walking, especially if you walk a little faster than normal, then stop at a viewpoint, is an ideal fat-burning activity. It's free, safe, easy, aerobic, calorie-burning, heart-conditioning, muscle-tone-improving, stress-relieving, and can help with a variety of illnesses including back pain, osteoporosis, respiratory problems, diabetes, arthritis, cardiac rehabilitation and so on. If it cost money, and was advertised as *'finger-licking good'* or some such old twaddle, we would 'buy' walking. As Lao Tzu said, remember that *'the journey of a thousand miles begins with the first step.'* Gentle exercise, of a two mile stroll in this book, could lead to longer walks at a faster rate. As to who should carry our these walks, it is difficult to give a definition of 'elderly', but the author is almost 57, and finds every walk in this book fairly easy and enjoyable. If anyone who classes himself or herself as 'elderly' and is unsure whether to attempt the walk, there are plenty of resting places. My advice would be to take someone with you on the first attempt, on a fine day, and see how it goes. As always with walking, you will find that your fitness, enjoyment and appreciation of the environment improve the more you walk. Some walks are unfortunately not suitable for those with wheelchairs or pushchairs.

Please find the time. Buy a pair of good shoes with adequate cushioning - it will be one of your best investments. Wear suitable clothing. As a family, whenever we walk, I carry a small rucksack with four rolled-up plastic cagoules (in case of wind or rain), my wallet, a camera, some squash in plastic bottles, crisps (and sometimes sandwiches for a longer stroll), and a plastic bag (for our 'rubbish'). Make a record of your walks. Make it an objective to cover all of the **52 weekly walks** in this book, including the **12 monthly walks** A-L along the coastal path, and develop some of your own around your home. Your health will improve, along with your outlook on life. Your metabolism will be raised, so you will burn off any calories more easily and quickly than a non-exerciser. You will live longer, and lead your family and children into better habits, with healthier hearts, lungs and posture. You may miss the latest 'East-Enders', or Richard and Judy's latest interview, or your children might miss a cartoon. Please think about it. What will you actually really *'miss'* if you take time to go for a walk? Try to make walking a regular event, perhaps starting on a Sunday afternoon with friends as a group. It is always easier when other people are involved - self-motivation is often difficult as we have so little leisure time these days. It is tempting to curl up on a nice, warm sofa, instead of facing a bracing breeze off the Channel in March. If you are committed with someone else, you will be far more likely to leave the sofa. I remember playing rugby (from the age of 11 to 40) that often I only used to drag myself along, so as not to let others down. And my memories of playing rugby in the snow against then-current English internationals will always stay with me.

The memories of a terrific walk, seeing spring flowers or a sparrow-hawk, talking with friends will be remembered long after any television programme. Another motivator might be to take a camera along. You will find areas of this beautiful countryside that you did not know existed, and want to revisit. You will gain knowledge when you realise that the landscape is littered with the traces of Welsh

5th and 6th century saints - when it was 'the Dark Ages' across Europe, the light of Christianity was only kept alight by the Welsh, in what has always been known as their *'Age of Saints'*. But mainly - and this is important - you will feel better, think better, sleep better and live longer if you exercise by regular walking. Few of us have manual jobs, or jobs which involve exercise. Our parents and grandparents could get away with unhealthy diets and 'cooked breakfasts' because they needed calories. They lived in cold houses, had no transport, had to walk to the shops and prepare meals every day, without any labour-saving devices. They had lives which involved constant effort and activity. How many of us can say the same?

If anyone undertakes the 52 Walks in this book over the course of a year, then that person will be fitter, healthier and wiser at the end of it. Families should be encouraged to walk every week - we do not spend enough time socialising and talking, with the pressures of today's workplace. Where possible, I have noted which walks are suitable for disabled and less mobile people. I would like to thank the tireless photographers, Martin Green and Cathy Crompton, both of whom also contributed greatly to my *'The Welsh Almanac'* and *'The Secret Vale of Glamorgan'*. If anyone wishes to contribute walks in Glamorgan to future books, please contact me. For any omissions or errors, I take full responsibility. Publishing deadlines, the pressures of finishing another book and the duties of my full-time job, meant that there was not the time to have other, better-qualified, people read the proofs of this book.

Another problem in putting this book together is the sheer density of interesting information upon the Vale and Cardiff - we have Roman sites; Iron Age sites; fabulous medieval churches (all on the site of the *'llannau'* of 6th-century Welsh saints); the second highest tidal rise in the world; rare plant and animal species (otters are back on the River Thaw, and peregrine falcons nesting on the cliffs); and the highest density of castles in the world. To keep this book down to a marketable price of £10.99, I have had to omit about 100 pages of information. There are Glamorgan Heritage Coast free leaflets which describe the range of birds we can still see along this strip of coast, despite the loss of the Cardiff Bay mudflats to the Barrage project - they include buzzards, sparrowhawks, kestrels, stonechats, various owls, kingfishers, fieldfares, lapwings, redwings, blackcaps, whitethroats, chiff chaffs, willow warblers, grasshopper warblers, wrens, green and spotted woodpeckers, swallows, swifts and martins, cormorants, curlews, redshanks, oystercatchers, turnstones, sanderlings, dunlins, plovers, shelduck and swans. Butterflies include the green-veined white, wall butterfly, dingy skipper, red admiral, small tortoiseshell, small heath, brimstone, orange tip, meadow brown, small copper, speckled wood, common blue, painted lady, ringlet, peacock, grayling, clouded yellow and gatekeeper.

Some of the walks I remember as a child are more difficult now, because of increased road traffic (and house-building), and these have thus have been unfortunately omitted. Please remember to leave your car in a place where it is easily visible, and leave no valuables in it. My family needs two cars to travel to work, and we always take the 'old banger' when parking rather than the newer car - such are the vagaries of modern society. Also, there have been several 'incidents' along paths such as the Taff Trail through Cardiff, so single women or children are always advised to walk in company. Hopefully, the more all of these paths are used, the less likely they will be to attract perverts, who will be more likely to be seen and reported. It is a terrible indictment of Britain today that safety has to be our first priority, when we should be enjoying our lives, and especially our leisure time, to the full. Some readers may believe that these comments are out of place in a book celebrating (and trying to preserve) the wonderful legacy of this rich coastal region, but the author grew up in a more innocent time.

My weekends, before I discovered rugby and girlfriends, were spent with my father, grandfather, friends or by myself gathering watercress, chestnuts, blackberries, hazel nuts, field mushrooms and bunches of bluebells, cowslips and primroses (before we understood the consequences) and traversing the Vale without a car, or a care in the world. We all had our 'secret' places where we knew there were mushrooms or bluebells or the like. Sometimes as a 9-13 year-old I could vanish from breakfast-time until it was dark. My generation has seen a terrible change in society - from an atmosphere of trust, of unlocked doors, of safe single women and children, to something very different. To return to the lighter side, I hope that all who read this book will be encouraged to undertake some of the walks. The Vale of Glamorgan, Bro Morgannwg, is my favourite place on earth, and I have worked and travelled all over the world. *Hiraeth* pulled me back, from a better job with greater prospects, to bring up my children in one of the most beautiful parts of Britain. If we appreciate what is around us, we can pass that on to our children and make the world a better place.

I have to thank Joanne Davies of ARWAIN, who helped make this book possible. The ARWAIN scheme, under the aegis of the Wales Council for Voluntary Action (WCVA) develops projects which help local communities. Hopefully, readers will think that this book fulfils ARWAIN's mission. Also of great assistance have been Dr Cliff Nelson and Christopher Jones-Jenkins of the Vale of Glamorgan Council. There were to have been full-scale maps of each walk, but this would have made the book too expensive, with another 60 pages having to be printed, and copyright fees having to be paid. An alternative would have been to publish sketch-maps, which are no substitute for the splendid OS Explorer 151 Cardiff and Bridgend map which is double-sided and only costs £6.99. Anyone who loves South Glamorgan should possess a copy of this map. The full-colour *Street Atlas of Cardiff, Barry and Penarth* is also extremely useful, and only costs £3.50 from most newsagents and bookshops. It also covers Wenvoe, Dinas Powys, Sully, Rhoose and Cowbridge.

Bro Morgannwg means the Vale of Glamorgan, and 'Y Fro' usually refers to the 'Southern' Vale, the land beneath the A48 Via Julia that stretches from Cardiff Roman Fort to Cowbridge (Bovium) and into Bridgend before carrying on to Neath (Nidum) and Carmarthen. North of the A48 is the 'Northern' Vale, leading into the region known as 'Blaenau', the 'edges' or beginning of the mountainous part of South Wales. The Southern Vale was deforested and farmed by the Silures, and was always the richest region of Wales, yet the most difficult to defend against constant waves of invaders - the Irish, Saxons, Vikings and Normans all attacked the area at some time, and it was the first toe-hold for the Normans after they cleared through to Cardiff. This book is concerned with the coastal area from Cardiff to Gileston, through the Vale north to Cowbridge, and back along the A48/Roman Road to Cardiff. Because of space and time limitations, some walks around Cowbridge and St Nicholas were not included, but will be placed in future books on Vale walks which will also include the Northern Vale and the Heritage Coastal pathways.

The Glamorgan Heritage Coast extends for 14 miles from Aberthaw/Gileston westwards, designated as *'Heritage Coast'* by the Countryside Commission and local authorities in 1972. The western limit is Porthcawl, and the eastern is Aberthaw Power Station. The public footpaths in the Vale of Glamorgan pass mainly across working farmland. Please use due consideration at all times.

1. Keep to the Waymarked Path.
2. Keep dogs under control.
3. Leave gates as you find them, usually closed.
4. Avoid damage to hedges, fences, etc.
5. Leave no litter.
6. Protect all Wildlife.
7. Respect the life of the countryside.
8. Do not pick wild plants.

Report any problems in the Vale of Glamorgan to the Rights of Way Officer (01446 704600). On roads, walk facing the oncoming traffic so that you can see and take defensive action if necessary. Never, ever, wear earphones - they are dangerous in the countryside and on roads. There are programmes of local walks by various societies. If you want to take up walking seriously, membership of The Ramblers costs £20 p.a. Telephone 020 7339 8500 for details or visit their website at rambers.org.uk. There are Ramblers Clubs for the Vale of Glamorgan, Caerffili, Bridgend, Penarth and Cardiff which are active. Cardiff Ramblers, on their website, give details of longer walks in south-east Wales. They are The Taff Trail (Cardiff to Brecon, 55-60 miles); The Coed Morgannwg Way (Margam Park to Merthyr, 36 miles); The Ogwr Ridgeway Walk (Margam Park to Mynydd y Gaer, 13 miles); Ffordd y Bryniau (Mynydd y Gaer to Caerffili Mountain, 21 miles); the Rhymney Valley Ridgeway Walk (Caerffili Circular, 27 miles); The Sirhowy Valley Walk (Newport to Tredegar, 26 miles); The Usk Valley Walk (Cerleon to Abergafenni, 25 miles); The Cambrian Way (Cardiff to Conwy, 265 miles); The Capital Walk (Sully to St Brides Wentloog, 38 miles loop); and the **Glamorgan Heritage Coast** (Southerndown to Aberthaw, 14 miles).

One must note here the problem of sand disappearing from our shoreline in South Wales. Campaigners believe that over 100 million tons of sand have been lost from Gower beaches alone by sand dredging in the Bristol Channel. The effects have been felt from St Mary Well's Bay and Jackson's Bay in the eastern Vale, all the way to Pembrokeshire. Possibly over a quarter of a billion tons of sand has gone, probably forever, and the disappearance seems to be accelerating at places like Port Eynon. The extracting companies may have Welsh names, but are all owned by English firms. They create hardly any jobs compared to tourism, and offer no benefit for local communities. After all the gold, silver, iron, lead, coal, and sand depletion has ended,

Wales is becoming a land of unwanted reservoirs, alien pine forestries and unsightly wind farms, all feeding its neighbour's vast needs. The Assembly **has** to act to stop dredging and save our coastline. The rich dredging companies employ their own 'expert' scientists to tell us that the coastline is not being affected. They are neither impartial nor scientific in their approach. Hundreds of thousands of Welsh people have seen their leisure resources being destroyed.

Finally, the Cardiff Ramblers website describes the **Glamorgan Heritage Coast** as *'one of the first two coastlines in Britain to be jointly designated as 'Heritage Coast' by the Countryside Commission and local authorities in 1972. The aims of the 'Heritage Coast' designation and of the GHC Project's work are to conserve this beautiful and unspoilt section of coastline, so that present and future generations may enjoy its natural beauty.'* The original objective of this book was to try and protect the continuation of this coastal walk for a further 16 miles eastwards into Cardiff, and 150 free copies of this book are being given to politicians and opinion-formers to try to stimulate interest in the project. The former South Glamorgan County Council had also proposed such a ***'Seascape Trail'***. The Cardiff Ramblers' website states that the proposed route from Aberthaw eastwards *'includes some lovely coastal scenery, such as Porthkerry, as well as, inevitably more built-up areas through Barry, Penarth and Cardiff. The new marina at Penarth, and the Cardiff Bay Barrage are modern developments that will help make this route possible.'* Please use all the walks described, and ask your local councillor/MP/newspaper editor to help in making this wonderful resource safe for future generations.

If you wish to follow the proposed **SEASCAPE TRAIL**, it consists of twelve short walks 4, 8, 18, 20, 25, 32, 33, 34, 39, 40, 46 and 48, lettered A-L in this book. From Cardiff you will be looking south-east to Clevedon; from Lavernock towards the Holm islands, and the headland of Brean Down; from Penarth the resort of Western-super-Mare is easily seen; from Barry you can see Watchet, and from Aberthaw, Minehead and the hills of Exmoor are in the distance. Small coastal traders used to criss-cross the Channel, for instance there was a daily boat from Aberthaw to Watchet, but the amount of shipping on the Bristol Channel has declined immensely in the last three decades.

A final note of warning must be sounded. The Vale of Glamorgan Local Environment Agency Plan notes that the Vale *'probably contains one of the highest concentrations of sites of archaeological and historic interest anywhere in Wales. These include a whole range of sites from burial chambers of the prehistoric period to the military installations of the Second World War. There are also a wide variety of important archaeological and ancient agricultural features such as those associated with the communications network, field patterns, hedgerows, ancient woodland and water management systems. There are many important Roman-British villas and settlements in the area, which are typical of Wales as a whole. Important medieval ("Dark Age") communities, with probably monastic origins, such as Llandough and Llancarfan also exist in recognisable form. These and other extant communities testify to the strong and distinctive Anglo-Norman influences of the early 12th century. A recent archaeological survey of the Thaw Valley has established a large number of new records and highlighted areas of interest at Flemingston.'*

Contemporaneously to this survey the author found a medieval chapel, probably on the 6th century St Tathanas's cell site, in the Thaw Valley, so we are still discovering our heritage. We have to try and protect such an area. Planners have already disfigured the Vale with not one, but three airports (Llandow, St Tathan and Rhoose), with their attendant buildings and influxes of population. All are expanding. Recent decisions on industrial policy mean that there will be more building in the Vale, more people racing their cars to work through its lanes, and ever more boxes being built upon the green fields of history. Politicians seem to think that displacing jobs is the same thing as creating jobs. The massive Atlantic Trading Estate in Barry is in the town with the fourth largest population in Wales, but is deserted. Do we really need more factories and yet more housing estates in Bro Morgannwg? Cannot we take the jobs to where the people live? Once something is lost - it is lost forever. Many of us remember the wonderful beaches and pools of Pleasant Harbour at Aberthaw. Now there are waste tips which will take 30 years to remove. Most of us remember the views across the Vale before the huge maintenance hangar was built at Rhoose. All of us will see the massive new hangar to be built at St Tathan. New housing will again have to be built for the 2000 army personnel and their families moving into the Vale. This author is not against progress, but politicians and their planners seem to measure progress by concrete boxes on green-field sites rather than the socio-econo-demographic indicators of their constituents. The Vale and its coastline has to be protected. The more people undertake these 52 walks, the more people will see the value of this unique facility for the people of south-east Wales. We take the treasures of the Vale and its coast, its castles, churches, pubs, Roman sites, burial chambers, leafy lanes, rivers, flora and fauna for granted. Having lived away from the area for thirty years, I have seen it radically changed, not for the better. The Vale and its coast is a wonderful resource - a green lung for the people of Cardiff, Penarth, Bridgend and Barry. Its preservation will be one of the main gifts that we can leave to our children.

Footnote: *The 52 Seascape Walks are meant to be taken in conjunction with the Ordnance Survey Explorer 151 Map of Cardiff and Bridgend, which shows all the footpaths, in far greater detail than would be possible for this book to show. All the walks may be easily undertaken without reference to this map, but knowledge of the terrain and places of local interest will be greatly assisted by its purchase.*

LIST OF WALKS

Capitals denote those walks which actually pass along the sea front and can be connected to form a continuous walk from Cardiff to Aberthaw/Gileston to link up with the existing Heritage Coast from Gileston to Porthcawl.

WALKS AROUND CARDIFF

There is plenty of information available upon things to do and see in Cardiff. These walks are added to give variety to the country walks, and because, for example, from the top of St John's Tower or Cardiff Castle, you can see the sea. Also, developments such as Lloyd George Avenue and Cardiff Bay are helping bring the

Cardiff Bay Barrage - Cathy Crompton

coast 'closer' to central Cardiff at long last. Walk 1 is included because it is possible to follow the coast almost into Newport from Cardiff. It is hoped that in future the **Glamorgan Seascape Trail** can be extended from Cardiff Bay to 'pick up' the Eastern Sea Wall Walk, and give us an unbroken path from Newport to Porthcawl. There is a planned East Bay Link Road to join Rover Way with Cardiff Bay. Some of the new road development around Cardiff Bay has no pedestrian pavements, and as this road will skirt the coast, it is hoped that pedestrian access can be effected by the planners.

WALK NO. 1: EASTERN SEA WALL - c.6 miles (10km) - the length and time depends on how far you wish to walk. The walk is flat and easy for all walkers, but there is often a fierce breeze blowing off the Bristol Channel. Not suitable for push-chairs.

Park in the Lighthouse Pub Car Park. You leave Cardiff on the old A48 Cardiff-Newport road at Castleton, turning right by the church, heading for Marshfield. (This remarkable Baptist Church is listed, was founded in 1756 and rebuilt with the Italianate façade in 1824). After about 3 miles, turn left at a T-junction along the B4239 for St. Brides Wentloog. After another 2 miles, take the first right just after leaving St. Brides and you will come to the pub car park, signed 'Live Music'. Do not go into the caravan park. Alternatively, follow the signs to Peterstone Wentlooge, park by the medieval church, and follow the footpath down to the sea wall.

There are wonderful views across the Bristol Channel and of the shipping in the estuary, plus the added advantage of many waders and seabirds. Take your binoculars. The walk passes

Cardiff Bay before the Barrage - Cathy Crompton

alongside a new golf course which has an artificial lake, on which you can often see swans, geese and ducks. The view westward is to Cardiff Docks, Penarth Head, Flat Holm and Steep Holm, and eastward to Newport Docks, Newport Transporter Bridge and the Power Station. On the wall of the Six Bells pub at **Peterstone Wentlooge**, which is easily reached from the sea wall, it shows the height to which the sea rose in the floods before the present sea wall was built. Many people died in *'The Great Flood of 1606'*. **St Peter's Church** at Peterston Wentlooge dates from around 1450 and is Grade I listed. It was restored in 1606 after the Great Flood of January 20th 1606, and is on a monastic site. Much of the area between the sea wall and the A48 is at, or just below sea level, and is drained by the complex network of *Reens* (linked ditches) into collecting reservoirs known as *Grouts*, from which the drainage water is let out into the sea at low tide. It is thought that the area was first reclaimed from the sea under the Roman occupation of South Monmouthshire and Glamorgan, around the 2nd century.

Pierhead building detail, Cardiff Bay - Martin Green

Heading east, the limit of easy sea wall walking is the old lighthouse at the mouth of the Usk which has now been converted into a guest-house and complementary therapy centre. **The West Usk Lighthouse** is unique in its short and wide appearance, and back in 1821 was on an island. It was decommissioned as a lighthouse in 1922. On the levels, there are small breeding populations of redshank, lapwing and curlew, and you may be lucky to spot a hare. A few reed warblers also breed around here. You can follow a road up into **St Bride's Wentlooge** for refreshments at the excellent pub there. St Brides Wentlooge Church dates from around 1450 and is Grade II listed. Like St Peter's, it has a plaque commemorating the Great Flood.

Heading west, you walk along Peterstone Great Wharf and **Rumney Great Wharf** to the mouth of Cardiff's Rhymney River. The road running parallel to the seawall is known as Broad Street, and on its north side Sluice Farm and Sluice House Farm remind us that this vast expanse of moorland, with many rare birds, needs active management to keep drained. The sea towards Cardiff is known as Cardiff Flats. We should also mention one of Cardiff's forgotten castles in this context. Next to St Illtyd's School in Rumney is Cae Castell, or **Rumney Castle**. The small ringwork was first mentioned in 1184, guarding the river crossing into Cardiff. A coin hoard of 1288-1289 shows that it was hastily abandoned when captured by the Welsh in that year. Excavations here have been the most extensive of any Norman ringwork castle in the British Isles, and it seems it was built with the first establishment of the Normans around the port and fort of Cardiff in 1081, or around 1093 when Robert Fitzhamon took Gwynllwg. **St Augustine Church** in Rumney dates from 1108, is Grade B listed and was enlarged in 1450. Nearby **St Mellons Church** is also Grade B listed, dating from 1360, but is said to be on a 2nd century site, and thus one of the oldest churches in Europe. Bishop Mellon, or Melloninus (257-311), was feasted on October 10th and 22nd, and was from Llanllewrig (Llanlleurwg) on the eastern outskirts of Cardiff, now called St Mellons. The first Bishop of Rouen after visiting Rome, he was bishop for 55 years. The Wentloog area around St Mellons was an extremely important centre at this time, and there is an old farm called Pont Mellon. **St Lleurwg** Mawr (Lucius Major, the Great Light) lived from c.137-c.201, the son of 'Old King' Coel ap Cyllin, and was said in the Triads to have been the original founder of Llandaff Cathedral, as well as St Mellons.

Note: The lordship of Wentloog (Y Waunllwch) covered the land from the Rhymney to the Usk, up to Breconshire, and was known in the book of Llandaff as Gunliuiuc. It may have been named after the 6th century king who became **St Gwynllwg**, however, the founder of St Woolo's Cathedral in Newport, and the father of St Cadoc. Around the Wentloog Levels, there was a Capel Meiryn at Castleton, which became a barn. At Marshfield, **St Mary's Church** was originally built in 1135 by Mabel, the daughter of Robert Fitzhamon. Marshfield was originally called Llanarthen, and Llanarthen Church, founded by **St Arthen** ap Brychan in the 6th century, was destroyed by the Saxons about 900AD. The church at **Michaelston Y Fedw** is medieval, dating from around 1200, and in the grounds of Druidstone House there is a ten-foot high menhir. The 2nd-century **St Medwy** (Medwyn) was said to be one of the very early saints, with Ffagan, Dyfan and Elfan, sent by Rome to Christianise the Welsh in 180, at the request of King Lleurwg, noted as the founder of nearby St Mellons. Michaelston-y-Fedw was formerly called Llanfedwy, and the Welsh church was burnt in the wars of the 11th century.

WALK 2 - CARDIFF CITY CENTRE - just over 2 miles (3.5km) but far more if you are 'exploring'. *Start anywhere - this is a full-day walk if you wish to look at the sights, suitable for pushchairs. If you want to spend time shopping in the arcades, and visiting the castle, museum and art galleries, you need two days. There is plenty of parking in central Cardiff, but it is best to arrive early. Saturdays are particularly difficult days to park. Sophia Gardens car-park is useful, off Cathedral Road, as it borders Bute Park, the Castle grounds and the Taff Trail.*

My preferred start would be at the **Millennium Stadium**, the home of what passes for Welsh rugby these days. Guided tours are available in this remarkable piece of architecture, from the entrance in Westgate Street. Exit right down Westgate Street, heading south, and turn right at the end. The bus station (due to be removed and/or remodelled) is opposite you, in front of the **Great Western General Railway Station**, itself an excellent building which has recently been restored. On your right, you will pass a **Tourist Information Office**. Carry on right, with the stadium to your right, past its south entrance, and head right again. Walk along the special boardwalk above the **River Taff**, following the stadium and then Cardiff Rugby Club's **Arms Park**, until you reach Castle Street. Divert right and cross the road to visit the wonderful **Cardiff Castle**. Make sure you go up the Norman tower for views all over Glamorgan, and also try to take the guided tour of the apartments. There are also two

Millennium Stadium at Summer Solstice -
Martin Green

military museums and a café here. Come out of Cardiff Castle and turn right, following the **Animal Wall**, with the Millennium Stadium on your left, and turn right into **Bute Park**.

There are lovely gardens here, and the remains of **Blackfriars Priory**. Walk towards the northwest corner of the Castle, cross the footbridge and follow the castle's North Wall until you come to the famed **Civic Centre** in front of you. Take the underpass and pass the **Law Courts**. You can now walk up Gorsedd Gardens Road, to see the **Welsh National War Memorial**, or visit the next building, the old **City Hall**. It is free to enter, and the debating chamber is open to the public. Note the marble statues of Welsh heroes on the first floor. Next door is the superb **National Museum and Art Gallery of Wales.** Cross the road to head back into Cardiff Centre, but take a slight detour left along Stuttgarter Strasse, and then right into the red-brick **Windsor Terrace**. This will bring you into **Queen Street**, the main shopping street in Cardiff. Its western continuation is called Duke Street, and then Castle Street, running parallel to the castle. Turn right into Queen Street, and on your left you will see **St David's Shopping Centre**.

Head into the shopping centre and turn right along St David's Way, then turn left along the site of the old Town Wall, and you will exit into Hills Street. Turn right, and you will come into a restaurant/pub/club/café area known as **The Hayes**. There is a lovely old wooden café here, and the underground Victorian toilets are worth a visit. The 'gents' urinals are Edwardian, with a 'bullseye' motif. On your right is the **Old Library**, now a venue for exhibitions, and in front of you two of Cardiff's finest department stores, James Howells and David Morgan. Turn left along the Hayes, and follow **Mill Lane Café Quarter** to the end of St Mary Street. Turn right up St Mary Street, past Wyndham Arcade and Caroline Street (once the home of Brain's Old Brewery) and turn right into the **Royal Arcade**. You will emerge again into the Hayes. Turn left and walk past the Morgan Arcade's twin entrances, then turn left into Wharton Street. Wharton Street comes out into St Mary Street. Turn right, and then right again into Cardiff's **Victorian Covered Market**. Walk straight through the two-tier market, and note the superb fish stall on the right as you exit. Turn left along Trinity Street, where you will see, and can visit, the medieval **St John's Church**. St John's Church has a café, and there are superb views from its tower. Turn left into Church Street, and then right again into St Mary Street (which is now called High Street in its most northerly section). Heading towards the castle, cross the road to enter **Castle Arcade**. Go through the Arcade and you will emerge opposite the **Castle** again.

WALK 3 - CARDIFF CITY CENTRE TO PARKS TO CARDIFF BAY - about 7 miles (11km) *Only parts are suitable for pushchairs and wheelchairs. Similar at the start to the last walk. Park centrally and make for Cardiff General Station. Over the next few years, the buildings around the station, of no architectural merit, will be redeveloped.*

From the station and bus terminal, head north and turn right on Wood Street. Pass the **Prince of Wales** pub (a Wetherspoons pub, formerly a theatre, and worth seeing inside), and cross the road at the traffic lights. Turn left up St Mary Street. The area on your right, behind the Albert pub, used to be Brains Brewery and is being redeveloped. On your right you will pass another Brains pub, The Cottage, with a

carved wooden front, and two excellent department stores, David Morgan and James Howells. Keep on heading towards **Cardiff Castle**. At the junction, cross the road and head left past the castle. On your left, before the River Taff bridge, you will see the Arms Park, home to Cardiff Ruby Club, and adjoining it, the magnificent Millennium Stadium, host to FA Cup Finals, the Rugby World Cup, and pop concerts. On your right you are walking along the **Animal Wall.**

Cardiff Bay sculpture - Martin Green

As this wall ends there is a Lodge House and a gate, which is the entrance to the castle grounds and Bute Park. They are open from 9am until dusk. Enter the park here and walk straight on. Where the path splits, go left. Keep walking on this path, keeping the River Taff on your left, and ignoring all paths on your right. (However, if you digress in from the river, you will see the **Gorsedd Circle** and the foundations of **Blackfriars Priory**.) On this side of the Taff, the parkland is known as Coopers Field, leading into Bute Park and Blackweir. On the other side of the Taff, the parkland is known as Sophia Gardens, leading into Pontcanna Fields and Llandaff Fields. The huge park is a wonderful facility in Cardiff's centre, practically unique among the world's capital cities in terms of its size in proportion to the city.

Carrying along the Taff pathway, on your right you come to a wrought iron sculpture clock and then a collection of green houses and large metal gates. Keep straight on this path and the river is now going away from you. About 100 yards past the greenhouses is a cross road on the walk, and take the path to your left. As you walk down this path you will keep the tree line to your left and a large open space to your right. Follow the path round, you will have the tree line on both sides now, continue on until you reach a weir (**Blackweir**).

Go through the metal gates and keep straight on, the river staying on your left. At the metal stile (there is a Tudor-style house ahead) turn right sharply and walk back down this pathway, signed Llys Tal-y-Bont. You will come to another stile (houses on your left, park on your right), go through this and continue on for a few hundred yards. Keep straight on and you come to an iron gate and stile which takes you into some car parks. Turn to your right and continue down this road keeping to the right, through the car-park. Across the road is a large building which is a nursing home. Keep straight on this pathway/cycle path and there will be a brick wall appearing on your left. Across the road is the Christian Science Church. You are now heading back to central Cardiff. At the traffic lights keep straight on. (Corbett Road is on your left, the northern limit of the University, Welsh Office and Civic Centre complex. Just left off Corbett Road is the lovely residential accommodation of Queen Anne Square.) You now pass the **Welsh College of Music and Drama** and some tennis courts on your right. At the traffic lights, cross over to the left, using the subway. This will bring you to the **Law Courts**.

The next building to the Law Courts is **City Hall**. Turn left to the War Memorial along King Edward VII Avenue, keeping the Law Courts on your left and City Hall on your right. Continue on down past the Police Station on your left and at the first cross roads there is a sign to the station. Turn right and the **Alexandra Gardens Park** is on your right. On the left side is the **Welsh Office** and opposite its doorway is the entrance to the park. Walk straight ahead to the huge **War Memorial**. You can either leave the park by the left hand exit which will take you into Museum Avenue, and as you leave the large building across the road is the University of Wales. Turn right and continue down this road to the end. The other choice is to leave the park at the bottom entrance and turn left then right on to Museum Avenue. At the end of this road, with the superb **National Museum and Art Gallery** on your left, cross the road and enter **Gorsedd Gardens**. Follow the pathway out into the road at the traffic lights. Cross to the centre and turn to your left and cross again into Stuttgarter Strasse, denoting one of Cardiff's twin towns. (Its western continuation past the Civic Centre to the castle is the Boulevard de Nantes). As you walk along here you will come to a crossing on your right and St Andrew's Church on your left. Cross here into the red-brick Windsor Place. Walk to the end, to the prime shopping area of Queen Street. Turn right along Queen Street, and at its end is a statue of **Aneurin Bevan**.

Turn left onto St John's Street, and the medieval **St Johns Church** is on the right. Continue straight on to Working Street, and on the left is the concert venue and restaurant of **St David's Hall**. Ahead is a statue and **The Hayes** café area. Carry straight on to the end of the shopping precinct. The Marriott Hotel is over on the right and the Ice Rink is in front of you. You are now in Hayes Bridge Road. At the traffic lights cross over the road and walk under the railway bridge (Bute Street) continue ahead for 100 yards and at Herbert Street turn left. Behind you are the new fountains of Tresilian Way. Keep on this road as it becomes Tyndall Street, heading towards the flyover. You will see footpath signs pointing to the right (**Dockside Walk**). Follow the path along the side of **Atlantic Wharf**.

At the end of the dock bear right towards roundabout. The new **County Hall** is to your right. Follow Hemingway Road west, and at the road junction, cross over Lloyd George Avenue and continue along Hemingway Road. After a few yards turn into Bute Street. On the right side you will pass the Baltimore Arms and the NatWest Bank. Opposite the Baltimore Arms is the **Butetown History and Arts Centre**. (At 5 Dock Chambers, Bute Street - the centre preserves and presents the lived history of Cardiff Bay, and has a gallery and exhibitions). At the traffic lights cross over

James Street, with Bute Place to the left, and carry on along Bute Street. Ahead of you is **Mermaid Quay**, with some excellent modern sculptures and facilities, and the heart of **Cardiff Bay**.

Heading left you see a large red brick building with a clock face, the magnificent **Pierhead Building**, and if you continue round you will see a white church which is the **Norwegian Church Centre**. Next to that is the **Lightship 2000** and the **Cardiff Bay Visitors Centre**. Or, at the end of Bute Street turn right, with Bar 38 on right hand side, continue on this road and you will see the **Techniquest Centre** on your left and on the right is a road called Adelaide Street. Turn right down here, with a school on your left. At this point you will have walked around 6 miles. At the end turn left, and at the crossing cross over to the Police Station. Keep walking straight on Clarence Road, going over the bridge and you will see signs for the **Taff Trail**. Turn right and follow the riverside path back north into Cardiff centre. At the next bridge cross over the road and continue following the Taff Trail signs, passing under railway bridge. Just 20 yards further, at the bridge just before the Millennium Stadium turn right and you return to the Railway Station.

WALK 4 - CARDIFF BAY 1 - 2 miles, suitable for all ages.

WALK A OF THE SEASCAPE TRAIL

You can easily park at the Bay, but it is much more difficult at weekends, and in summer, as it is such a terrific place to visit. Coming from Penarth, Barry or the motorway, Cardiff's Butetown Link Road across the Bay leads to an underpass, before which you exit at the sign marked Techniquest. A twin-storey carpark is just on the left, next to Mermaid Quay. From here road-train trips can take you along the Barrage, every hour. If you carry on through the underpass, you can park at Atlantic Wharf Leisure Village, or try to find somewhere along Harbour Drive. There is a shuttle train from Queen Street station which accesses the Bay, and plans for a public system to run down the new Lloyd George Avenue. Alternatively, you can walk along the footpath on the West bank of the Taff to the Bay, and back along Lloyd George Avenue. The Bay itself is now a 500 acre lake on the site of the mud-flats, and the area in front of the cafes and shops of Mermaid Quay is known as the Inner Harbour. There are dozens of places to eat and drink.

Cardiff Bay sculpture
Martin Green

Starting from the car-park in Stuart Street, turn right heading west, and right again up Adelaide Street. Cross James Street and enter **Mount Stuart Square**. The **Coal Exchange** here was the site of Britain's first million-pound deal. A remarkable building, it was intended to be the first Welsh Assembly, and a

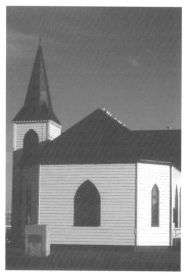

Norwegian Church, Cardiff Bay
Martin Green

bomb-proof underground carpark defaced its frontage. There are plans for sympathetic redevelopment of all these superb Edwardian buildings, including a nearby famous but semi-derelict pub, the Big Windsor. Carry on past the Exchange, and turn right into West Bute Street, and right again to bring yourself back into James Street. The area around here used to be known the world over as **Tiger Bay**, with flourishing jazz clubs and the oldest black community in Britain. The difference between the 'old' Cardiff and what you are about to see is astonishing. Turn left into James Street, and cross Bute Street/New George Street and you will see a large roundabout and set of fountains, called **The Flourish**. If you have time, visit the **Butetown History and Arts Centre**, opposite The Baltimore Arms in Bute Street. On The Flourish, there is the modern building of **Crafts in the Bay**, which is well worth a visit, displaying the finest in Welsh craftsmanship. You can also access **Atlantic Wharf Leisure Complex** with its cinemas, bowling, brewpub and restaurants from here. Come back along James Street, and turn left into Bute Crescent. From here you can enter **The Oval Basin** with its great stainless steel fountain. The new centre for the arts and music, the Wales **Millennium Centre** is under construction to your north. Head east towards the **Pierhead Building**. You will next pass the excellent modernistic NCM Building, its marble frontage shaped like the prow of a boat. Now carry along the waterfront to the **Norwegian Church Arts Centre**. Next, stroll to **The Cardiff Bay Visitors' Centre**, a silver 'cigar-case' known affectionately as **The Tube.** The green here is called Britannia Park. Make for the red lightship, **Lightship - Goleulong - 2000**, which is free, open to the public and serves snacks. Carry on along Britannia Quay, alongside Roath Basin, and the **Welsh Assembly** is on your left. You will come to a bridge separating Scott Harbour on your left from Roath Basin (Captain Scott sailed from Cardiff on his ill-fated expedition). There is often a cormorant fishing around here. Walk past the site of Bute East Dock Basin, keeping Roath Basin on your right, and you will see on your left Junction Dry Dock and cross the bridge over to the well-designed apartments of Adventurers Quay. An entrance to **Roath Dock** is the channel on the south-east side of Adventurers Quay. Roath Dock also leads into Queen Alexandra Dock, which then leads into the open sea at Cardiff Flats. The Barrage, with its fish weir and locks, is only used by pleasure boats and yachts. Commercial shipping enters Cardiff Docks via the Queen Alexandra Docks. Retrace your steps past the Pierhead Building and the Oval Basin and you will come to **Mermaid Quay**, fronting the **Millennium Waterfront**.

From here you can take **boat trips** to the Barrage, the Ely River, up the Taff to the Millennium Stadium, and to Penarth Marina. The Bay has turned to fresh water, now the sea has been excluded, and you may see bubbles rising in the water. Pipes have been laid to oxygenate the water and encourage new freshwater plants and animals. Once established, the plants themselves will oxygenate the water and encourage wild life to populate the bay. The ecology of the lake will change dramatically over the years, as the area was once tidal mud flats favoured by waders. The Rivers Ely and Taff flow into the new bay, which was formerly called Penarth Flats. This author felt that the Bay would silt up rapidly over the years and need regular and thorough dredging, to the detriment of any freshwater ecological system. The Bay's planners believed that the former silting of the Penarth Flats and Cardiff Docks was due mainly to the action of the River Severn. However, as of January 2003, Cardiff Council are now putting out to tender *'a major dredging and shore protection scheme in the area known as the Inland Bay, Cardiff Bay, together with adjacent lengths of the River Ely and the River Taff.'*

There are terrific restaurants and bars around Mermaid Quay. Carry on walking and you will see a Harry Ramsdens Fish and Chip Restaurant, and after that **Techniquest**, at the head of three old graving docks. Carry on along to the spectacular **St David's Hotel**. Looking west, you can see Windsor Esplanade, a favourite place for sea captains to buy their houses, and the new Cardiff Yacht Club. The walk across the Barrage from Cardiff Bay to Penarth is not quite completed as this book goes to print. The public rights and landscaping have to be effected at its eastern boundaries, to join up near the present Visitor Centre.

WALK 5 - CARDIFF CASTLE TO LLANDAFF CATHEDRAL - 5 miles (8km), easy walking. *Start from Cardiff Castle or Llandaff Cathedral. Parking can be difficult at Llandaff, however. Parking in Sophia Gardens car-park, off Cathedral Road, puts you on the West bank of the Taff. Cross the modern bridge to Bute Park and head north away from the castle.* Simply follow the Taff north from the Castle Grounds along the footpath to Llandaff Cathedral. You can return on the other side of the river. You can take a picnic, or there are pubs and restaurants in Llandaff Village.

Cardiff Castle - this is a series of castles, beginning with the huge Roman fort which you can see, dating from the 1st century AD. Two further Roman forts were built on the site. *Caerdydd* lay on the Roman Road between Caerleon and Caerfyrddin (Carmarthen), which passed through Bovium (Cowbridge) and Nidum (Neath). Much of the Roman masonry was incorporated into the 11th century Norman fortress on this strategic site, from where the conquest of Glamorgan was planned. The remarkable shell keep on its motte, surrounded by a moat, gives a superb view over Cardiff. On the site of Fitzhamon's 1091 wooden keep, it was built by Robert the Consul in the 12th century. The castle has had a turbulent history, being a prison for Robert Duke of Normandy (the rightful King of England), and with Ifor Bach, Lord of Senghenydd scaling its walls. Llywelyn Bren was imprisoned here in 1317 before being illegally hung, drawn and quartered by the Despensers. Owain Glyndŵr attacked the castle when he burned the town and sacked Llandaff Castle. Jasper Tudor, the great hero of the Wars of the Roses, was given the castle by a grateful Henry VII, and upgraded it. It was captured by Cromwell's army, and passed through the Herberts to the Bute family. 'Capability Brown' laid out the grounds, and the Butes made the castle into a superb Gothic fantasy, using William Burges as architect. When it was given to Cardiff City Council in 1947, it was thought to be the longest continually-inhabited building in Britain.

Llandaff Bishops Palace - The high walled remains of the fortified palace now form a pleasant park outside the Cathedral - it was destroyed by Owain Glyndŵr in the early 15th century. The twin-towered gatehouse probably dates from the early 14th century.

Llandaff Cathedral - From the peaceful village green, walk down the steps to the cathedral on the river-bank. The site dates from the 6th century, and St Teilo's Holy Well still runs here. During the Civil War the church was used as a tavern, and was in ruins in the 18th century. The 19th century cathedral was badly damaged during the Second World War bombing of Cardiff, but has been magnificently restored, with Epstein's wonderful *Christ in Majesty* bridging the nave. The Cathedral is dedicated to St Teilo and St Dyfrig.

St Teilo, who died around 580, was feasted on February 9th, and later February 20th at Ffair Wyl Deilo at Llandaff and Llandeilo Fawr, and also on November 26th and June 11th. He is patron Saint of horses and apple trees in Brittany, and born near Penally. He was taught by Dyfrig, and founded the college of Llandaf which was called Bangor Deilo. Teilo died at Llandeilo Fawr, from whence came the fabulous Chartulary which was later appropriated from Llandaf by Lichfield Cathedral. It is now known as the Book of St Chad. Teilo was supposed to have been the second Bishop of Llandaf, and St Euddogwy (Oudoceus) was his nephew. In 1850 his tomb was opened in Llandaf Cathedral and his staff and pewter 'crotcher' discovered. Thirty-seven churches are associated with Teilo in south and mid-Wales. The relic known as Penglog Teilo (Teilo's Skull) has now been installed in its own niche in Teilo's chapel in Llandaf. The stolen Book of St Chad contains the **earliest known written Welsh**, except for that carved on stone. Throughout the Middle Ages, oaths were taken on Teilo's tomb.

Llandaff Cathedral is associated by **St Dyfrig** (Bishop Dubricius c.465-c.546) who was feasted on November 4th. It seems fairly certain that he and his disciples moved west after the battle of Dyrham, when Gloucester, Bath and probably Caerwent were destroyed by the pagan Saxons. Their monasteries in Ergyng and Ewyas were wasted, and they sought refuge at Llandaff with St Teilo, and at Llanilltud Fawr and Llancarfan. It was claimed that Dyfrig crowned Arthur. Dyfrig retired to Enlli (Bardsey Island), but a Norman bishop of Llandaf had his bones translated to Llandaf in 1120 for the greater honour of his cathedral, where he was one of the four titular saints. His reliquaries (his head and one arm encased in silver) drew pilgrims until the Reformation. They were removed in 1538 and lost. Tennyson called him *'Dubric the high saint, Chief of the church in Britain'*. The Book of Llandaf states that Dubricius *'summus doctor'* was appointed archbishop of all of *'Southern Britain'*, being elected by the king and the whole *'parochia'*, with his see being based at the monastery of *'Lanntam'* (Llandaf), founded in honour of St Peter, with the consent of King *Mouricius* (Meurig). Meurig was Arthur's father.

WALK 6 THE TAFF TRAIL - LLWYBR TAITH TAF

Walk 5, above, is the first section of the Taff Trail, a mainly off-road cycle path and footpath from Cardiff up the Taff Valley, and into the Brecon Beacons National Park to Brecon. Largely traffic-free, the 55 miles pass through industrial heritage sites as well as areas of woodland and hillside. Most of it is in easy gradients, and parts can be attempted as and when one wishes. A full set of 6 leaflets on all the walks interconnecting the Taff Trail's 55 miles is available from the Taff Trail Project, Groundwork Merthyr and RCT, Fedw Hir, Llwydcoed, Aberdare, Mid-Glamorgan CF44 0DX (01685-883880)

WALK 7 ROATH PARK and LAKE - 3 miles - easy for all walkers

It is usually easiest to park at the northern end of the lake, although parking is available on many of the roads around both park and lake. Cefn Onn gardens, further north, also make a splendid walk. You can hire a rowing boat.

Simply walk around the lake and through some splendid displays of a vast variety of shrubs and flowers. Roath Park is the best of all the city parks. The walk can be started from any number of places. The Scott Memorial is situated at the south end of the lake, and around the island at the north of the lake can be seen a variety of bird life. At the south end of the lake, are more gardens, and the Conservatory costs about 60p for entry. There you will find a variety of exotic plants, African whistling tree ducks, lizards, tropical fish and some terrapins. There is a café and refreshment stalls around the lake, and plenty of benches.

WALK 8 - CARDIFF BAY TO PENARTH MARINA - about 6 miles round trip
WALK B OF THE SEASCAPE TRAIL

From Penarth Marina, it is easy to access the Barrage when the path is open, and cross to the bay, but remember that there will nearly always be a fresh wind. From the Bay, it is assumed that the start-point will be near the 'Tube' Visitor Centre.

This walk and cycle-path is not yet completely open. The walk will be across the barrage itself to Penarth Customs House and Marina. Work has to finish on its eastern end to link up with Cardiff Bay. It should be open by 2004. From the end of the walk at the old Customs House in Penarth, a new walk is being built around Penarth headland to lead towards Penarth Esplanade and Pier.

Footnote on Cardiff Walks

The Bay link road passes the site of Caerau Castle Ringwork and St Mary's Church. This site has been scandalously neglected over the years. The Normans placed a motte and bailey castle inside an Iron Age hill-fort, and the ruined and desecrated 13th century church lies next to the castle's bailey. There are fabulous views across the Channel, the Ely River, Cardiff, the Garth Mountain and towards Castell Coch. The church is Grade II listed but is crumbling, with the tower finally succumbing to lack of maintenance, and collapsing in 2000. Most people in Cardiff do not even know of the existence of this site.

Concrete caissons under construction in old dry dock in Cardiff

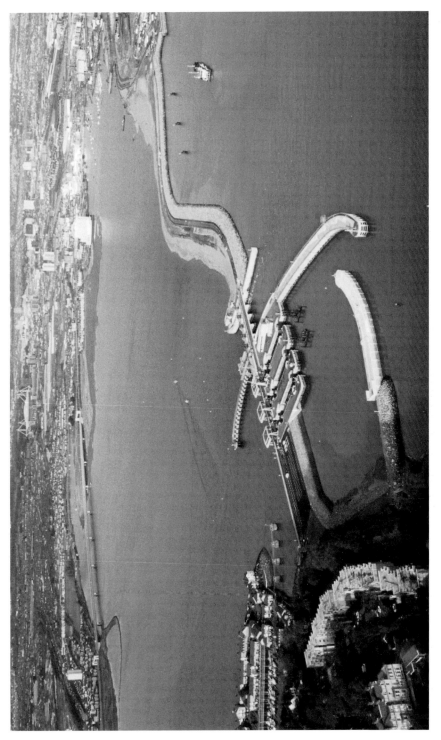

The completed barrage at Cardiff Bay

WALKS IN AND AROUND WENVOE AND WRINSTONE

The following walks are recounted in more detail in *'Wenvoe - Past and Present'*, published by the Wenvoe History Group in 2000 (ISBN 095392310X). There is a strong sense of civic pride in this old village, just a few fields away from Cardiff's western boundary of Culverhouse Cross, and it has won the *'Best Kept Village in the Vale of Glamorgan'* award twice in the 1990's. **Culverhouse Cross** is now regarded as a driving nightmare by those of us who live west of Cardiff, after successive 'out-of-town' developments, roundabouts and traffic lights have been imposed by town planners with a minuscule knowledge of traffic flows. There was a 'culver' house', a large dovecote here, opposite the Culver House pub, near the Western Cemetery.

Iolo Morganwg postulated a 6th-century female named **St Gwenfo**, but the recorded history of Wenvoe village really begins in Norman times. The adjective Gwen (female) or Gwyn (male) means 'white', and as such also means 'blessed' or 'holy'. Many of the 'Whitewell's' scattered across Wales are Anglicisations of Welsh holy wells. Several Welsh saints had the prefix of Gwen or Gwyn. The 7th century Gwenfrewi [Winifred] has the oldest pilgrimage well in continuous use in Europe, at Holywell. The 6th century St Gwynlliw, a Gwent prince and the father of Cadog, had his *llan* in Newport, Monmouthshire. St Gwynlliw's Cathedral has been sadly Anglicised to St Woollo's. However, Wenvoe was called and pronounced in fairly recent times 'Gwaun-fo', which may be its origin rather than the site of the saint's *llan*, or holy place. Gwaun means moor, or meadow, and the 'waun lawn' of Wenvoe Castle preserves this place name via a Welsh 'soft mutation' from gwaun. It could thus be a corruption of 'gwaun-fawr' or great moor. 'Gwaun-ffo' means the moor of flight, and 'Gwen-ffo' would be blessed flight. There does not seem to be a well close to the present church, so if there was an original holy cell or llan, it may have been near the Tarrws Well on the east side of the village. However, water runs next to the present church. The pre-Norman name seems to have been Tre-Golych (Town of Golych) and before that Villa Guocof, possibly signifying a Roman site. Celtic churches were often based on Roman sites. An 1833 Survey gives two derivations of Wenvoe - Gwynfa and Gwynfai - the former means 'paradise'.

WALK 9 - WENVOE VILLAGE TRAIL - about a mile - 20 minutes

This is a short walk, suitable for anyone. The main road through the village was known as the Port Road, indicating the importance of Aberthaw as a port, from pre-Roman times. Since the A4050 was built in the early 1930's (the author's grandfather worked on it), the original Port Road is now known as the Old Port Road, running parallel with the main Cardiff to Barry 'Port Road' bypass. (This bypass cut Ty-Pica and Tarrws Farmhouses off from their fields). *There is ample parking on the road in the village, and an excellent pint of Brains to be had at the Wenvoe Arms, near St Mary's Church.*

If we start our walk at **St Mary's Church**, one will notice its gateway, built in 1930 to commemorate the last inhabitant of Wenvoe Castle. Laura Frances Jenner had died in 1926 - Jenner Park football ground and Jenner Road in Barry are named after this important Vale family. The church is a medieval gem, dating from the 13th century and with an embattled tower with three bells. (More information on all the Vale's remarkable medieval churches can be found in Geoffrey Orrin's book). The church may well be on a much earlier site. The majority of Welsh saints' churches were rededicated by the Normans to Mary and the apostles. Only by the existence of old place-names can we sometimes associate a 6th-century Welsh saint with a later church. (See the author's *The Book of Welsh Saints*). There is a churchyard cross, a carved rood-screen complete with cross, and a beautiful decorated reredos. The grave of Mary Morgan, near the tower, states she was 109 years old when she died. The large yew tree is between 500 and 700 years old. Opposite the church entrance door one can see the Old Rectory, now a nursing home for the elderly. Next to it, the rectory's old coach house is now a residence. The grassy area opposite the Church Entrance Gate is the **Village Green**, where there was a village pond until it was filled in, in 1932. The red telephone box here is the only listed building in the village apart from the church. The War Memorial consists of a slab from the Alps Quarry and unusually includes the names of those who fought and well as those who lost their lives.

The Church Hall is opposite the road from the Jenner Gate, built in 1894 on the site of a thatched cottage. Up until 1900, the majority of Vale cottages were thatched, and most Vale villages still contain at least one or two. On the north side of the hall is the 'Old Wheelwright Shop', a shed which has also been used for coffin-making. Walk past the **Wenvoe Arms** (a fine place to finish your stroll), which has been a pub officially since 1786 at least, and is probably on the site of an older tavern. There is a record dating from 1766 of a Wenvoe Innkeeper's wife (her name was 'Cecil' Goderick) abusing her servant maid. The coat of arms hanging outside the pub is that of the Jenner family. At one time there would have been several 'inns' in the village, each brewing its own beer. Carrying on, across the road you will see a cul-de-sac signed *'Old Market'*. Until the 1940's a thriving sheep and cattle market was held here every other Tuesday. On that side of the road there is also a thriving village shop, Springfield Stores. The house opposite, on the corner of Springfield Close, used to be the village stores, closing in 1996, and its outbuilding was the village bakery. Next to the old village store is the old Police House, and then the Schoolmaster's House. On your left, as you carry on walking is the Wenvoe Community Centre, previously the old village school. Behind it is the Village Library. Opposite the Community Centre is the Village Hall. The new Gwenfo Primary School can be now seen on the right, a fairly typical piece of 1970's shoe-box architecture.

Carry on walking , past the public playground, to where Tarrws Lane turns left up a small lane. On this corner, one can see in front heading east, the car-park to the Wallston Castle pub, 'Beefeater Restaurant' and 'Travel Inn'. This is not on the original site of Wallston Castle, but where Sunnydale Nursery used to exist. There is an excellent garden centre still at Wenvoe, however, accessed off the Port Road near the golf club entrance. Before turning left up the lane, look at the building opposite, on the corner of Old Port Road and Nant Isaf ('Lowest Stream ' - Wenvoe would have been virtually monoglot Welsh until the 1860's). This is Tarrws House, on the site of Tarrws Farm, and the field opposite (now built on) was known as the Rope Yard. Perhaps tarred ropes were laid our here to dry from the 'Tar House'. Walking up the hill, the Tarrws Well is on the left, and at the top of the hill one can see a high bank, which is spoil from the disused Whitehall Quarry, which was worked from 1931 to 1976. If you wish, divert and walk towards the entrance of the quarry, where you will see a tree-lined mound on the left screening its entrance.

On the right was the location of **Wallston Castle**, originally a Norman motte and bailey castle built as the French moved out from their Cardiff Castle stronghold into the Vale, with fortified sites at Leckwith, Caerau, Wrinstone, Wallston and Dinas Powys. Each castle across the Vale was usually built within the sight-line of another, so that Welsh attacks to regain their lands could be spotted more easily. A stone 'Edwardian-style' castle replaced it, and its last vestiges were used as a store-room for explosives and a garage, before it was unfortunately razed to the ground to accommodate stone-crushing machinery. 1939 records show quite considerable remains, but the castle would have been robbed for dressed stone over the centuries (- the author's house contains a Norman arch from West Orchard Castle in St Athan). Additional material now covers Wallston Castle's foundations, and the area is planted with trees.

Back on the Wallston Road, heading west, the little village of Wallston was once separated from Wenvoe. *'In 1933 the local population was around 50, and the oldest inhabitant ruled as 'Mayor' of the small community. Like most country villages the area had no piped water or sewage system, relying on the Tarrws Well for fresh water, and a communal cesspit served most of the cottages.'* On the right one will see the **Zoar Presbyterian Church**, rebuilt in 1839, where all the Calvinistic Methodist services were once in Welsh, and some of the oldest properties in the village are around here. At the junction of Pound Lane on your right, Upper House is over 300 years old. Carry on until you return to St Mary's Church. This gentle walk can be added to, by taking the following walk to Wenvoe Castle.

WALK 10 - WENVOE CHURCH TO WENVOE CASTLE - around 2 miles, plus a half-mile diversion if wished - about an hour. *There are 2 stiles, which can be avoided if necessary.*

Another gentle stroll, starting at the church entrance and heading up Wallston Road, then taking the first turning on the left to Clos Llanfair (The Close of the Holy Place of Mary). This new estate was built on a site used by Anstee's Nurseries to grow plants, of which a beautiful Tulip Tree remains. (The author vividly remembers how this nursery used to throw out all its old stocks on a site in woodland near Wenvoe Castle. Often there were usable bulbs, corms, and young plants growing on the site. My father and I used to walk up from Cadoxton on a Sunday with brown paper carrier bags [there were no plastic carriers in the 1950's] and fill them with 'treasures' for our garden. We even used to take home mole-hill earth from the golf-course. Garden centres, as we know them today, did not exist). Anstees in those times supplied flowers and plants all over Britain, and its main selling site is now the Wenvoe Garden Nursery.

Walk through this estate, and cross a stile into a field, bearing left following the fence and hedge, alongside a ditch which drains water into Wrinstone Brook. You will soon pass a lawn on your left with an oak, in the garden of the Rectory. Passing through a gap in the hedge, head for the electricity pylon. Next to the junction of the boundary

Wenvoe Church - Cathy Crompton

fencing, for the garden centre and Port Road, there is another stile. (Alternatively, one can walk from St Mary's Church back to the A4050 and along the Port Road to the Wenvoe Garden Centre). Turn right on Port Road alongside the garden centre, past the small roundabout, past the turning to Burdonshill and garage workshop, until you come to **Castle Lodge**. This was the entrance lodge for **Wenvoe Castle**. Turn in towards the golf club. The main drive to the castle crosses a greensward known as the Waun Lawn, with plenty of oak trees. The Wenvoe and District Agricultural Show used to be held here or in the local area, from around 1889 to 1969, with ploughing, hedging and ditching contests. (Wales is remarkable for its different styles of hedging, or 'pleaching'. The Museum of Welsh Life at St Ffagans has some interesting tools and pictures of different techniques). After a small pond on the left, pass between two square stone piers. On the left, **The Bothy** was at one time the home of the Wenvoe Estate gardeners. There is the possibility of a diversion here. Just before The Bothy, there is a public footpath to the left, across the golf course, which after 400 yards or so will give a fine view of the castle. Returning to The Bothy, after another 200 yards on the castle drive, the road divides. Straight ahead is the golf club car-park, and on the left one can see the stable block for the castle.

This area now belongs to the golf club. If you wish to walk around the castle perimeter, please request permission. Wenvoe Castle was designed by the great Robert Adam, and built in 1776-1777 for Peter Birt, probably on or near to an existing medieval castle. Normans originally owned the manor of Wenvoe, including the Flemings who built Flemingston Castle. Via the Earl of Pembroke, by Tudor times the castle had passed to Edmund Thomas of Wenvoe (c.1570-1637). In 1594 he was recorded as the leaseholder of *'the castle and ditches of Wenvoe'*. He built the great mansion known as Wenvoe Castle, probably on the base of a medieval castle, which itself was probably on the site of a recorded motte and bailey precursor. Edmund became High Sheriff of Glamorgan, but to clear debts his family sold the estate in 1774 to a Yorkshire industrialist, Peter Birt. His daughter married a Jenner, and the Jenners lived in the castle until 1726. Even in the 1900's there were 40 workers employed on the Wenvoe Estate. Adam built the castle in a *'Roman fortress style with a castellated roofline and a long three-storey south front'*. Only the east flank, no longer castellated, remains after a fire in 1910 and demolition in 1926. The stable block was designed by Heny Holland, who was actively working on Cardiff Castle in the 1770's. The landscaped park was largely the creation of Sir Edmund Thomas, between 1733 and 1767, and included four separate lawned areas, with a grotto and serpentine canal, the remains of which form a water hazard on the golf course. The golf club took over the remaining buildings in 1936.

Return from the castle to The Bothy, and take the left path to the top of Burdonshill. Follow the beech-lined track, and to the south one can see across the Severn to Exmoor. At the junction turn right down Burdonshill, where many of the servants of the estate used to live. (One can instead head left at the junction to St Lythan's burial chamber, or head straight on to take the St Lythan's and Twyn yr Odyn walk noted below.) Pass the last house on the left and a small parking area, and look for a stile in the hedge on the left. Diagonally cross the field towards Wenvoe Wood, with views to the south and west towards Wrinstone Farm. At the bottom of the field is a path between the houses leading back into Clos Llanfair and to St Mary's Church.

WALK 11 - WENVOE CHURCH TO ST LYTHANS CHURCH AND TWYN YR ODYN
- about 3.5 miles - about 1.5 hours. *Medium difficulty, lots of stiles.*

From St Mary's Church, walk up Wallston Road, passing on the left Clos Llanfair, Church Rise and Is-y-Coed (Below-the-Wood), and then turn left up Pound Lane. The first house on the left is Coed-y-Ffald (Pound Wood), and next to it is the old **village pound**, where stray animals were kept. At the top of the hill is a bridle track on the right. If you wish, there is a small diversion straight up the road in front of you to see Wheatley Hall on the road to Poundfield Farm. Wheatley Hall was previously known as Dan-y-Lan (Under-the-Slope), and was formerly the Wenvoe Wood gamekeeper's cottage before being vastly extended. Turning back to the bridle path, now on the left, one can see Steep Holm and the Somerset Coast on looking backwards. At the top of the path, before it heads down again, an ivy-covered wall on the right is all that remains of an old house known as Y Clwyd (The Gate, or Hurdle. It could also mean The Roost). Follow the path to Whitehall Farm. Behind the farm a 300 yard detour on the right will allow you to look down into the bowl of **Whitehall Quarry**. Return to the outbuildings of the farm, and take another shorter diversion right up the bridle track

St. Lythan's Church - Cathy Crompton

to the site of The Yackla, once a thatched cottage and then a bungalow which was demolished in the 1970's.

Turn back towards the farm and then turn right towards Bryn (Hill) Lodge, at the edge of the woods. Cross a stile on the right of the house and follow the garden boundary to another stile and follow the track alongside **Wenvoe Wood**. As the track widens, you will see a stile on the right into a field. (The wide track leads on to Burdons Farm). Cross the stile, follow the field hedge on the left to the next corner, and cross the stile to a lane lined with pine trees. (Alternatively you can miss the visit to **St Lythan's Church** by not crossing this stile but following the alternative route to your right). Follow the pines to a stone stile on the left leading into St Lythans Church. This is an ancient holy site, although the church only dates from the 12th century. Instead of St Bleiddian (Lupus), it was probably originally dedicated to the 6th century Welsh **St Elidan**, who was feasted on June 16th, but on September 1st at St Lythans

A charter copied by the Book of Llandaf records that the *church of Elidon* was granted to Bishop Euddogwy by King Ithel ab Athrwys. Llaneliddon is the Welsh for St Lythan's, and the Anglicisation of the mutated 'dd' is easy to understand. St Lythan's in Welsh was later known as Llanfleiddian Fach to distinguish it from Llanfleiddian Fawr, or Llanblethian-juxta-Cowbridge. This latter village was also once called Llan Elidan or Llan Leiddan, so there is no Bleiddian or 'Lupus' attached to either village. There is a Norman font, and on the south wall are two ape-like gargoyles. The nineteenth century gravestones in Welsh, in this village just outside Cardiff, remind us of how quickly the Welsh language was wiped out in Glamorgan. There is a walled area around **St Lythan's Well**, near the church entrance. All of the 5th-7th century churches of 'The Age of the Saints' in Wales were built next to wells or a fresh water supply. This era was known as 'The Dark Ages' over the rest of Europe, as pagans virtually wiped out Christianity everywhere except Wales.

Leave the church, turning right down the small lane, taking care to stop for passing traffic. At the next crossroads, you can cut the walk short by turning right to The Yackla and Whitehall Farm and returning to Wenvoe. To the left at the crossroads is the entrance to the Wenvoe BBC Transmitter Station, which began television transmissions in 1952. The present aerial is 791 feet high (241 metres in imposed Euro-speak). One can take this lane past the reservoirs which serve Barry and get onto the Downs overlooking Cardiff and the Channel. Go straight over the crossroads, however, and the fields towards the TV aerial mast were once Wenvoe Aerodrome. You will pass allotments and a playing field on the left, turn left past the site of Osmond's Quarry (filled in, in the 1970's), and you are in the village of **Twyn-yr-Odyn**.

The meaning is Lime-Kiln Hill, but there is also a legend that it was the burial mound (hillock, twyn) of a Viking chief named Odyn. The small village grew from 4 families in 1844 to 20 families in 1891 and just 21 in 1997. The tiny village pub, **The Horse and Jockey**, has been considerably extended since the author's youth, aided by the move of HTV from Pontcanna to new studios just below Twyn-yr-Odyn. Apart from water collected in rain-butts, the local supply until 1940 had to be transported from Wenvoe's Tarrws Well. Turn right past the Horse and Jockey, which serves excellent meals, and past the row of cottages, and one sees a **Welsh Baptist Chapel**, dating from 1821. People were baptised by total immersion in a pool under its floorboards, and it became a private residence in 1956. The last burial here was in 1946, but the gravestones which had not been destroyed by quarrying were broken up, which seems to be sacrilegious,

Past the chapel, Rock House was the village shop. The track past this house takes you to the entrance of the filled-in Greenwood Quarry on the left. Turn right on the road up towards Hill Terrace, built for quarry workers, with a Victorian post-box set in the wall just beyond. From the footpath past the terrace, take a kissing gate into a field, with the 18th century Ty Luc (The House of Luke) on the left. From the kissing gate Alps Quarry can be seen over the valley towards Cardiff, where equipment is kept for Wenvoe Quarry. A million tons of stone are excavated each year, and there are also old iron ore workings on the site. Cross the next stile, into a field known locally as the Orchid Field or the Sledging Field. The track leads to a stile before a new access road dating from 1995 and which was used to fill in Whitehall Quarry. (You can head back to Whitehall Farm this way). Cross the road and another stile, with Samuel's Wood on the right. A few yards and we pass the site of **Wallston Castle** on the left, and follow the path through woods to another stile which leads on to Wallston Road and back into Wenvoe.

WALK 12 - WALK FROM WENVOE CHURCH TO WRINSTONE (and Beauville)

About 2.5 miles. *Time about an hour - very muddy in Winter months. Medium difficulty. Lots of stiles.*

From St Mary's Church pass the Wenvoe Arms, Springfield Stores and the Community Centre to turn right into Station Road, along the school hedge to the footbridge over Port Road. Carry on along Station Road, past playing fields on the right (which formerly belonged to Cardiff's private school, Monkton House). Cross **Wrinstone Brook** and carry on past the 'new' Ty-Pica Farm on the right. The old Ty-Pica farm is opposite the church and was cut off from its fields by the Port Road bypass (A4050). Cross the footbridge over the old railway line from the Rhondda and Rhymney Valley coalfields to Barry Docks, where Wenvoe Station has been converted to a private house. Passenger traffic ran from 1896 to 1962. Carry on along the road to a T-junction, taking care concerning traffic, and bear right.

One can either carry on along the road, or bear left along the footpath, where there are excellent views of Wenvoe. One can bear left to Michaelston-le-Pit, or bear right to carry on with the described walk. This path can get muddy. (Before that there is also another path heading left, heading thorough Cwm Slade to The Lawns.) This footpath joins back with the road after 800 yards or so, and one walks towards Wrinstone Farm and then on to Beauville Farm (the latter with seascape views). One can walk towards Beauville Farm and on to Dinas Powys, or bear left just before Wrinstone and head towards Michaelstone-le-Pit and the salmon leaps. The church of **St Michael and All the Angels** at Michaelstone-le-Pit was first mentioned in 1254, and is Early English in style. **Wrinstone** was once a medieval village, first noted as Wrencheston or Wrenchestun (the tun or manor of Wrench). In the 13th century it belonged to the de Gloucesters, then the de Reignys, and then to the de Raleghs (relatives of Sir Walter Raleigh). The de Raleighs built Cwrt-yr-Ala (Court of Ralegh) near the salmon leaps with stone taken from **Wrinstone Castle**. Wrinston belonged to the Earl of Worcester, but in the English Civil War was given to Horton's Brigade, after their victory at the Battle of St Ffagans in 1648. It then was bought by one of Cromwell's greatest supporters, Colonel Philip Jones of Fonmon Castle. By the 16th century there were 9 houses at Wrinstone, with a castle or manor house. From 1536, the castle was noted as having only one tower remaining and its tenant, Thomas David, was several times summoned to Manor Court, for failing to repair the castle. Many coins, dating from the reign of Edward I have been found around the current farm-house, along with musket balls. William Thomas noted the eagerness in 1767 of the overseer of Wrinston woods to have offenders (male and female) whipped in churchyards for cutting wood. In 1765 Thomas also recorded the use of the *'skymmetry'* or *'skymmington'* at Wrinston. Morgan Daniel's wife had abused him, so she was subjected to *'noise and riots'* in a mock trial, with neighbours acting the traditional roles of Maid Marian and the Sheriff of Nottingham. This little hamlet, just west of Cardiff, still had monoglot Welsh speakers in 1764, as evidenced when Charles Batt of Wrinston married an English girl in Bristol, neither knowing the other's tongue.

St Gwrin (6th - 7th century) was possibly the saint associated with Wrinstone, and was celebrated on November 1st (All Saints Day), and on May 1st at Llanwrin. According to Iolo Morganwg, Gwrin ap Cynddilig ap Nwython ap Gildas founded Trewrin, or Wrinstone. Many Roman coins and artefacts have been found at the deserted village and fields around Wrinstone Farm. Many, if not most of the 900 plus Welsh saints from the 'Age of Saints' were associated with Roman sites. The presence of Roman artefacts may mean that there was a villa on this site.

Turn right past the farmhouses and barns, and enter the field via the gate. Turn right and take a line across the field heading just to the left of the Wenvoe Aerial. Cross the stile, turn left and head diagonally across the field to the far corner. Pass under the electricity cables, and over three stiles in quick succession to cross the old railway line. Go over the wooden bridge over Wrinstone Brook, then head straight over another four stiles to the tunnel under the Port Road. It was built for the cattle from Ty-Pica Farm to cross to the fields after the Port Road was constructed. You are now back at the church.

WALK 13 - WENVOE WEST CIRCULAR - RAMBLERS WALK TO BURIAL CHAMBERS AND DUFFRYN GARDENS

About 6 miles (10 km) - not difficult, but plenty of stiles, and can be muddy.

From St Mary's Church, Wenvoe, walk into Wallston Road and turn left into Clos Llanfair then into a short cut de sac on the right. Look for the paved path in the left corner. Follow the path to the rear of the houses and go through a gap the in fence into a cultivated field. Follow the right-hand edge of the field for 200 yards, and look for a gap in the hedge just before the field path turns sharply left. Go through the gap into a small wood and to a visible stile ahead. Go over the stile, turn left and walk across the field in the direction of an electric pylon to reach a stile in the far right corner of the field. Cross the stile into Burdonshill Lane, turn right and walk up the hill passing houses on both sides to reach a kissing gate on left leading onto **Wenvoe Golf Club**.

Wenvoe castle - Cathy Crompton

Keeping to the right hand edge of the fairway, walk west following way-mark posts. In 250 yards turn right onto a clearly defined downward path into **Goldsland Wood**. Follow this path around to the left with a hedge to the right to reach a stile on your right, which leads into a small field. Walk diagonally to another, clearly visible, stile and then a further stile/gate. Cross both stiles into a large field. With the hedge on your left, walk to the next stile and gate, then to a further stile and gate. Cross the stile and walk north west, with the hedge to your left initially, but gradually moving right to cross one stile and then very soon through a field gate Then pass through another gate into a metalled farm yard, **Maes y Felin Farm** (Mill Field Farm). Walk through the farmyard and on to the driveway to reach a visible stile ahead. Cross the stile and then the field, bearing slightly left, to reach a kissing gate which leads to the road. (Look for the **St. Lythan's Neolithic Burial Ground** standing stones as you walk across the field).

Turn left at the lane and walk to a T-junction in 150 yards, where you turn right, sign-posted Dyffryn Gardens. Walk for 800 yards, passing North Lodge, the entrance to **Dyffryn Gardens**. Ignore the footpath sign on your right immediately opposite North Lodge, but look in 120 yards, for a stile on right, also with a footpath sign. Cross the stile, and walk up a gentle rise aiming slightly to left of Wenvoe T.V. transmitter mast, to reach a group of tall trees on the left, and then to a stile in the left hand corner of field. Cross the stile, turn right and follow the right hand hedge to a second stile/gate. Cross this stile and continue along the hedge on the right to yet another stile ahead and then to yet another. Cross over this stile, and pass an electricity pylon on your right walking towards the still visible T.V. transmitter.

Where the hedge turns right, carry on ahead into a shallow wooded hollow, and then walk up a slight rise to reach a hidden, small metal gate. Do not go through this gate. Turn right and go through a wooden gate onto a clearly defined path through **Coed Nant Bran Wood** (Crow Stream Wood), and in 500 yards you will reach a stile and gate. Cross the stile and follow the hedge to the left to reach **Lodge House Farm** ahead. (At the time of writing the public footpath is obstructed at the farm's perimeter fence. Should this still be the case, make your way to the left of the fenced barn to reach a tall metal gate on the right just beyond a second gap in the hedge). Go through the metal gate onto the driveway (a public right of way) and walk south to the road. Cross the road and cross over the stile. Walk ahead with a hedge to your right to a second stile, cross this and continue ahead to a metal gate in the hedge ahead. Turn left before the gate and walk with the hedge to your right to reach a lane via the gate/stile exit from the field.

In the lane turn left, walk along the clear path through **Wenvoe Wood** for 350 yards to reach a stile, which leads into a field with a bungalow to the right. Continue ahead to a second stile, in the right-hand corner of the field. Cross this stile and on to another stile leading into a small fir plantation. Go through the plantation. passing an electricity line pole, to reach a stile which leads to a field and thence to a track to Wallston. At the track turn right, then immediately left onto a concealed path to the left of a stone wall by the house. Follow the path with the wall to the right, and pass the rear of outbuildings on your right, before gradually descending to the entrance to **Whitehall Quarry** (disused) via stone steps. Turn right, cross the visible stile and walk along the road (Wallston Road) for 800 yards back to St. Mary's Church.

WALK 14 - WENVOE CIRCULAR - RAMBLERS WALK by Norman Slater

About 8 miles (13km) - many stiles - can get muddy

From St Mary's Church, walk north up the main street (Old Port Road) past the shops and turn right into Station Road West (the station went 40 years ago). Walk over the main road (Port Road) via the footbridge, then continue up Station Road East for 100 yards. After "Springfield" bungalow turn left onto a path leading to a visible gate,

next to which is a ladder stile. Go over the stile and walk diagonally right to a small copse in 40 yards. Then follow the hedge to your right for 100 yards, to reach a stile in the hedge/wall. Cross this stile and with the hedge to your right, walk 250 yards to the stile ahead. After crossing this stile go through a gate to the right, leading to a bridge over a disused railway.

Salmon leap, Michaelston-le-Pit - Cathy Crompton

At the end of the bridge continue into the field ahead and then bear left (north-east), to reach a gap in the corner of a hedge. Going through the gap, aim for a stile ahead.The stile leads onto the road near **Alps Farm**. Turn right and walk south-east along the road for 800 yards to a road junction (with good rural views towards Wenvoe and Barry). Immediately beyond the road junction, look for a stile near an electricity grid pylon.

Go over the stile and walk up the rise to another stile in 100 yards. From this stile follow the left-hand hedge at the edge of a wood, to reach another stile in the left hedge in 100 yards. Go over the stile and, with this hedge to your right, walk to a second stile on the right and re-enter the field. To your left, another stile leads into a wood with a clear narrow path descending to another stile, which exits from the wood into a meadow. Aim ahead for the wide track (The Lawns) at right angles to the path from the wood. At the track turn right and walk south-east for 1.5 miles to the outskirts of the village of **Michaelstone Le Pit**. (in 500 yards the walk may be shortened by a half by turning right at another wide track going uphill. This takes you to Wrinstone Farm and a waymarked route across fields back to Wenvoe).

Continuing the full walk, look for a weir and pool (**Salmon Leaps**), on your right, opposite a cottage, in about 800 yards. At the end of the pool turn right at a gate and stile to cross a stream, on a bridge to reach a wide track going south. Follow the track between cultivated fields via 3 stiles/gates into a wooded valley (**Cwm George**). Walk through and out of the cwm in 450 yards via a kissing gate. Just beyond the kissing gate turn right over a stile, and then in 30 yards over another stile, which ascend a path through a copse to the edge of **Dinas Powys golf course**. (The way described over the course is a public right of way throughout). After the stile at the edge of the golf course turn left and follow the hedge around to reach the clubhouse on the left.

Follow the waymarks for 40 yards near the clubhouse, towards the houses ahead. Then turn right and walk for 800 yards north-west following waymarks to a wide ascending track which leads to a gate and a road (One O'Clock Gate). Turn right and follow the quiet road for about a mile and a quarter to **Beauville Farm**. At the farm take the stony track descending slightly right outside the farmyard wall. Follow this winding track for 400 yards to reach **Wrinstone House** on the right, immediately after passing over a metal bridge across a stream. Pass the house and ascend to **Wrinstone Farm** in 40 yards on the left. Go through the farmyard with the farmhouse front to the right and look for a gate in the furthest right corner. Go through the gate into a field with 2 electricity lines crossing in parallel. Aim right for 2 adjacent sets of electricity poles and then to the nearby hedge. With the hedge to your right, look for a gate ahead. Pass through the gate and bear right towards the visible stile opposite. Cross this stile and then 2 more in close proximity which leads to the disused railway crossed earlier.

Look ahead for a footbridge and stile which leads to another stile 40 yards ahead. Then follow a clear wide track with a hedge to the left, to another stile in the left hand corner of the field. Yet another stile awaits in 15 yards. Immediately after this stile took for a wide gap in the left hedge with a footbridge. Go through the gap and turn right to follow the stream on your right for 150 yards, to reach a stile to the right in the fence. Cross the stile and a footbridge in front of water culverts. Cross the second stile at the opposite end of the footbridge and turn immediately left over a (final) stile to pass through the **tunnel** under the main road into a housing estate (Venwood Close). Walk directly out to the T-junction with the main village street and turn left to return to the Wenvoe Arms or St. Mary's Church.

WALK 15 - SHORT WALK EAST OF WENVOE

A short walk of 4 miles to the East of Wenvoe and a longer walk of 7 miles to the West can be combined into a figure-of-eight of 11 miles. The going is fairly flat, made up of country lanes, footpaths and woods. It includes two excellent examples of pre-historic burial chambers. A similar route to the longer walk is the Ramblers Walk, Wenvoe West Circular.

From **Wenvoe Village Hall** follow the public footpath sign, towards the pedestrian footbridge down Station Road West. Go over the footbridge and proceed down the country lane opposite, past playing fields and then pass British Soil Ltd. on your right Take the bridge which crosses the disused railway line. The lane narrows and winds until you get to a T-junction with a large electricity pylon towering overhead.

Turn right along the road, and after 30 yards by a metal gate and telegraph pole on your left take the stile into a field. Follow the remains of an old track across the field aiming for a gate and stile on the edge of the trees, and following the line of the electricity cables overhead. Cross over this stile, and then keep to the left-hand edge of the field. At the end of this field, and just to the right of the line of the cables, take the stile on the edge of the wood. Go through the wood in the direction of the yellow footpath sign, and on the far edge take another stile into a field. Ahead you will see a track crossing and a prominent dead tree – aim just to the left of the tree. When you reach the track, turn right and proceed along it. Ignore a turning off to the right after which the track becomes a metalled road. About 10 minutes after joining this track the road starts to descend with a metal fence on the right. The last house on the right is **Cwrt-yr-Ala**. Looking to the right you will see a stretch of water marked on the maps as the **Salmon Leaps**.

Take the metal kissing gate to the right and double-back along the path with the water on your left. You could see a Kingfisher along here. At the end of the water a wooden stile takes you into the trees. Follow the path to another stile and keep ahead with the stream on your left. Cross another wooden stile. Gradually the path starts to ascend. Cross a stile on the edge of the trees, into a field and aim for the right-hand edge of a stone wall, where there is a stile alongside a metal gate. Go over the stile and drop down to the road, turning right and then after 20 yards left into the Farm following the waymark sign. (An alternative route here is to keep along the road which brings you back to where you were earlier in the walk and retrace your steps to Wenvoe). Pass **Wrinstone Farm** on your right with a wooden fence on your left. Just past a telegraph pole, head slightly right with the farm buildings on your right, and the route takes you past a gate and into a field.

Head down the field aiming to the right of the double electricity poles in the middle of the field towards a metal gate. Look out for an electrified wire which unfortunately often runs across the middle of the field. Just beyond the metal gate is often very muddy, although after 20 yards the conditions improve. Follow the yellow waymark and after the gate aim diagonally right, towards a gap in the hedge, and roughly in line with the transmitter on the horizon. Just to the left of the gap is a boardwalk and stile. After this stile aim in roughly the same direction, but just to the left of the transmitter, towards a stile this side of some trees. After this stile take a second one 20 yards further on and a third one the same distance beyond. This takes you into a field and 30 yards beyond is another stile at the far end of a short wooden bridge. Keep ahead across this field to another stile 50 yards beyond.

Head towards the left-hand corner of the next field and another stile. Be careful, because within 10 yards, the path goes to the left across a wood and metal bridge. Immediately turn right heading down a path enclosed on either side with trees and a stream just on your right. Keep ahead across the field until you get to the end – you will hear the traffic just the far side of the hedge. In this corner of the field take the stile to the right by the stream. Cross the stream and take the stile on your left, down a concrete tunnel. The path becomes paved and emerges onto a road. Turn right and immediately left towards a red telephone box with the church of St Mary's to the left of this. At the T junction turn right passing the Wenvoe Arms on your left, then the village shop on your right to return to the start.

WALK 16 - LONG WALK WEST OF WENVOE

7 miles (11 km) - up to 3 hours - can be muddy

With your back to the **Village Hall** head down the road towards the tall Chestnut trees, with the school on your right. As soon as you reach the trees, turn left into the park which you cross, aiming for a road with houses on either side, Grange Avenue. Go down Grange Avenue to a T-junction. Cross the road, turn right and then immediately left into Pound Lane. Head up Pound Lane, ignoring a stony Bridleway to the right (we return down this at the end of the walk). The road descends and then ends by a house. Aim for a green metal gate to the right of the house at which point you will see a path off to the left going behind the house. Take this path which, after passing the house, goes into the trees. Ignore a rough track from the right, keeping ahead. At the edge of the wood you come to a wooden gate and stile which you cross, and then go left along the rough track.

After a little under 10 minutes walking along this track you pass farm buildings and housing on your left, to reach a metal kissing-gate on your right, on the edge of the golf course. Head down the right-hand edge of the fairway with the hedge on your right. After a while you will see a waymark sign pointing diagonally right, which takes you towards some trees and through quite tall bracken. The path curves to the left, with a wire fence on your right, to reach a wooden stile. Cross this and go left towards another stile just this side of a rough track.

Go right up this track for 40 yards, past a metal gate on your left, and then turn left into the field by a waymark sign. Head down the left-hand edge of this field, descending then ascending, until you reach a metal gate with wooden stile on your left. Cross the stile and continue along the left-hand edge of the next field, with electricity pylons prominent to your right. On the brow of the hill take the wooden gate to the left of a metal gate, and keep ahead following the waymark direction towards a house. On clear days there are good views to the left across to the West Country. Cross another wooden stile and aim for a metal gate to the right of a red brick wall ahead. Go through this and aim for another metal gate by a white garage. Head down the drive passing the house on your left until you get to a stile. If you look to the left across the field, you will see the prominent **St Lythan's Burial Chamber**. The right of way goes across the field just to the right of the stones to a kissing gate in the hedge. Go through this onto the road and then turn left.

The cromlech that stands at St Lythan's (not far from the superb **Tinkinswood** site and magnificent **Dyffryn Gardens**), has an ancient raised circle of oak trees near it, with a stone in the centre. St Lythan's Cromlech once was around 90 foot long with an average width of 35 feet, with the chamber we can see facing out of the eastern end. There may be a path that can be delineated from Tinkinswood through St Lythan's to the ancient pillow mounds now covered up by Barri's Atlantic Trading Estate. Like many other burial sites in Wales (such as Michaelston-y-Fedw), the St Lythan's cromlech is known as *'Gwal y Filiast'*, or *'Llech y Filiast'* which modern translations tell us is the *'Lair of the Greyhound Bitch'*. The capstone measures 14 feet by 10 feet, and the field in which it stands is called the *'cursed field'* because little will grow there. It has always been used for sheep rearing in the author's lifetime.

Keep down this lane, ignoring the junction to the right sign-posted to Dyffryn Gardens and in a little under 10 minutes you come to the picturesque houses of **Dyffryn Village**, with a prominent stone wall on your right. Just past the letter box on the right, turn down the lane to the right and within 10 yards turn right again, following the waymark sign and on to a wide grassy avenue with tall trees to the left. The route follows the overhead electricity cables. You are passing the house and grounds of Dyffryn Gardens to your right. Cross a wooden stile by a metal gate and head towards the gap in the trees ahead. Keep straight ahead through the metal gate, and across the field towards the trees in front. You pass two oak trees in the field and just beyond is a stile. Take this and head down the path with wooden fences on either side. Cross a wooden stile and head uphill, straight ahead past some fallen tree trunks to another wooden stile and go ahead aiming in the direction of the large electricity pylon.

Go over the next wooden stile and then immediately left through a kissing gate to visit the magnificent **Tinkinswood Burial Chamber**. Just the other side of Duffryn House and Gardens from St Lythans is this Long Barrow, with the heaviest capstone in the British Isles, possibly in Europe. Twenty-four feet long, fifteen feet wide and three feet thick, it weighs around 46 tons. About 200 people would have been needed to move it into position. It is known as a 'cromlech', from the Welsh 'cromen' (roof) and 'llech' (stone). This area is known as 'Dyffryn Golwg', the 'Vale of Worship'. Somehow, morons have given planning permission for a huge electricity pylon next to this remarkable site. Courses upon cultural appreciation should be mandatory for the faceless bureaucrats who make such decisions. There are other Neolithic remains nearby as well as ancient field systems. Tinkinswood is also known as Castell Carreg, Llech-y-Ffiliast, Maes-y-Filiast and Gwal-y-Filiast. Dating from around 4000BC, the wedge-shaped cairn contains a rectangular stone tomb-chamber, which contained at least 40 people of both sexes (identified from 920 pieces of bone). The tomb was used right up to the early Bronze Age. There are many legends about the cairn.

Go back though the kissing gate to pick up your original direction across the field, aiming slightly right towards a stile set in a hedge. Follow the direction of the waymark through a field with a wire fence converging from the right. When you reach the fence, go left and then take the stile on your right, which is level with the end of the field on your right. Go along the left-hand edge of this field for 40 yards to reach a stile and metal gate under a tree on your left. Cross the stile and then aim slightly to the right towards a gap in the hedge ahead. As you get closer to the gap, you will see a wooden stile in the hedge to the right under a tall tree. Keep ahead through the field. You will see a white house ahead, and to the left of this is a double metal gate. To the left of this gate is a single metal gate and to the left of this a stone stile which you cross to reach a road heading north to **St Nicholas**. Go left, crossing the road to walk along the pavement. (You can detour into St Nicholas village to see the medieval church, if you wish).

The pavement becomes a path with metal railings on your left and stone wall on right. When you reach the main Cardiff-Bridgend road, turn right along the pavement passing the old Police Station on the right Just past the white house called Los Andes turn right passing The Garth house on your left. Go over a cattle grid, and by some farm buildings the track goes to the left. Here you are heading to the right of the distant transmitter and to the left of two tall electricity pylons. The path then curves right heading towards the nearest pylon with views to the right across the **Bristol Channel**. When you get to the end of the field with a pylon just to the right, look to the left to find the stile in the corner of the field. Cross this, and then turn right through a metal gate. Head to the left of a dead tree stump, aiming for the top left-hand corner of the field with a wire fence converging from the left. Just beyond a metal gate in this fence, you will see a waymark sign and stile. Take this to cross the fence and head through the gap in the trees ahead, just to the left of the distant transmitter. Just before a metal gate ahead which leads into a field beyond, turn right to follow the waymark sign which points towards a path through the left-hand edge of the wood.

Take this path until you reach a stile to the right of a metal gate, now keeping along the left-hand edge of the field towards a house in the distance. As you reach the perimeter fence of the house, follow the waymark sign to the left which crosses into the next field. Turn right with the fence now on your right, over a stile and then through a metal gate on to the drive to the house. Turn left down the drive, passing the house on your right, until you reach a road. Head for **St Lythans**. Where the road curves right, look left and take the stile which brings you into the churchyard of St Lythans Parish Church. Pass to the left of the church and leave the churchyard by a stone stile which takes you onto a track. Turn right and just before you reach some metal gates, go left down a conifer-lined path. Cross a stone and wooden stile to emerge on to a field. Head down the right-hand edge of the field towards the trees. At the end of the field is a stile by a metal gate. Cross this and turn left along the track through the trees with wire fence on right. Go over a stile by a house, down to a second stile by a wooden fence. Go on to the drive and turn left. You can either go down the drive until you meet the rough road ahead by the farm house, at which point turn right. Alternatively, take the stile on your right on a path which winds through a small conifer plantation (look out for concealed tree stumps) to reach a stile on the edge of a field. Cross the field following the line of the overhead telegraph wires to reach a stile at the far end and emerge onto a rough road. Turn right passing the house on your left and follow the rough track uphill and then downhill to reach **Pound Lane** which you came along earlier. Turn left and retrace your steps across the park and then right to the start.

WALK 17 - SAINT NICHOLAS (SAIN NICOLAS) - TINKINSWOOD - DYFFRYN GARDENS - ST NICHOLAS

Moderately difficult walking - some of the fields have gradients, there are stiles, and the 5 mile (8 km) walk should take around 2.5 - 3 hours, plus any time spent in Dyffryn Gardens. In other words, if you take a picnic to Dyffryn, or use its restaurant, it is a 'good day out'.

Two of the above walks can add Dyffryn (Valley) Gardens to the itinerary. Its café is open for all but the winter months. *Instead of parking at St Nicholas, you can park the car in Dyffryn Gardens, and walk along the road south to St Lythan's Burial Chamber, and then return to Dyffryn and walk the road north to Tinkinswood Burial Chamber.*

Park near the medieval **St Nicholas Church**, on the north side of the A48 in the village, and return to the A48. The church is probably on a Celtic saint's site, as Nicholas was one of the Normans' favourite saints. Turn left on the A48, and after a few yards cross over and turn right down the lane sign-posted Dyffryn. Head downhill, and after about 150 yards cross a stile on your right. *(However, if the conditions are very wet, stay on the lane until you see the sign for Tinkinswood Burial Chamber on your right, and cross a field uphill towards it).* Walk ahead, heading slightly diagonally left across the field to follow a line of trees. Cross the stile and head left, but soon leave the hedge and walk uphill to a stile near a gate. Generally, the path from the lane to Tinkinswood is in a direct line south. Turn right along the hedge to a stile, and then follow the fence. The corner of the field now bends away to the left. At this point keep walking in a straight line along the footpath, bearing slightly right towards a stile.

Keep going straight on, to come to the **Tinkinswood Burial Chamber** on your right. The 'Severn-Cotswold' type of cairn was built about 6000 years ago, and is one of the finest Neolithic tombs in Europe, yet it seems hardly known. It was excavated in 1914, and is probably the Vale's finest treasure. *(If conditions are poor, head back east to the lane, and turn right to pass the entrance to Dyffryn Gardens, until you come to a junction. Turn left, and not far on your right you will see the sign for St Lythans Cromlech).* Go back through the kissing gate and cross the stile. Carry on, heading slightly right to the stile in the far right-hand corner of the field. Head half-right to another stile, then straight to the next one. If you carry on the footpath, heading south all the time, you will skirt the western boundary of Dyffryn Gardens and come out in the picture-postcard village of Dyffryn, with the moated site of the original Dyffryn House. Turn left up the lane, ignore the turning for Dyffryn Gardens on your left, and keep heading uphill on the lane.

About 200 yards after the Dyffryn Gardens turn-off, you will find the sign and entrance to **St Lythans Burial Chamber** on your right. This portal dolmen. It is more open and exposed than the magical, craggy area around Tinkinswood, and is one of the author's favourite places in the Vale, especially the mysterious tree circle just south of it. There are more standing stones and tumuli in this region. Return back down the lane and take the right-hand turning towards Dyffryn Gardens. After 700 yards you see the main entrance.

Dyffryn Gardens - The Grade I listed Edwardian Gardens are free to visit in winter, and otherwise cost £3 for adults, £2 for OAP's and children and £6.50 for a family ticket. Ring 02920 593328 if in doubt. Parking is free. Dyffryn Gardens are being restored to the pristine days of my childhood via a Heritage Lottery Fund grant. Work on the great Arboretum and statue restoration is on-going. There are woodlands with remarkable trees from all over the world, including the original Acer Griseum collected by *'Chinese'* Wilson. There are lawns, water features, seasonal beds, garden walkways, greenhouses, and feature garden rooms such as the Grade II listed Pompeian Paved Court and Theatre Garden, enclosed by yew hedges and walls. A good half-day can be spent pottering around the estate, but the house with its wonderful wood-panelled billiards and snooker room is not open to the public. It is an ancient site, originally owned by the Bishops of Llandaff for 800 years, later belonging to the Button family, and then the Pryces. In 1893 the house was rebuilt when owned by John Cory, and the magnificent gardens were laid out in 1904 by Thomas Lawson. The site dates from the 7th century, being given by King Iudicael to Bishop Euddogwy of Llandaff. There is a fairly complicated system of footpaths to return you on alternative routes across country from Dyffryn to St Nicholas, but the author prefers to stroll up the quiet lane back.

WALKS IN AND AROUND PENARTH

Penarth is known as *'the Garden by the Sea'*. Linking the elegant town and the seafront are a series of parks and gardens, but it is a fairly steep climb from the seafront to the town centre. Since 1926, the Esplanade has been overlooked by the Italian Gardens and their palms, with views across to the Pier, Flat Holm, Steep Holm

Penarth Pier - Cathy Crompton

and Somerset. At the eastern base of Penarth Head is the former port, and the origin of Penarth's prosperity, built between 1859 and 1865. Its wasteland has been now turned into a beautiful marina, with attractive waterfront homes, and full of the latest yachts and cruisers. From the Marina, one can see the huge workings of the Cardiff Barrage and the new inland lake of Cardiff Bay. Regular water-buses take you across to the restaurants and bars of Cardiff Bay. The cycleway and pedestrian walk across the Barrage to Cardiff has not yet been completed, which will link Penarth and Cardiff. Work is going ahead on the walk from Penarth Marina and the end of the Barriage, around Penarth Head, to link up with the Esplanade and Pier.

WALK 18 - PENARTH MARINA, PENARTH HEAD TO PENARTH PIER AND ESPLANADE

WALK C OF THE SEASCAPE TRAIL

Around a mile (1.5 km) - flat but there will probably be steps over the groynes. It is not known at present if wheelchairs/push-chairs will be able to use the path.

The new pathway from Penarth Marina, around the headland to Penarth Esplanade, is being constructed as this book is being written. The ugly multi-storey concrete car-park on the east of the Esplanade has been demolished. You will see pink alabaster in the cliffs which are under St Augustine's Church on Penarth Head.

WALK 19 - STEEP HOLM

From Penarth Pier, at least once a year the 'Waverley' steamer crosses to the island of Steep Holm, and one can make a circular tour of the island. You can book from the Information Office at the Pier Entrance. *Not suitable for those less mobile. There is a sharp climb to access the island, and disembarking and embarking on the island involves a 'scramble' across rocks. Wheelchair access is virtually impossible, but one can stay on the boat and go on a cruise while other passengers are allowed to explore the island. Walking around the island, you will probably cover about a mile or so.*

The Steep Holm defences were begun in 1866 and completed in 1868. At the same time, Brean Down, Flat Holm and Lavernock Point were fortified, forming a defensive line crossing the Bristol Channel protecting the principal ports of Bristol, Cardiff and Newport. This fortified island in 1882 had 10 seven-inch guns, each weighing 7 tons, and a

Penarth Marina - Cathy Crompton

barracks which could take 50 men. Some of the guns can still be seen. It is presently a **Nature Reserve**, and was used in World War II, being re-fortified with Coastal and Anti-Aircraft batteries, with 4 six-inch guns. The army first moved out in 1901, and again in 1945. Steep Holm is about 49 acres, with an average height above sea level of 200 feet, bordered by precipitous cliffs. The **fortifications** on Steep Holm consist of six small parcels of land which run around the cliff top perimeter path, with an average distance between each of about 200 yards. Each gun battery has its own underground magazines for shells & cartridges. Most of the Victorian batteries have suffered from damage caused by the refortification of the island during the Second World War, although all but one of the batteries still have their 7-inch cannon lying near them.

It is a **SSSI**, with spectacular views in all directions to the Severn Bridges, Weston Bay, and the North Somerset, Devon & Welsh coasts.

A five mile boat trip lasting about an hour, from Penarth (or Weston-super-Mare), lands visitors on a rock and pebble beach. Occasionally the smaller Weston vessels link up with the Waverley or the Balmoral paddle steamer to take some of their passengers ashore, because the larger vessels are constrained by their draught. Once ashore, there is a zigzag ascent through a small sycamore wood to the island's plateau 256 feet above sea level. For those seeking the opportunity to observe & appreciate flora & fauna of the island, there is an abundance of rare plants & other lush Mediterranean vegetation waiting to be discovered. Like Flat Holm, it has wild peonies and a variety of sea birds. Muntjac deer graze the island.

Archaeological investigation has produced evidence of a Roman presence here. The Vikings used the island in 914 and are the earliest confirmed residents of the island. *The first British historian*, the 6th-century monk **St Gildas**, who trained at Llanilltud Fawr, stayed on both Flat Holm and Steep Holm. (St Gildas is remembered all over Brittany, but only in Britan at Llanildas, which then was known as Y Wig Fawr, and is now Wick, near Llantwit Major). The earliest ruins on Steep Holm are that of the medieval priory. This was founded on a Celtic site by Augustinian canons in the 12th century, as a cell and retreat. In 1832 a house was built on the island just above the landing beach. This was to later become the island's inn, the ruins you pass on the right as you head up from the beach.

Penarth Beach - Cathy Crompton

There were six emplacements built in 1867 and they were given some of the largest and last muzzle loaded guns made. It also has the distinction of being the only Victorian heavy battery in Britain that still has its cannon. As mentioned above, the 7-ton cannons remain on or near their original batteries - two of the cannon are scheduled **ancient monuments**. In World War II, Bristol & Cardiff Docks & the various aircraft factories in the West were major targets for enemy bombing. As a result, hundreds of soldiers were drafted on to the island to build & man 6 inch coastal gun emplacements & searchlight posts. The Kenneth Allsop Memorial Trust took over the charitable administration of Steep Holm during the period 1974/5 in memory of the well-known broadcaster & naturalist. On the island the renovated **Victorian barracks** is used as a Visitors Centre, with a small museum, café and souvenirs. All in all, with the boat trip and the island's attractions, it is an excellent day out.

WALK 20 - PENARTH TO LAVERNOCK (LARNOG, LLANFYRNACH?) TO COSMESTON LAKES TO PENARTH

WALK D OF THE SEASCAPE TRAIL

Easy walking - 2-3 hours. About 4 miles (6 km) from the cliff car-park and miniature golf-course in Penarth, and a half a mile more from the Pier. Not suitable for push-chairs or wheelchairs.

It is not easy to park on the esplanade or anywhere near the pier, and there is a steep hill from the end of the esplanade heading westwards. Thus it is probably better to start from the café and car-park on top of the cliff. Walk along the cliff path past some houses on your right, and you reach a rougher path between trees, still following the cliffs. As you see two luxury houses, you are approaching **Lavernock**. At low tide, you can drop down to the beach here, and cross to St Mary's Well Bay across the pebbles and sand.

At Lavernock turn right up the lane, past the **medieval church** which is dedicated to St Laurence, but was possibly Llanfyrnach. The parish church of

Penarth coastal path heading west - Cathy Crompton

43

Penarth Custom House - Cathy Crompton

Llanfrynach, near Cowbridge in Glamorgan, was dedicated to the 6th century Irish saint, who established the first church on this site. **St Brynach** died around 570, and was also known as Abbot Bernach, Byrnach and Branach, feasted on April 7th. He was chaplain and instructor to King Brychan, after whom Brecon is named. His association with Penlline (Penllyn, also formerly called Llanfrynach) and Llanfrynach near Cowbridge seem to indicate that Lavernock could well have been one of his foundations, renamed by the Normans. At Lavernock, **Marconi** sent *the first wireless telegraph message across water*, to Flat Holm in 1897, and there is a commemorative plaque on the wall outside the church.

Heading on up the lane, Marconi Holiday Homes Park is on your left. The walk to St Mary's Well Bay is across the stile on your left, just after the entrance to the holiday park. You can refresh yourself here at the **Marconi Inn**, which is open to the public but closed in winter. To go to Cosmeston, carry on up the lane to the B4267 (Penarth-Sully road) and cross the road to a stile. Once over the stile, walk across the field, with the reconstructed village of **Cosmeston** on your right. Cross a stile near a gate and turn right on the track. Carry along the track, ignoring other paths and cross the long bridge separating Cosmeston East and West lakes. Then, after 40 yards, turn right along a broad track, past the children's playground to the Visitor Centre. Leave the carpark, bearing left from the Visitor Centre, then recross the B4627. Turn left on the pavement, and after 500 yards turn right on a road that crosses the old Penarth-Barry railway line. At a junction bear right, then shortly left along Stanton Way. Walk ahead until you reach the path at the top of Penarth cliffs, then turn left to the car-park.

WALK 21 - PENARTH TOWN TRAIL 1 - PENARTH PIER > WINDSOR GARDENS > PLYMOUTH ROAD > STANWELL ROAD > ALEXANDRA GARDENS (from the Penarth Society)

About 2 miles, suitable for most people, but a bit 'hilly' between the esplanade and the town.

Walk to the end of the **Pier**, which was built in 1894. The tide often goes out beyond the Pier as the range between high and low tides in the Bristol Channel is the second largest in the world. Turn to face the seafront. On your extreme left is Lavernock Point, the southern limit of Penarth Bay. Rising to about 200 feet on your right is Penarth Head, the 'garth' (meaning hill or enclosure) that probably gave Penarth its name. 'Pen' means 'head', and Pen-garth is mutated to Penarth. Legend also associates Penarth as being the headland of the fabled king Arthur. 'Arth' is Welsh for bear, and Penarth might also mean the Bear's head, which is the name chosen by the new Wetherspoon's pub in Penarth town centre. Around Penarth Head, protected from westerly winds, lie the mouth of the River Ely and Penarth Dock, now developed as a Marina. The expansion of the coal trade led to the rapid development of both town and dock in the second half of the nineteenth century.

St. Augustine's Church - Cathy Crompton

To your left, near the slipway at the bottom of Cliff Hill, is a Victorian building with spiralled pillars and a cast iron veranda balustrade. Now a listed building, this has been the **Yacht Club** since 1883. The inshore lifeboat is housed in the flat-roofed pavilion nearer to you on your left. Next comes the Edwardian terrace (1904) with decorative iron balustrades and a tower at both ends. The lower floors of these terraced buildings are now restaurants with living accommodation above.

Almost ahead of you on the **Esplanade** is a block of flats known as Windsor Court, built in 1963 on the site of Balcony Villa and Rock Villa. To the right is another Victorian building, now a pub, which until a few years ago housed the swimming baths. It is built of local blue lias stone with carved bathstone window surrounds and pilasters. Next to it is the unlovely modern development on the site of the 1887 Esplanade Hotel, which had been badly damaged by fire in 1977. Until 1905 a ferry went across the mouth of the Taff to Cardiff Docks from a movable landing stage in front of these buildings. Further to the right is Seabank Flats and, in the trees above the multi-storey car park, **The Kymin**, an 1870's house owned by the Town Council with grounds recently landscaped for public use.

As you return to the Esplanade, notice the fan designs and border patterns on the Pier's cast iron railing and the Esplanade's original lamp standards between the Pier

Penarth Pier - Martin Green

and the Yacht Club. There was no continuous sea wall in the nineteenth century; the promenade was built in 1883 and widened by twenty feet in 1927. Leave the Pier, cross the Esplanade and turn left in front of Windsor Court, the restaurants and the **RNLI Station**. You can now see the **Italian Gardens** laid out in 1926 on the site of a building once used for storing bathing machines. Walk up the steps, turn right, climb the metal steps to the flat roof and continue into **Windsor Gardens**, up the flight of concrete steps. Turn left, pass the bandstand and cross the path into the continuation of the Gardens, laid out in 1884. On your right are the modern houses of Marine Parade built in the gardens of the Victorian residences of coal owners and ship owners, whose prosperity was linked with Penarth Dock. As you leave Windsor Gardens pass the Lodge where visitors had to pay an admission charge until 1932 when the Earl of Plymouth gave the grounds to the public.

Pause on the pavement of the main road. From the opposite side of Cliff Hill, a coastal path continues along the eroding cliffs to Lavernock Point. The two islands in the Channel, **Flat Holm** and **Steep Holm**, both have Viking associations. The nearer Flat Holm is a nature reserve and gull colony. Part of the City and County of Cardiff, it has been farmed for at least seven hundred years. The lighthouse was established in 1737. There is a ruined nineteenth-century cholera hospital and a barracks that was used during the last war by coastal defence artillery-men. In May 1897 Marconi achieved his first radio transmission over water when his Morse message, *"Are you ready?"* was transmitted from Flat Holm and received by an 110-foot mast on the farm at Lavernock Point. A commemorative plaque can be seen there in the front wall of St Lawrence's Church. Continue on the pavement round the corner towards the junction of Marine Parade and Alberta Road. Here you will find a Victorian seat, post box and fire hydrant. Continue up Alberta Road and cross Plymouth Road into Alberta Place directly ahead. Plymouth Road is named after the family that owned much of the land in Penarth. In about a hundred yards you reach a continuous grassed area which from 1887 until 1968 was the extension of the Cardiff-Penarth Railway to Barry *via* Lavernock, Swanbridge, Sully and Cadoxton. There was a halt platform here at Alberta Place. Walk towards the old railway bridge, turning right just before it to go down Sully Place.

Cross Plymouth Road and walk down Tower Hill — between 54 and 56 Plymouth Road. You soon pass on your left Tower House, the former **Coastguard Station**. The terraced cottages below were built for the coastguards. Turn left into Marine Parade at the bottom of Tower Hill, turn left again into Holmsdale Place and return to Plymouth Road. Turn right and walk up Plymouth Road. The three-storeyed semi-detached houses are not quite on the scale of Marine Parade but they represent the spacious stone-built residences of the well-to-do in the 1880s. Beyond 12 Plymouth Road is Roxburgh Garden Court, built on the site of James Pyke Thompson's house "Roxburgh". In 1888 Thompson built an art gallery on land previously occupied by a the thatched farmhouse of Taylor's Farm. He named it after the painter J.M. Turner and used it to house part of his private art collection which was opened to public view. **Turner House Gallery** is now part of the National Museum of Wales and is open every day except Monday. Opposite the Gallery is the former Penarth railway station's down platform, built in 1878 but now a garden centre and petrol station. Between Turner House and the Glendale Hotel is a path (known locally as the **Dingle**) which leads down to the seafront. The Lansdowne block was built in 1886 by Frederick Speed of Shepton Mallet who also built the 1904 terrace on the Esplanade. Continue walking up Plymouth Road. The next turning point is Rectory Road. On the corner is **Penarth Library**, opened in 1905 with a gift of £4,000 from the Carnegie Trust. On the opposite side of the main road (Stanwell Road) is **Washington Buildings.** In 1922, Captain W.H. Bevan converted the then Penarth Tutorial College

Demolished car park, Penarth front - Martin Green

into an hotel, which he named the Washington in the hope of attracting American visitors. In 1936 its tennis courts became a cinema and the present shops were built around the cinema's car park.

Walk to the end of Rectory Road past **Penarth Lawn Tennis Club**, founded in 1884. For the town centre roundabout (the starting point of the Inner Town Trail) turn left into Windsor Terrace. To return to Penarth Pier, turn right into **Alexandra Park**, named in 1902 after the wife of King Edward VII. Bear right on the higher path and walk down through the park on any of several paths, all leading eventually to the Esplanade where you began your walk.

WALK 22 - PENARTH TOWN TRAIL 2 - TOWN CENTRE TO PENARTH DOCK
(from the Penarth Society)

About 2.5 miles (3 km), but again quite hilly.

Penarth has one of the finest concentrations in South Wales of Victorian buildings and architectural styles. Many of the terraces and large detached properties were built of local materials: lias limestone quarried on the site of Cwrt-y-vil playing fields (off Lavernock Road) and brick made of local marl at two sites in Cogan. (There were remains of a castle at Cwrt-y-Vil). This walk begins at Penarth town centre roundabout. Opposite **Windsor Arcade** (1898), now a listed building, is the National and Provincial Building Society. Passing Lloyds Bank opposite, also a listed building, begin walking up Albert Road. To the left, on the corner of Ludlow Lane, stands the former **Crown Post Office building**, which was built in 1936 and which, together with the pillar box, has been listed as of special architectural or historic importance. The Post Office building has recently been extended over the site of what was the Solomon Andrews Hall, the Hippodrome. From 1887 until 1929, when it was destroyed by fire, it was used for meetings, films, variety shows, and productions by the Penarth Operatic Society. Continue walking up Albert Road. The **Methodist Church** was opened in 1906. Higher up, on your left, Belle Vue Court is now in residential use, but was the town's first fire station and the offices of the Urban District Council. The next building, **Albert County Primary School**, a listed building, was the first Board School in the town when it opened in 1876. On the opposite side of the road stands one of several red telephone boxes that have been listed in Penarth.

At the top of **Belle Vue Park**, opened in 1914, turn right. Like the Edwardian terrace on the sea front, **Belle Vue Terrace** is a unified block with pointed roofs at numbers 1, 7 and 14. Continue walking towards the Grade I listed **St Augustine's Church.** You are now at the highest point in Penarth, about 220 feet above sea level. Due to its prominent position, it is the *only church in Britain to be mentioned on sea navigational maps.* The 90-foot saddle-backed church tower is well known to seamen in the Bristol Channel and is a prominent landmark from many viewpoints far inland. For centuries this was the site of a religious settlement, dating back to a foundation of the Austin Canons around 1200. Designed by **William Butterfield** and financed by Baroness Windsor, the church replaced a much smaller building in 1865-66, and is *one of the finest Victorian churches in Britain.* The interior is particularly noteworthy for its organ, and for use of coloured brick. Three relics of the old church are preserved: a long, flat, thirteenth-century stone with an elaborate carved cross; the fourteenth-century churchyard cross brought indoors to minimise the ravages of the weather; and a prayer desk made from the former chancel gate. However, there is an appeal for urgent restoration which is needed to the fabric of the building. A pillar surmounted by a harp marks the grave of the composer *Dr Joseph Parry*, Professor of Music at Aberystwyth. His most famous composition was the beautiful *'Myfanwy'.* Wing-Commander Guy Gibson, who led the famous *'Dam Busters'* Raid in May 1943, was married here. Set into the wall just past the church gate is an ornate cast-iron drinking fountain. Continue along Church Place South, and cross the main road to enter Penarth Head Lane at the side of 57 Clive Place.

At the end of this lane you are standing about 200 feet above sea level, on the Penarth headland, the *Garth*, that probably gave Penarth its name. This is probably the most spectacular local **viewpoint**. On a clear day you can see the towers of the Severn bridges near Chepstow. Ahead are the Penarth Head buoy and the Outer Wrach buoy marking the dredged channel entrance to Penarth and Cardiff. The **Cardiff Bay Barrage** can be seen, with a great view of Cardiff's new waterfront developments. In 1984 a sponsored charity football match was played on Cefn-y-Wrach (Ridge of the Witch) sandbank. You can see Penarth sea front, the 1894 pier, and Lavernock Point. The two islands in the Channel are *Flat Holm and Steep Holm*. On the Somerset coastline opposite Penarth are Clevedon and Weston-super-Mare. Return along Penarth Head Lane, turn right into Clive Place, and walk down St Augustine's Crescent.

At the bottom of St Augustine's Road, the imposing building used to be the *Penarth Hotel*, opened by the Taff Vale Railway in 1865, for a business and seafaring clientele. It was eventually given to the National Children's Home and Orphanage Society. Turn left into John Street. This was the first type of terraced house to be built in Penarth. Similar use of lias limestone and local brick can be seen in Queen's Road, Salop Street, and Ludlow Street. The *Clive Arms* was the first pub of the "new" town that sprang up with the development of Penarth Dock. Turn right down Maughan Terrace. These three-storey properties were seamen's lodging houses, and no. 12 was the Dock Hotel. Cross the main road with North Cliffe Cottage on your right and continue down hill to the **second viewpoint** of your walk.

Ahead of you, is the new barrage and Cardiff Bay. On your left is the basin of **Penarth Dock**, now transformed into a marina development that has won a Civic Trust commendation. There used to be a swing-bridge to the far side of the dock and to the subway. For 63 years, until it was bricked up in 1963, the **Ely Tidal Harbour Tunnel** gave pedestrian access to Ferry Road on the Cardiff bank of the river Ely. It was opened in 1900 (built in 1899) and a toll-keeper collected a penny from

Penarth Pier - Martin Green

pedestrians, two pence for a bicycle, and 4 pence for a pram. Horses were also allowed through. The first building on your right is the **Custom House** (1865), now thankfully being renovated. Note the Royal coat of arms on the stone clock-tower with its cast-iron weather vane. This was the site of Penarth Head Inn, said to be owned by the eighteenth-century smuggler, Edward Edwards. The next building is the **Marine Hotel**, another Taff Vale property. Note the unusual mansard roofs and the French windows with the initials TVR on the guard rails of the balconies. Both buildings are listed. The lifeboat station was at the rear from 1883 to 1905. From the far side of the Marine Hotel look up at the wall from the shore to the Northcliffe House cliff-top summer house. Retrace your steps up the hill, right along Paget Road, formerly called Dock Road.

The cobbles and triassic marl steps of Ferry Lane (the first left on the far pavement) are a reminder of the path that used to continue down the fields on your right to the chain ferry. Between Ferry Lane and Hill Street, which is also cobbled, the pavement is on a raised platform. Then, until the aptly named Steep Street, note the housing style with bay windows and short steps to a front door set back above the pavement. You are still walking above the curve of land into which Penarth Dock was fitted and which was opened in 1865. A record of 4,660,648 tons of coal were exported in 1913. General cargoes were handled on the far side, but both sides of the dock had coaling staithes and some stone piers remain. There were four moveable steel tips on the far side of the basin, and it was claimed that they were so fast-loading that a boat could be turned round on one tide. Brunel's Great Britain — the first ocean-going propeller driven iron steamship — left from no. 9 tip in February 1886. This proved to be her last voyage. Caught in a hurricane off Cape Horn, she took shelter in the Falklands and lay there until 1970. She was then brought back to Pembroke Dock and then Bristol, and is on display in the dock where she was built. After the post-war decline in the coal trade the dock closed in 1936, but re-opened for war service with the Royal Engineers and the United States Navy, being especially busy in advance of D-Day. Climb to the end of Paget Road and turn right.

Continue walking along Harbour View Road. At the end of the last Harbour View block of flats is the **third viewpoint** of your walk. After about thirty yards, stand on the highest point of the path leading down to an adventure play area. On your right is the expanse of Cardiff, with the river Ely ahead of you winding its way inland. On the left of the river is the railway to Cardiff, and above it, on the curve, a modern block of flats in two-tone brick (Elizabethan Court) next to the oldest building in the area. Part of **Cogan Pill House** (now a Beefeater pub and restaurant called Barons Court) dates from 1554. In clear weather you can see the turrets of Castell Coch above the River Taff gap and, in the far distance, towards the hills of the Glamorganshire coalfield. It was this coalfield whose exports were the main reason for the construction of Penarth Dock near Cogan Pill, a tidal creek of the river Ely. Less than a mile ahead of you is the village of Llandough*. (The landmark saddle-backed tower of **St Dochdwy's Church** is to the left of the former 18th-century farmhouse of Great House Farm, now demolished, the site of a Celtic monastery. The remains of a Roman villa were discovered near there during house-building in 1979. The church is a Grade II listed building, dating from the

Lavernock cliff walk, looking back to Penarth -
Terry Breverton

12th century and within the grounds stands an ancient monument, the **Irbic Cross** in the form of a Celtic Cross, with the cross-head vanished.)

Towards your left Andrew Road rises from Penarth Leisure Centre in Cogan towards Dinas Powys. Further to your left is the estate built on the sloping fields of Cornerswell Farm. On your extreme left, above the site of two former brickyards in Cogan, are Tennyson Road, Kipling Close and the other *'poets corner'* streets of Penarth. Retrace your steps as far as the first gap (after flats 65-68). Turn right and after about sixty yards follow the paved path bearing left. Then, after making two sharp right turns down the steps, enter Hill Terrace. Cross the road to the right of Holy Nativity Church (opened 1894) and walk up Windsor Road. Pass the Police Station (1864) and cross the bottom of High Street. Monty Smith, at the junction with Railway Terrace on your right, has premises adapted from the Windsor Kinema.

Cross the bottom of Arcot Street. Several roads in Penarth commemorate a local link with the Clive of India family, for instance Cawnpore Road, Clive Crescent, Plassey Street, Ludlow Street and Paget Road). **Windsor Road** was originally residential, but towards the turn of the century a 'town centre' was created with shop conversions. The use of the houses' front garden space achieved projecting shop fronts without sacrificing a wide pavement. The original 19th-century upper floors remain clearly visible. Notice, for instance, the ornate roofs and embellishments above David Morgan, Olivers and Lo-cost. The Solomon Andrews horse buses for Cardiff left opposite from the side of the St Fagan pub. You have now returned to the town centre roundabout where the walk began. In Plassey Street is the fine building of the Welsh-speaking Bethel Welsh Independent Chapel.

*If you walk up to **Llandough Church**, you will find the Celtic Cross of Irbic in the churchyard. The llan of Llandough was founded by St Cyngar in the 5th century, on a Roman site, like so many of the early Welsh churches. His feast days were November 7th and 27th, but March 7th at Llangefni and May 12th in Brittany. He was also known as 'Dochdwy', the teacher, from the Latin Doccuinus, and this is the origin of Landough. The ten feet high pillar **Irbic Cross** is similar to one at Llandaff, and it is elaborately carved out of Sutton stone from the ancient quarry near Ogmore.

50

There are figures of people on all four panels of the rectangular pedestal, but the cross-head has disappeared. Llandough was a 'clas', or mother which grew into a noted monastery, but was eclipsed eventually by the spiritual growth of Llancarfan and Llanilltud Fawr, and the political growth of Llandaff. The present church dates from its rebuilding in 1866, when the old medieval church was dismantled and re-erected as St James at Leckwith. Alongside St Dochdwy's was Great House Farm, scandalously demolished despite a great petition in 1974. It was on the site of the Celtic monastery, and underneath its floor was found the body of a soldier and his horse, with the visor and lance given to the Museum of Wales. The ancient farmhouse was eventually demolished on the orders of the BP Property Fund, despite doubts about their legal rights. Farm visitors could see the cheese drying room hollowed into rock, and how cheese, butter, milk and dried pork were prepared. Wool was sent from the farm to the old Leckwith Hill Woollen Mill. Part of the purpose of a book like this is to make people care enough, not to let such financially-motivated vandalism happen again. What is lost, is lost forever.

Cyngar's foundation at 'Llangenys' in Glamorgan is probably Llandough-juxta-Cardiff, formerly known as Bangor Cyngar and Bangor Dochau. In 1979, the Glamorgan-Gwent Archaeology Trust undertook emergency excavations at Llandough, uncovering a substantial Romano-British villa, with evidence of 'Dark Age' activity. The site was then used as a monastic grange in the Middle Ages. Originally a late Iron Age farmstead with a defensive ditch and round timber huts, the Roman villa was constructed around 120-130 AD. In the early 3rd century it was extended and an elaborate bath complex was added. The iron collars that connected the wooden hot water pipes were still intact. By the middle to late 4th century it had fallen out of use and was used as a burial ground. This was probably Cyngar's monastic site – many other early saints are associated with Roman sites as the local Roman-British nobility took them over. Part of the villa was still standing in the 13th and 14th centuries, and a medieval dovecot was also found in the buildings. This exciting complex is now covered by a series of identical boxes known as modern housing. Archaeologists, with very limited funds, were only allowed eight weeks to excavate the site before the bulldozers charged in. There was also a British camp to the south-east of the Church, within 400 yards of which hundreds of human bones were discovered, probably denoting a battle between the native Welsh and the Norman settlers here. This author believes that there was a castle at Landough at some time, which has probably been built over.

Note: **PENARTH TOWN TRAIL 3 - 'DOCK TOWN' (from the Penarth Historical Society) is available at the Penarth Tourist Information Centre on the Esplanade.**

WALKS IN AND AROUND DINAS POWYS

This is an ancient site, associated with Arthur and the kings of Glamorgan and Gwent. The **Iron Age Fort** at Cwm George has earthworks from the Dark Ages, and the nearby castle was possibly the final stronghold of Iestyn ap Gwrgan, the last Prince of Glamorgan, who was defeated by Robert Fitzhamon's Norman invaders. **Dinas Powys Castle** in its current form dates back to 1190. There is a path from Letton's Way near St Peter's Church in Mill Road, up to the castle on its right-hand side. This castle site was used by a succession of settlers or invaders over the centuries. One end of the hill had been fortified in the early Christian period by a bank and ditch dating from the 5th to the 7th century. Arthur is associated with the area at this time, and rich pottery finds from these times have been excavated. In the Norman period a new bank and ditch were added The entrance at Dinas Powys Castle was on the north-west side, with a timber gate at the end of the passage. It may have been Iestyn ap Gwrgan who refortified the site in the wake of William's conquest of England. The castle was strengthened later by the addition of banks and ditches, now forming a formidable stronghold. This was probably carried out by the Normans as they cut through the southern Vale in the early 12th century. The castle has recently been bought privately. Although still known to 'locals' as the Village, Dinas Powys is the fourth largest community in the Vale of Glamorgan with a population of 8,790. Dinas means fortress or stronghold.

The parish **Church of St Andrew's** dates from the 12th century. It was originally a Celtic Church, with the first stone church being erected in 1040. The tower was added in 1400. The population of Dinas was static at about 300-400 until the second half of the 19th century, when there was an influx into this thriving rural community, including a big contingent from the West Country. The small green in the centre of the village is known as the **Twyn**, and the War Memorial was built in 1935. There are three old pubs near the green, The Star, The Cross Keys and The Three Horseshoes The latter was the home of Dewi Wyn o Essyllt, the *'White Bard'*, who is

St. Andrews Church - Cathy Crompton

commemorated in St Andrews Churchyard. His is the pink marble pillar inscribed in Welsh, one of very the few Welsh dedications at this lovely church. **The Common** is a popular recreation area, and home to Dinas Powys Rugby Club. There is an annual **Dickensian Fair** in early December.

St Andras was feasted on October 1st and 2nd locally, and he was the 6th - 7th century founder of the parish church of Dinas Powys, which is situated a mile west of the Common at St Andrews Major, on the lane to Wenvoe. He was the son of Rhain Dremrudd ap Brychan and brother of St Nefydd. (Presteigne used to be called

Llanandras after him). Llandow is in the parish of St Andrew's Minor in Glamorgan, about fifteen miles west of Dinas Powys. The font of the nearby ruined church of St Andrew (Andras) is in Llandow church, just a half mile away, and this place was formerly called Llanandras, like Presteigne. This saint is virtually forgotten, but his Feast Week could easily be restarted in Dinas Powys in the first week of October. The author's 'The Book of Welsh Saints' gives plans for reinstituting feast days and weeks across Wales for its 900 saints, for year-around economic and cultural regeneration. The present St Andrew's Major Church was probably built in the 13th century by the de Sumeri family.

WALK 23 - DINAS POWYS - MICHAELSTONE-LE-PIT

Not suitable for wheel-chairs or push-chairs - plenty of stiles - about 5 miles (8 km).

The walk takes in a delightful wooded ravine, a staircase of weirs, agricultural land (but beware of some very muddy patches), a brief contact with a golf course and passes near the ruined Norman castle, an Iron-Age settlement and an old Manorial Mill. Part of the route is a much used circular walk, well-waymarked for most of its route. A short cut can be made to reduce the distance walked by about 1.5 miles.

Park near **St. Peter's Church** in Dinas Powys, and head off Mill Lane into Heol y Cawl (Broth Lane). Walk up the steep lane, pass Ebenezer Church shortly, then turn right into Highwalls Road, which leads to Dinas Powys Golf Club and car park. Go to the rear of the clubhouse and at the first tee turn right, and follow the hedge as it turns left around the green. In about 50 yards, at a golf club notice, turn right, over a stile to descend via 2 more stiles in quick succession, to the entrance to **Cwm George**, a wooded ravine.

Turn left to enter the valley, via kissing gate/field gate and walk past a row of beech trees on a wide track. In about 500 yards, towards the western end of the cwm, opposite a steep limestone cliff and on top of the wooded hill to the right of the track, is the site of an **Iron Age Hill Fort** and settlement whose defensive banks are quite well defined and worth exploring. The wood here is called Coed Clwyd Gwyn (White Gate Wood). Walking on up the slight incline (ignoring the stile to the right) go through a stile/gate to follow the old **Cwrt yr Ala** estate driveway through cultivated land with a fence to the left. **Michaelstone le Pit** can be seen to the right and Leckwith Hill beyond. **Leckwith** is probably a corruption of Llechwedd, meaning slope or hillside, and there are plenty of walks in its woods, with wonderful views over Cardiff and the Channel. In Michaelstone, **St Michael and All the Angels' Church** dates from 1100. Cross a second stile in 150 yards and a further stile/gate after the same distance to reach the road, via a bridge crossing the Wrinstone Brook. At the road turn left and walk for 150 yards to reach, on your left, a kissing gate entrance to a series of weirs known locally as **Salmon Leaps**. There is a sign, 'Private. No Fishing' but there is a right of way throughout. Go through the gate and follow a clear waymarked path alongside the man-made weirs, part of the Cwrt yr Ala estate. The house (private) lies above the rise to the right.

Cross a stile into a wood in 400 yards and follow the path as it ascends briefly and then turns slightly left before continuing ahead, into an initially denser part of the wood. Follow the clear path which borders the Wrinstone Brook on the left for about

Lavernock Church - Cathy Crompton

600 yards until the path rises to leave the wood at a stile leading into a small meadow. Turn left from the stile and walk to another easily seen stile. Cross the stile and turn right along the concreted driveway of **Wrinstone Farm** with Wrinstone House behind you. Once beyond the short driveway entrance turn right onto a wide stony track. In 400 yards, just beyond 2 pairs of adjoining wooden electricity line poles, turn right onto a similar track going east. As you do, you find yourself almost at the top of the hill. Look back and enjoy the views of Wenvoe village and its woods and hills. This track soon descends in winding fashion to join, in 600 yards, the unsurfaced road which links Michaelstone le Pit with **Caerau** (and its Iron Age Fort, and medieval church and Norman castle) to the north. At this road however, turn right and walk 60 yards to a stile on the left opposite a field gate. *(At this point the walk could be reduced by about 1.5 miles by walking further along the road to pass the entrance to Salmon Leaps to rejoin the stile/gate, opposite the driveway to Bullcroft Farm, which allows one to cross the footbridge over Wrinstone Brook and rejoin the walk at the italicised note later in this text).*

If you are still set on doing the longer walk go over the stile and continue, via a second stile opposite, diagonally right across the field to a third stile in the right hand hedge, near a gate. Cross this stile into the field on your right, turn left and walk down, crossing the field diagonally right to another stile, soon seen in the facing hedge. Go over this stile and its attendant metal footbridge. Look for a wire fence 60 yards opposite (there is no recognisable stile), cross it and look for another fence slightly to the right in 60 yards. Cross the stile here and follow uphill the hedge on your left (this is Coed y Ddylluan Wood - 'Tylluan' means 'Owl') to reach another stile in 100 yards. After crossing this stile look for a rustic stile in the facing hedge. Having crossed this stile and with the hedge to your left, walk to another in 200 yards in the hedge ahead. Cross this stile and walk to a visible barn to the right with the hedge on the right. With the barn to your right go through a facing gate.

Turn diagonally right to a nearby, waymarked stile and cross to walk immediately across the metalled road into the driveway of facing cottage. The public footpath is not marked but goes to the left of the cottage, then through the back garden and out via a wicket gate into a field. The lady of the cottage is very pleasant and provided that you respect her privacy by quickly, carefully and quietly traversing her property, she will not object. Follow the hedge downhill to the left and cross a stile to reach yet another stile and footbridge in 50 yards in the left hand hedge.

Having crossed this bridge, walk diagonally over the field. Follow the line of the telegraph poles, past a small clump of trees towards the easily seen cluster of buildings which constitute Home Farm. The gateway is normally extremely muddy.

Walk through the farmyard to the gate on the right which leads onto the road. Turn left then immediately right to a group of former forestry houses. Turn sharp right onto a track fronting some of these houses. In 15 yards turn left onto a narrow but clear path, between the hedges of 2 adjacent houses. Cross the stile/gate at the end of this path into a field. Turn slightly right and follow a wide green sward to a stile/gate which leads onto the road, ignoring the stile and footbridge seen soon in the field to the left.

Turn left and walk 150 yards along the road to reach the gate leading to the footbridge over the **Wrinstone Brook** crossed earlier in the walk. (*This is the point where the earlier shortcut is noted*). Retrace your steps to the first stile/gate, do not cross the stile but walk to the left along a clear track with a fence/hedge at each side to reach another stile/gate shortly. Cross this stile and with the hedge to the right walk to another in 500 yards. When over this stile keep the hedge to the right to reach another stile in 350 yards which leads onto a track (Cwm Drive). Go over the track onto a path, then in 20 yards over/under a sort of stile. The path is bordered by a fence on the left and a ditch on the right. Pass commercial glasshouses on your right to reach a stile/gate in in 250 yards. To the right, and above on the hill, lie the hidden ruins of **Dinas Powys Castle** dating back to 1190. (The site can be visited, but care must be taken, from Lettons Way, near your start point). Cross the stile to walk the last 100 yards back to the start point. (On the right, beyond the Cadoxton River, a glimpse can be had of the **Manorial Mill** (c.1426), now a private residence. The stream turned part of an extensive mill leet, since dried up, following the disuse of the mill.

WALK 24 - DINAS POWYS - LAVERNOCK

About 5 miles (8 km). This walk passes Old Cogan Church (St. Peters), Old Cogan Hall and takes in part of the Cosmeston Countryside Park at Lavernock. The park has an information centre, a cafeteria and a very authentic medieval village, all open every day. Park in Dinas Powys. The Cardiff Road passes through the village towards Barry. Coming from Cardiff, there are traffic lights, and on your left Dinas Powys Infants School. Murch Road is this road, past the school, off Cardiff Road.

Walk up Murch Road, then into Murch Crescent ahead for 800 yards to pass St Cyres Comprehensive School on your right and then walk along a surfaced lane ahead. Follow this lane to its exit into Sully Road at a T-junction. Turn left then in 200 yards turn right into road leading to **Old Cogan Church** and then **Old Cogan Hall** where one joins a wide track which leads into **Cosmeston Country Park**. Old Cogan Church has Saxon herringbone stonework.

In 800 yards look for wide grassy areas on both sides of the track

Dinas Powys Castle - Cathy Crompton

with a stile and gate in each. Take the left one and descend a short slope to a stile by a gate. Cross the stile and walk diagonally right, going down and back up a fold in the ground to reach a narrow path, which roughly follows a stoned surface water drain on the left. Aim for a clearly visible stile which leads to a wide path around the park's lake. Turn left and follow this path clockwise around the lake passing the park entrance onto a wooden boardwalk.

In 130 yards take a right fork on the boardwalk to reach a service road dividing the lake. Turn left and walk to 2 stiles facing each other, just beyond the road leading to the mediaeval village. Take the right hand stile, and with hedge to your right walk through the narrower of 2 gaps in the facing hedge into a second, inclined field. Bear slightly left and walk up the slope to reach a stile in the hedge on the left. Go over the stile and over another immediately on the right. Walk right keeping just below the mound on the left to reach a gate. Go through the gate, and with the hedge to your left, walk to a clearly seen barn. Go to the right of the barn to a stile leading to the junction of Cog Road and Sully Road.

Turn right and walk along the Sully Road for 450 yards to a single cottage on the left. Just beyond the cottage (**Cog Bridge**), go through the gate on the left and walk diagonally right heading for the corner of the field. Walk through a clear gap in the facing hedge and turn left to the stile ahead. Cross the stile and walk up a short incline to a second stile ahead. Over this stile and with the hedge to your left, go to another stile which leads into a small copse. Go through the copse on a clear path, which leads into a field with a ditch across the path. Keeping the hedge on your left, cross the ditch and then a clearly visible fence. Once over this fence (or nearby gate), you reach another part fence. Cross this, or go around it, to reach a stile in the left corner which leads onto **Cross Common Road**.

Turn left, pass a bungalow on the right, and, at the left hand bend in road turn right into a driveway. Leave the driveway by going onto a grassy track on the left which runs between a hedge and a line of trees. Follow the clear path, descend and rise from a hollow, crossing an old mineral line. Keep to the clearly defined track, which descends through a small wood to reach the Murch housing estate. Turn right along Longmeadow Drive and walk to a small shopping centre. Turn left at the junction with Murch Road and follow this road to the traffic lights at the junction with the Cardiff-Barry Road.

WALKS IN AND AROUND SULLY AND COSMESTON

Sully Island - Cathy Crompton

Sully is a long, narrow village, spread along the shore of the Bristol Channel between Penarth and Barry, seven miles from Cardiff. The beach at Sully is mainly rock and pebble with sand at the low water line. A unique feature is **Sully Island**, which is connected to the mainland by a rocky causeway, which is only uncovered at low tide. The currents around the causeway are treacherous as the sea attacks the island from the Bristol Channel. On the opposite side of the Channel is the Somerset coastal town of Watchet, and out in the Channel are the two islands of Steep Holm and Flat Holm. Steep Holm is a bird sanctuary and Flat Holm is designated as a nature reserve. Although Sully is largely a relatively modern village, the area around the parish church of **St. John the Baptist** is obviously much older. The Romans certainly passed through Sully, although they left few traces - no roads or encampments. However, a burial on Sully Moors around 300 AD which included Roman coins indicates that Romans were an influence on the area. The Norsemen also formed settlements in the area from the first half of the 9th century. Many local place names are of Scandinavian origin and there are remains of a Danish fort or camp on Sully Island.

With the Norman conquest, Reginald de Sully obtained the Manor of Sully around 1093. Little is known of him, other than that he probably came over with William the Conqueror from France, and was given large estates in Devon. The present church dates from around this time and was dedicated to St. John the Baptist. The current church fabric dates from around 1426. By the middle of the 13th century the de Sully family held Sully, Wenvoe and Llanmaes. Reginald built **Sully Castle** which was the smallest castle in Glamorgan. It occupied an area behind the church of about half an acre which was until recently still called Castle Wood, but has been built upon, with the development called Rookery Nook. Occupation of the main castle ceased around the mid-14th century, probably as a result of the extinction of the de Sully family. Some traces still remain in

Sully Beach - Cathy Crompton

St John's churchyard. About 100 yards west of the church is the site of the original 13th century village, and north of **Sully Inn** are the remains of a **medieval moated manor house.** Sully was for centuries a busy trading port, but silted up. There are several lime kilns in the area, including one on Ashby Road, and the remains of a 17th century mill can be seen at **Old Mill House** on Cog Road.

Old Sully House stood near 'The Captain's Wife' pub but was demolished. In the 19th century the community was almost entirely agricultural and the population was between 150 and 200. At Sully, the 19th century English vicar, a W.D. Conybeare, was responsible for substituting the English language for Welsh in the services, although Welsh was the predominant language of the parish. Characters at this time were known as Nan y Gof Gwyllt (Mad Nancy, *'a wild, swearing, bitter tongued sort of woman'* according to William Thomas), and Howel yr Aur (Howel the Gold). This language suppression was repeated all through Wales in the nineteenth century, supported by the heinous use of the *'Welsh Not'* in schools. By 1920 the population had increased to 550, but in the last 40 years Sully has grown substantially and is now mainly a dormitory suburb of Cardiff, with a population of around 5,000. At Swanbridge, opposite Sully Island, **The Captain's Wife** has altered considerably for the worse since it became a pub around 1978, and is now owned by a chain - a cross between a burger bar and a children's playground, unfortunately. The pub stands near the site of Old Sully House, and was tenanted by a sea captain who decided to take his wife on board ship with him. At sea she died, but the captain hid her death from the crew, putting her body into a box. They believed that a corpse on board was even more unlucky than a woman. Arriving back at Sully, he secretly rowed the box at night to his house, and hid it so that a coffin could be made for a decent funeral. When the coffin arrived, the body had disappeared, and she haunted the site dressed in black. When the inn was being built, the skeleton of a woman was found buried in the woods, given a Christian burial, and the ghost vanished.

WALK 25 - LAVERNOCK TO SULLY ISLAND VIA ST MARY'S WELL BAY
WALK E OF THE SEASCAPE TRAIL

Lavernock Point - Terry Breverton

About 3 miles (5 km) round trip - not suitable for push-chairs or wheelchairs. On the B4267 heading from Penarth to Sully, pass Cosmeston Country Park on your right and turn next left down a narrow lane towards Lavernock Point. There is Parking on your left, before the church. The path down from the church will lead you back along the coast to Penarth to the east. From Lavernock Point, you can access the beach via a steep path, and carry on west at low water to St

Mary's Well Bay. Once you round Lavernock Point, the walking across the beach is easier, as there is more sand, and stone 'pavements' containing fossils.

Head back up the road from the car-park towards the Marconi Club and Holiday Home site, and you can access the **Lavernock Point SSSI** of 15 acres by the kissing gate into the field, just north of and adjacent to the Marconi Inn entrance. Cross a stile through an gap in a hedge on

Lavernock Beach - Terry Breverton

your left. The public footpath runs through the reserve. Another three stiles then give access to a fenced paddocked area. There is an inland unimproved meadow and a cliff-top field of limestone grassland and scrub. Plant species include Yellow-wort, Dyer's Greenweed, Adder's-Tongue Fern, Cowslip, Common Twayblade, Common Spotted-Orchid, Bee Orchid and Greater Butterfly-Orchid. There are many species of butterfly, and Yellow Wagtails, Firecrest, Brambling and Redpoll can be seen at certain times of the year. From Lavernock Point, there can be seen unusual vagrant sea-birds, such as Manx Shearwaters, Skuas, Common Scoter and terns.

Heading west on the footpath, you will see the substantial remains of a World War II camp. The path now leads west along the coast, to a World War II Lookout Post on the point overlooking St Mary's Well Bay. The path now used to run along the southern edge of the Caravan Park, but has tumbled into the sea - there is no way

through to the beach, unless you can scramble down the cliffs (which are very wet in winter), just inland from the lookout post. Unless you can access the beach, the walk ends here. From **St Mary's Well Bay**, one used to be able to access St Mary's Well Bay Road, near Ball Rock and **Ball Bay**, and follow the coast road past Swanbridge House, alongside **Swanbridge Bay**. However, the access lane is now dangerous and blocked off. If you can get onto St Mary's Well Bay,

St. Mary's Well Bay - Terry Breverton

fishermen have tied an orange rope to help you access the damaged footpath leading to Swanbridge Road. However, you take this route at your own risk. Perhaps the Vale council can repair this access in the future.

The three bays, particularly St Mary's Well Bay, used to be far more sandy in the past. The road at Swanbridge is blocked off to cars, where it has eroded in the past,

Lavernock WWII camp - Terry Breverton

and you now enter The Captain's Wife car-park which is opposite Sully Island. The sea defences here are 'private', and unsightly. From here, you can walk up the lane from Swanbridge into Sully Village, or carry on walking towards **Bendricks Rock**. One can access Ball Bay and adjoining Swanbridge Bay by scrambling across the foreshore rocks, but it is dangerous. It is difficult to see how the coastal path can be reinstituted along here. An alternative route from Lavernock to Swanbridge is to take the lane north from Lavernock Church, past the Marconi Inn, and turn left on the footpath that leads through Sutton Farm. Marked on the OS maps, this joins up with the Swanbridge Road. Alternatively, carry on up to the main road, turn left and follow the verge until the next left turn, Swanbridge Road. The old Golden Hind pub on Swanbridge Road, just after the caravan park, is being converted to luxury flats. Just past this is the old footpath to the beach, which leads to the orange rope mentioned above. You can see a ruined house in the woods on your left. This has beach access but is private property, and seems to be in the process of renovation. When you walk past the wonderfully situated Swanbridge House, you will see that the old Swanbridge Farm has been converted to luxury houses. Please do not cross to **Sully Island** if the tide is coming in. If you see people crossing they are probably fishermen intending to stay on the island for several hours. If in doubt, do not cross. The best time is probably as the sea is just uncovering the causeway, but it is quite slippery. Take care also on the Island - there are steep cliffs on its north

Lavernock Point WWII fortification - Terry Breverton

side. Sometimes you can sit on the sea wall, and watch the tide coming in from the east hitting the tide coming in from the west, and forming remarkable patterns of currents and wave forms.

WALK 26 - COSMESTON TO SULLY CIRCUIT (from Cardiff Ramblers)

This takes about 4 hours at a slowish pace, and is about 3.5 miles (5.5 km). Instead of Cosmeston Lakes car-park, you can also park near St John the Baptist's medieval church in Sully to begin this walk. A level, easy walk, but farm gateways will be very muddy after rain, with boots definitely required.

Go from Cosmeston car park to the nearest lakeside. Turn left and take the boardwalk passing behind the cafe and where the boardwalk forks, go left. Shortly after the end of the boardwalk, the path meets a wide cross track. There are views over the second lake from here. Go left, following the track for 100 yards, and then go over stile on your right with footpath sign.

Walk half-left uphill, keeping just to the right of some old walls. Then go through a gateway ahead at a field corner. Keep to the left edge of the field as it curves to the right and then to the left. There are views on the right over **Cosmeston Lakes**. Look out for a partly hidden stile on the left, about 100 yards before the fence at the end of field. Go over the stile to your left, then immediately turn and go over a second stile/old gate, which brings you into corner of next field.

Now head diagonally left uphill towards some small hillocks on the skyline. Pass to the right of these. Two gates are now ahead. Go through the one on the right. Then keeping to the left field edge, walk to the right of the barns and leave the farm at a stile in the corner of a field, near the farmhouse. Walk down the farm entrance drive

to the road. Cross to the road opposite, sign-posted 'Sully-Barry'. Walk this road for about 500 yards towards Sully. There is no footpath, so take care, especially on bends. Continue on this road, **Cog Road**, through the village for about 750 yards, ignoring side turns. Look out for **Sully Inn** on the left, and 50 yards beyond keep to the left hand pavement, as it curves left in front of the medieval church. Walk past the bus shelter and, 50 yards beyond it, cross the road

Sully Church - Cathy Crompton

and take a signed footpath at a kissing gate. Take this path to **sea front**.

Go left over the shingle beach in front of houses, soon joining a coastal path, near an old boat slip-way. The attractive view ahead now shows three islands; from the left, **Flat Holm, Sully Island (Ynys Sili)** and **Steep Holm**. Keep to the coast path for about a mile as, on the landward side, you pass houses, sports-field, boatyard and more houses. A large sports-field is ahead. Keep to the perimeter path of this, above the beach. Some 50 yards before the fenced caravan park look out for large wooden post and remains of an old metal stile/gate on your seaward (right) side. Go right and down steps to the beach. Keeping to the left, walk for 200 yards over fairly flat, but broken and in parts slippery, rock and then go up the stone steps to a cafe and **Swanbridge** car park/promenade. (*Please note that if the tide is high and it is preferable to avoid this beach section, then keep to the sports field path, pass to the left of the caravan park and join the road where fence ends. Go right and then down the road to Swanbridge.*)

It is possible to walk over to **Sully Island (Ynys Sili)** from here at low tide. But check tide times carefully, as the island is usually only accessible for about 2-3 hours either side of low water, and the incoming tide is very dangerous. You can easily be cut off from the mainland for 8 hours by the vicious tidal race. There are several rare plants on the island, such as bee orchid, adders-tongue and sea spleenwort. On the east one can see the ramparts of a small **Iron Age Fort**, known locally as the 'Danish', or **'Saxon Fort'**, from the time when pagan invaders were trapped here in 650, when their ships were burnt. Roman coins have been found on the island, notably a hoard of gold and silver in 1899. It is popular for fishing off the southern rocks, and conger eel, silver eel, bass, cod, whiting, dogfish, pouting and thornback ray can be caught.

Walk east across the car park, keeping to the coast until you reach a small gateway which takes you onto the coastal road. Go up, keeping to this road for about 1.5 miles to the B4267 Penarth-Sully road. Cross this road to the track opposite, and there are **Cosmeston Park** notices on gate. Walk on and the recreated **mediaeval village** soon appears on the right. Take the metalled lane on your right, signed 'to the village', and then, unless you want to visit the village, go left at the village entrance, over the bridge and boardwalk to return to the car park. If you are enjoying your walk, it may be easily extended by use of the paths around both lakes. Refreshments are usually available at cafes at Cosmeston and Swanbridge, and inns at Sully and Swanbridge.

WALK 27 - COSMESTON TO OLD COGAN TO PENARTH (similar to COSMESTON LAKES TO DINAS POWYS TO SULLY CIRCULAR which is in the Valeways leaflet)

7 miles (12 km), about 2.5 hours - this route can be very wet in winter, across Sully Moors. More information is given on Cosmeston in the next walk. This Ramblers Walk skirts the three main settlements of the Eastern Vale - Penarth, Sully and Dinas Powys. It starts and finishes at splendid Cosmeston Lakes Country Park, although you can park at other places like Sully to start the walk. Although never far from pubs, cafes and villages, the route meanders through tranquil farmland. Boots are advised on this route, as parts can get wet and muddy - especially on Sully Moor, which is prone to winter flooding. The whole of the Vale of Glamorgan is covered by Ordnance Survey Explorer Map 151 (Cardiff and Bridgend, 1:25,000 scale) and you may find this helpful. The Penarth Society's Town Trail leaflets can be purchased from the Town Council offices at West House, Stanwell Road. George Thomas' book 'Around Old Dinas Powys' provides both a history and some interesting walks in the area

Cosmeston Medieval Village - Cathy Crompton

The desolate wasteland of the former Downswood Quarry, which closed in 1970 after 80

Cosmeston Lakes - Cathy Crompton

years' operations, was transformed into a 210-acre country park by the Vale of Glamorgan Council. On its fringe lies one of South Wales' most unusual tourist attractions - **Cosmeston Medieval Village**. This is a careful reconstruction of how the hamlet would have been in 1320, before plague and climate change left it deserted. In nearby fields, the route passes a medieval dovecot which originally housed 1,000 birds to provide meat and eggs for the Lord of the Manor's table. Little remains of **Sully Castle**, behind the hospitable Sully Inn (or of a moated manor house to the north) but the nearby church, **St John's**, dates back to the 13th century. It is hard to believe that this pleasant village was once a busy port trading cattle and pigs with Ireland - and a reputed haunt of smugglers. A short diversion from the route takes you to **Dinas Powys**, with good pubs and a history disappearing into the mists of time. The Iron Age fort at Cwm George has links with the Arthur legend and was the final fortress of Iestyn ap Gwrgan, last of the Princes of Glamorgan. The picturesque ruin of Dinas Powys Castle dates back to Norman times. On the walk back to Cosmeston, spare time, if you can, to visit peaceful **St Peter's Church**, Old Cogan - possibly the oldest standing church in Glamorgan. Its herringbone masonry dates it back to Saxon times. The western part of the nave and the south porch are 16th century. Listed Grade II, it was built around 1100 on the site of an earlier church. It was restored by the 3rd Marquis of Bute in 1894. A further diversion from here can take you into Penarth itself - a result of the Victorian coal-boom, when rich Edwardians adopted it as their favourite escape from the Cardiff grime. Boasting a century-old pier, fine parks, cafes, pubs, and even its own Bullmastiff Brewery, the town will be welcoming many more visitors when the walk from Cardiff Bay Barrage opens shortly.

Start behind the Cosmeston visitor centre, and bear left along the boardwalk, keeping to the left at the fork. Turn left at the end. As you go past **Cosmeston Medieval Village**, you will see a Public Footpath sign on your right. Cross the stile and bear diagonally left across the field - keeping to the right of the excavated **medieval dovecote**. Take your time on this section of the walk - the ground is very uneven. As you walk up the rise, there are pleasant views in every direction. Go through the gap into the next field, then follow the hedge. After a few hundred yards, take the double stile through the hedge. Cross the field diagonally, just below the remains of the quarry on the crest of the hill. Go through the gate and follow the farm-track. Skirt to the right of the barn and cross the stile, and pass through the farm gates. Cross the triangle past the recently-restored **Cog Well** and follow Cog Road to Sully - passing the old **Cog Farm**, which has recently been converted into a number of luxury dwellings. The original farmhouse was built in 1813-1815 as a model farm to replace seven local farms. Motorists drive fast along this narrow road, so keep well into the right-hand side. About 50 yards before the Sully Inn, turn right down Ashby Road. Take the stile on the left and head across the field to a distant second stile, which is slightly to the right of the gate. Cross the little stone bridge, then bear diagonally to the right to a more substantial bridge. After crossing it, bear slightly to the left diagonally across the field, to the waymarker post. Walk parallel to the watercourse, to the stile leading to the road. Turn right along the road-side ditch to 10 yards beyond the 'sharp bend' sign. Clamber up the bank and cross the busy main road with great care, to the little bridge opposite.

Turn right over the stile and follow the water-course across a number of stiles. After a section of track between hedges, the path emerges at the edge of the playing fields. *(NB: You can divert to **Dinas Powys** from here by continuing alongside the playing-fields until you emerge on the main road, then turning left, crossing the railway-bridge, and taking the left-hand turning immediately afterwards into the village, where there are pubs and other amenities).* From the playing-fields, go through the gate, cross the main road at the refuge, and turn right along the main road for about 100 yards. Turn left down the (signed) **Cog Moors** Water Treatment Road access road. A few hundred yards on the left, take the stile and walk

Lavernock Beach - Terry Breverton

up the hill. Turn right after the stile and follow the hedge to the waymarker post. Facing the post, strike out across the field at 'five to the hour' into a sort of 'ear' coming from the left corner of the field. Follow the 'ear' to a stile at its top end. Walk down the path to the right through the thicket into a field. Cross this and go through a narrow gap, where you will see the rear of a waymarker. Cross directly over the next four narrow fields before going over a stile into a yard and over a further stile onto Cross Common Road.

Turn right and follow the road around a couple of bends - ignoring the Public Footpath on the right. Just past a right-angled bend (and before a bungalow called The Breeches), the path cuts off to the left through open gates. Follow it between the hedges and along the left-hand side of the field and through the middle of the next, narrow, field to the stile. Continue along the path over the next stile and on up the lane. At the Sully Road cross-roads, turn left, then take the next turning right. Walk past the ancient **St Peter's Church** and **Old Cogan Hall Farm**. Follow the main track down through Cosmeston Lakes Country Park. Skirt to the left of the main lake to your starting-point. *(If you want to link this walk to Penarth, just beyond Old Cogan Hall Farm, a path doubles back behind the farm to your left. If you wish to cut through to Penarth, follow this and cross the field to Cedar Way. You can then cross Redlands Road/Lavernock Road and you can follow either Cornerswell Road or Stanwell Road into the town.)*

WALK 28 - COSMESTON NATURE TRAIL - SHORT WALK (from the Cosmeston Lakes - Guide to Country Walks leaflet)

Around a mile (1.5 km), about 45 minutes of easy walking without stopping. Suitable for wheelchair users, families with pushchairs and the elderly.

COSMESTON LAKES COUNTRY PARK - PARC GWLEDIG LLYNNOEDD COSMESTON

With a variety of habitats covering over 210 acres of land and water, 100 of which are designated a SSSI, the meandering wood-side and lakeside pathways of Cosmeston make a fine afternoon or morning stroll. The Downswood Quarry on this site supplied high-grade Liassic limestone to Penarth Cement Works, which operated from 1890 to 1970. Underground springs created the lakes and wetland here. The following walks are taken from a leaflet produced by the Vale of Glamorgan Council, but the author well remembers the fields of orchids between Old Cogan and Cosmeston, before the deserted quarries were made into a parkland. The park is just outside Penarth, on the 'low road' to that leads to Sully then Barry. Telephone 029 2070 1678 for any details of events during the year. Car parking and entry to the park is free, and there is a visitor centre, café and public conveniences. Nearly opposite the entrance are the old quarry offices, now turned into a pub. Parking and use of the park are free.

COSMESTON MEDIEVAL VILLAGE

This is sited on one of the largest medieval excavations in Wales, and has been reconstructed to show how the village existed in 1320. Cottages, barns, a bake-house and pig-sty have been built upon their original foundations. Established by the Norman knights, de Costentin, the settlement was hit by climatic change and the Bubonic and Pneumonic Plagues of the 14th century. Medieval re-enactments and fairs here are always a fun day out, where you can often ask a 14th-century 'doctor' his prescription for your ailments. Regular tours are held for a modest admission charge.

Start from the information panel next to the gate on the right of the toilet block, and turn left onto the boardwalk. This crosses a marshland full of birds and flowers. There are Reed Buntings here, and no less than six species of Warbler can be seen or heard in the summer. Yellow Flag Iris abounds, and the rare Greater Spearwort has established itself. In winter you may be lucky to 'flush out' a Snipe, and the extremely shy Water Rail may be spotted. There is a picnic area where you can watch the birds on the East Lake. There are grey squirrels about, which some people like, although this author is of the school of thought that

Old Cogan Church - Cathy Crompton

places them as *'rats with good PR'*. Turn right on the Main Path, and on your left there are observation points over the **West Conservation Lake**.

In the summer there are many species of Dragonfly and Damselfly hovering around. You can see Moorhen (black, bobbing, red beak), Coot (black, bigger, white beak) and Mallard Duck the year round. Goldeneye Duck and Pochard over-winter here. In the West Lake, swans are resident

The lookout, St. Mary's Well Bay - Terry Breverton

and build their nests every year. Great Crested Grebes can be seen diving. You may be lucky to see the spectacular Kingfisher perched on a ledge below the bridge looking for small fish. Carry on over the bridge between the lakes, and the hedge on either side contains Hawthorn, Blackthorn (with sloes in September), Elder, Hazel and Sycamore. These enable fauna such as Weasel, Fox, Common Shrew and Bank Vole to exist here.

Turn right after leaving the bridge, and follow the path around the **East Lake** passing Barbecue Sites and the Adventure Playground. Carry on around the lake until you reach a Conservation Area, fenced off to protect rare species. In Spring and Summer you can see here Primroses, Bee Orchids and Common Spotted Orchids. Walking on, you reach the commemorative stones at the end of your walk.

WALK 29 - COSMESTON BROOKSIDE RAMBLE

There is a leaflet available at the visitor centre for this walk, which is about a mile in length. It is essentially similar to the Shorter Walk above, but after looking at the remains of the **Dovecot**, do not carry on the main path. After the footbridge instead turn left over the stile and follow **Sully Brook** downstream. In winter you may see Redwing and Fieldfare, and Green Woodpeckers, Buzzard and Sparrowhawks are fairly common around here. Enter Cogan Wood past the fallen oak, and turn right on the main path until you take a left at a junction. You will see the West Conservation Lake, and you are back on the walk mentioned above.

WALK 30 - COSMESTON NATURE TRAIL - LONG WALK (from the Cosmeston Lakes - Guide to Country Walks leaflet)

3 miles (4.5 km), about 1.5 hours. Not suitable for wheelchairs or pushchairs.

Start at the information panel next to the gate on the right of the toilet block, and then turn left into the park, following the boardwalk across the **Marshland** area. In the summer months one can see Purple Loosestrife, Greater Spearwort and Southern March Orchid here, and later in the season the vivid yellow Fleabane or the pink Greater Willowherb, which both attract butterflies such as the Small Tortoiseshell or

Red Admiral. The boardwalk meets the Main Path, which leads you between the Western Conservation Lake and the Eastern Lake, north to Old Cogan. At this junction you have a wonderful view over the **Western Conservation Lake**.

Turn left on the Main Path and cross the wooden footbridge. On your left you will see the remains of the medieval **Dovecote** belonging to Cosmeston Manor. This originally housed 1000 birds to provide meat and eggs for the Lord of Cosmeston. Carry on westward along the path, and you will see many species of water fowl, including Dabchick, Tufted Duck, Heron, and in winter Gadwall and Wigeon. The path veers right and downwards and there is a small hollow on the left which floods for several months of the year. It is the habitat of Common and Palmate Newts. Carry on and a valley appears on your left. Walk up this valley, and in summer you will see Common Blue Butterflies on the yellow Birds-Foot Trefoil.

The small **Dragonfly Pond** is an SSSI because 13 species of Damselfly and Dragonfly breed there. Facing away from the Dragonfly Pond, walk up towards stone steps, heading to a stile over a wooden fence. The landscape now turns to a Limestone plateau, with a rich calcareous grassland, which is diverse in plant species. Here in season you may see feeding butterflies such as Small and Large Skippers, Speckled Wood and Peacock. Head straight ahead through Cogan Wood, which is mainly comprised of Hawthorn, Ash, Oak, Spindle and Elm. The woodland is managed, with glades opened up to allow flowers such as Bluebells, Red Campion and Lesser Celandine to thrive.

On meeting the gravelled path, follow it right until you exit the woodland, and go over the stile into **West Paddock**. Here there are rare grasses and flowers, such as the Bee Orchid and Southern Marsh Orchid. The paddock is grazed selectively to improve species diversity. Walking to your left towards the gate partitioning the paddocks, head for the stile. Cross over and turn right until you see a stile on the left. This leads you into **East Paddock**, which has Oxeye Daisy, Pyramidal Orchid and Common Spotted Orchid growing wild. It is the haunt of kestrels seeking voles, shrews and mice. Cross the paddock to the opposite stile and turn right, with the lakes in front of you. Walk alongside the Conservation Area, and past East Lake, then turn left on the gravelled path back to the main car park.

WALK 31 - SULLY ISLAND TO BENDRICKS ROCK
WALK F OF THE SEASCAPE TRAIL

Around 3.5 miles round trip (6 km). The beach is not suitable walking for those less agile, and the path towards Bendricks Rock can get quite muddy in winter.

Dinosaur footprints were found on the rocks (Sully Ledge Beach) heading west from Sully beach in 1979. The Bendricks, just east of Barry, South Wales, is the only known Upper Triassic dinosaur footprint site in Britain and the most extensive dinosaur trackway site in the country. Prior to 1996 all the trackways discovered both in the Bendicks and elsewhere in South Wales were of animals walking with a bipedal gait but in the autumn of that year a quadrupedal trackway was found, on the surface of a fallen block at the eastern end of the section, below high tide level. Due to the thickness of the bed in which the quadruped trackway was preserved, and the

Wrecked boat on Sully Island - Martin Green

problems that cutting and storing large slabs of footprints pose, the decision was taken to attempt to take a mould of the trackway in situ, from which permanent casts could be made. They are exhibited at the National Museum of Wales.

From **'The Captain's Wife'** pub car-park, you can either cross the foreshore past the caravan camp, and quickly pick up the path, or head on up the road from Swanbridge towards Sully, turning left into a field after the camp, and then walk south-west back to the official coastal path along Sully Bay. On your right you will then pass some houses fronting the sea, and after a few more minutes the path leads through trees, following the coast. You pass the old **Sully Hospital** on your right, disused for some years, and a beautiful building on an enviable site, which hopefully will be put to a use which does not involve resettling refugees. This is situated on **Hayes Point**, after which you will see **Bendricks Rock**. The path becomes fragmented here, due to wave action and lack of maintenance, and there is a broken slip-way. Bendricks is a popular place with anglers, and used to be a popular place for bathing, but has lost a great deal of sand over the last twenty years. Be careful of the mud where the re-routed Cadoxton River meets the sea. In front of you, heading into the sea off Black Rocks, is the **East Breakwater** of Barry Docks. On the road that runs parallel with the coastal path from Sully, Hayes Road, are the remains of an 1830 windmill. From Bendricks it is quite fiddly to get to Jackson's Bay, the next stage of the proposed Seascape Path.

WALKS IN AND AROUND BARRY

The author went to Cadoxton Infants and Junior School, and to Barry Grammar-Technical School for Boys, before leaving the area for thirty years. To return is to see a place that was rich, has been neglected, but is now climbing back to its former prosperity. The current Vale of Glamorgan Council has a plan to implement **interpretation boards** across the town, showing walks and points of interest,

Barry Old Harbour - Cathy Crompton

similar to the scheme that it placed in Penarth. The Town Hall, after around two sad decades of neglect, is to be restored, and the adjacent **King Square** made once more the focus of the town, with the awful red-brick fountains removed to enable market-stalls to set up and draw custom into the town. The 1906 Library will be upgraded and return to its location next to the Town Hall, again drawing people towards the natural town centre. A new road will cut across from Broad Street to ease access to **Barry Island**, which itself has undergone massive restoration to the promenade. The High Street Traders' Association has worked hard to make High Street and Broad Street an alternative shopping centre to Holton Road and King Square. The old Coastguard Station on the island will be renovated. The new **Barry Marina** has made the docks a facility rather than an eyesore. There have been major mistakes in the past, but the future seems brighter for Barry, as the fourth largest centre of population in Wales after Cardiff, Newport and Swansea.

Although Barry was recorded as an important port in 1276, the town as such really only came into existence with the docks built by David Davies of Llandinam to bypass Lord Bute's Cardiff Docks' monopoly of the coal trade. Between 1889 and 1914, the new railways from the valleys' coalfields to the new docks ensured that Barry grew exponentially. In 1913, the 11,000,000 tons of coal exported was a world record, for the export of coal from a single port. Before 1884, Tregatwg, Cadoxton, was the largest village, followed by what is now known as 'The Old Village' near Romilly Park, Merthyr Dyfan and a scattering of farmsteads such as Holton in between. In 1881, the population of Cadoxton was 303, and another 197 people were living in Barry, Merthyr Dyfan, part of Sully and Barry Island. In 1884, work began on Barry No. 1 Dock, building the causeway that united Barry Island with the mainland, and by the grim year of 1914 the population of Barry had risen to 38,000. Infill building, of many poor-quality council estates, since World War Two, has led to a very uneven standard of architecture in the town, and a rise in population to around 50,000 people. Little has been written on Barry in the past. In 1921, Thomas Ewbank and A.W. Storey of Cadoxton Boys' School wrote *'The Geography and History of Barry - with Welsh Folk Lore and Traditions.'* In 1954, Stan Awbery MP wrote *'Let Us Talk of Barry'*, a 104-

page booklet, and the author still retains his battered copy. Then in 1984, 'The Centenary Book', an excellent 496-page hardback, edited by Donald Moore and with contributions by local people, was published. It is this author's intention to write another book upon Barry, when time permits, within the next 3-4 years.

There was mass immigration into Barry when the docks were built - the author's great-grandfather walked with his family from Kent to find work, and his son married into the Hyatts, one of the old families living in Cadoxton for many years. Until around 1850, Welsh was the major language in these small communities, and the few Welsh names left in the area are all related to the former settlements. Porthkerry is a derivation from Porth-Ceri, the Gateway of Prince Ceri, referring to its importance as a port before landslips. Pencoedtre is the settlement at the top of the wood, north of Tregatwg, the place of St Cadog. Cadoxton-juxta-Neath was known as Llangatwg, the holy place of Cadog (Cattwg), otherwise the old name may have well been Llangatwg. Merthyr Dyfan is the place commemorating the shrine or martyrdom of St Dyfan. Barry Island was Ynys Peirio, the island of St Peirio, and Barry seems to have come down from St Baruc, whose 6th-7th century church was on the island. Cwm Cidi means the Valley of the Black Dog, through which Nant Talwg

Flat Holm: The Lewis Alexander - Cathy Crompton

(Bubbling Stream? 'Talog' means jaunty, but the author can find no reference to Talwg) cuts its way down to Porthkerry. Barry Brook flows through Cwm Barri (Barry Valley). Biglis comes from Llys Mawr, meaning Big Court (Big Llys), a manor on Sully Moors on a Romano-Celtic site. The Old Court Monastery at Biglis is illustrated in old books. On the coast, Bendricks is another amalgamation from the original Welsh, Pen being mutated to 'Ben'. The original name was Benrocks, or Head of Rocks. Similarly, Cold Knap comes from Cold Cnap (Mound, or Head). Coed-Capel-Wood at Merthyr Dyfan literally meant Wood-Chapel-Wood, pleasing both Welsh and English Communities. Coed Bryn-Hill Fawr be the golf-course again was an oddity, meaning the Great (Mawr) Hill-Hill Wood. Cae Coed Erw (Woodfield Acre) lay next to Maes-y-Cwm Wood (Field in the Valley Wood). Coed-yr-Odyn Wood means 'Wood of the Lime-Kiln Wood', again a bit of nonsense as the English translation is repetitive, and adjoins Porthkerry Woods. Several field names remain Welsh such as Cae Elmen, and Cae Ffynnon on Biglis Farm. The holy well next to Merthyr Dyfan church was probably once dedicated to Dyfan, but is now named Ffynnon Mynwent (Churchyard Well), and there was a Ffynnon Wen (White Well) supplying Colcot Farm. Gwaun-y-Nant (Meadow by the Brook) had built upon it Brickyard Terrace, and Davies Street was erected on Erw-Ty Ffynnon, the Acre-House Well. Tynewydd Hill leads from King Square to the Tynewydd pub, a 'New House' built for the Farmer Thomas of Barry Island. So, underneath the fabric of the Victorian-Edwardian town of Barry is a Welsh heritage. It has a Norman castle, two medieval churches on Christian sites

Flat Holm Lighthouse - Cathy Crompton

dating back at least to the 6th century, a Roman port building, medieval remains of a lost village, the site of a monastery, two sandy and one pebbly beaches, and a port which was for a short time the busiest in the world.

We must remember that saints founded most of our communities, always near a well or fresh water, and often on Roman sites. The Vale of Glamorgan, because of the Roman influence and settlement, is littered with the 'llannau' of Wales 'Age of the Saints'. **St Baruc** died before 577, not later, as the plaque on his chapel states. He was **feasted in Barry** upon September 26th and 27th, and on November 29th. However, the great holiday and Feast Day in Barry for centuries was the last Monday in July, so another saint might be remembered. St Samson's Day is July 28th, and his links with Barry Island monastery may mean that Samson of Dol was the original saint celebrated here. One of St Cadoc's disciples, Baruc died returning to Barri from Echni (Flat Holm Island). Cadoc had forgotten his codex, and sent Baruc and St Gwalches back to fetch it, but they drowned. On the plaque outside **St Baruch's Chapel** we read: *'We are told that in the year 700 the friars and monks left their Celtic monastery (Llancarfan) and walked to Barry Island, as it was then their custom, periodically to retreat from the world for up to six weeks to pray and meditate. They took a boat from Barry Island to Flat Holm to seek solitude. On returning to Barry Island they discovered that they had left the saints' enchiridon (handbook or codex) behind. St Cadoc sent St Baruc and St Gwalches back to retrieve the book. While recrossing they were drowned. The body of St Baruc was recovered and buried on the island. Baruc was revered as a saint for many miles around and people came flocking to the island to see his burial place, which they regarded as sacred. A chapel was built here called St Baruc's Shrine.'* However, as Cadog died around 577, we cannot accept 700 as Baruc's date of death. The nave measures about 20 feet by 11, and the chancel is just 11 by 9 feet.

Nell's Point was until the 1960's an unspoilt headland, with **St Baruc's Holy Well**, ruined medieval buildings, prehistoric burial mounds and the ancient St. Baruc's Chapel. Philistines allowed the building of Butlin's Holiday Camp, upon this land given in perpetuity by the Earl of Plymouth for the leisure of the townsfolk. On the opposite, unspoilt **Friar's Point** there are surviving prehistoric mounds. In 1999, the holiday camp was demolished to make way for housing, the only such development on a headland in modern Britain. The deeds deposited with the council pertaining to the gift of Nell's Point to the people of Barry seem to have been destroyed. Great numbers of women visited **Ffynnon Barruc** (St Baruc's 6th century holy well) on Ascension Day, washed their sore eyes in its water and dropped a pin in it. It also cured King's Evil, fevers and headaches. Butlins were allowed by a quiescent Barry council to 'tarmac' over the well to make a space for an extra car to park in a 300 bay

71

car park. Another well at Barri Island was known as the **Roman Well**, and was surrounded by a deep retaining wall when the docks were built. Votive pins and Roman coins were found in it. Just in the last thirty years at some time a café/pub was placed upon it. The author remembers it as a source of mystery, somewhat rather different feelings than the local council. There was also a **monastery** marked on 19th century maps of the island, and its foundations

Nell's Point, Barry Island - Cathy Crompton

were north of Baruc's church. A chapel recorded in 1237, sited about 100 yards west of Friars Point House has been washed into the sea, and **Friars Point House** was built on the site of the old Marine Hotel. Other old ruins were found near the railway station. In 1890 **Barry Island** was still cut off from the mainland. It had been an uninhabited nature reserve before the building of a causeway and Barri Docks, by David Davies. In the sixteenth century, **St Baruc's Chapel** was the only building on the island. Gerald of Wales described the church, and noted the wondrous rock or 'blow-hole' on Nell's Point which made the *'sounds of blacksmiths at work, the blowing of bellows, the strokes of hammers and the harsh grinding of files on metal.'* The little church was remodelled in the fourteenth century, as pilgrims travelled to St Baruc's shrine at least until the Reformation. John Leland in 1540 commented upon its effects on the amount of pilgrimage there. The holy well was full of bent pins thrown in by pilgrims who had sampled the healing waters. This followed the old Celtic custom of offering bent daggers and swords to the water gods. The well also appears to be the only one in Wales that was used for curing hangovers and alcoholics. How many other councils would allow a 6th-century well and a 'Roman Well' to be lost forever?

Footnote: St Cattwg's or **St Cadoc's Church** in Cadoxton-juxta-Barry, and **St Dyfan's Church** at Merthyr Dyfan are both fine medieval churches worth visiting, especially if one can gain access on a Sunday. Next to the old Three Bells pub, St Cattwg's is not included in these walks, but will be included in a future book on Barry. It dates from around 1150, was first recorded in 1254, and is Grade II listed. One other notable building in Cadoxton is *The Court* near Gladstone Road, which used to be known as **Old Court Monastery**, and which has a medieval dovecote.

WALK 32 - BENDRICKS ROCK TO BARRY DOCKS TO JACKSONS BAY

WALK G OF THE SEASCAPE TRAIL

This is about 4 miles (6.4 km). There is a problem here for those wishing to carry on along the coast, as Barry Docks are private property, belonging to ABP. The author used to criss-cross these docks as a youngster, as did all local people. Access has been restricted more and more over the past few years, partly because of fears of vandalism, and partly because of the problems of insurance. Docks are dangerous places, even one used as little as Barry, and the port authorities do not wish to be sued if someone, who is technically trespassing, is injured.

Jackson's Bay - Cathy Crompton

As we can no longer access the docks, passing the huge Ranks flour mill and the swingbridge to get to Jackson's Bay, we have to swing inland, up through the Atlantic Trading Estate. The shabby trading estate is being updated, and lies over a Bronze Age settlement with pillow mounds. You have to take Wimborne Road straight across the roundabout, with the cul-de-sac of terraced houses, Bendrick Road on your left, and Hayes Road on your right. This road crosses docks property, so stay on the pavement with Number 2 Dock on your left. Do not turn off to the left along David Davies Road after you pass Number 2 Dock, but carry on. The pond on the right has been known as Tom Edge for generations. At the junction turn left and head up the new road **Ffordd y Mileniwm**, Millennium Way. On your right you will see a statue of **David Davies** in front of the magnificent old **Docks Offices**, now used by part of the Vale of Glamorgan Council. There was an attempt a few years back to demolish this remarkable building, which seems unbelievable. The redbrick offices have a theme of the 'Four Seasons', with 4 floors, 7 lights in the traceried fanlight window, 12 panels in the porch, 31 steps on the Portland stone staircase you can see from the entrance hall, 52 marble fireplaces and 365 windows.

Nearly all of the infrastructure of the Edwardian Docks has been demolished. In front of the Docks Offices is the statue of *'Dai Top-Sawyer'*, David Davies, the inspiration behind the docks and railway, who is featured in the author's *'100 Great Welshmen'*. The sculpture is by Alfred Gilbert, who designed the statue of Eros in Picadilly. On your right you will see Morrisson's, the new supermarket. The whole area of Barry Marina is developing rapidly. There is a second road planned to access Barry Island, heading across waste land from Barry, near here. If you carry on along the waterfront, you are not allowed to turn left and cross Powell Duffryn Way to access Jackson's Bay and Barry Island any longer. Instead, you must carry on straight across a footpath (often flooded in winter) to the auxiliary carpark at Barry Island. (*If you head on under the Harbour Road to the main carpark and head for the far corner, you will emerge at the western end of Barry Island, ideal for walking down Friars Point*). If, instead, you turn left on the carpark access road, then right on Clive Road, you shortly come to a roundabout and the heart of **Barry Island** is straight across from you, past the funfair. The fair is on the site of an abbey and priory dating from 1132, possibly on the site of the old Celtic monastery of St Peiro. A monastery is marked on old maps of Barry near the railway station, and some sources say that the great St Samson of Dol served his novitiate here in the 6th century, not Llanilltud Fawr

(Llantwit Major). If you now wish to go to Jackson's Bay, turn left from the roundabout, heading up Plymouth Road, past the **Marine Hotel** (Brains beer) on your right, and descend down Docks Road. Barry Docks is out of bounds on your left, but you can follow the new footpath on your right, past Barry Yacht Club and harbour, into Jackson's Bay.

The 6th century **St Peiro** was the son of Caw (or of St Gildas ap Caw), who succeeded Illtud as head of Llanilltud Fawr on Illtud's death, but only survived a day before being succeeded by St Samson ap Amwn Ddu. Llanfair y Mynydd, now called St Mary's Hill, near Bridgend is also his foundation. He is possibly buried at Llanilltud, and the original name of Barry Island, Ynys Beiro, was named after him prior to Baruc's death there. The *'Insular of Peiros'* (Ynys Beiros or Byr) had a monastery where Samson was taught, and it seems that the monks later joined those at Llanilltud. A monastery was marked on old maps of the island before the docks were built at the entrance to a tunnel by the present railway station. There was also an 'abbey church' on Barry Island where St Doeninas, settled from Somerset, before moving on to Llandough-juxta-Cardiff where he used to be commemorated along with Cyngar (Dochdwy). A 'Roman' kitchen was also excavated upon the island. Samson left Llanilltud monastery for *'a certain island lately founded by a certain holy presbyter called Piro.'* St Dyfrig was also supposed to have spent Lent regularly on the island and met Samson there.

Bishop **Samson of Dol** (born 485, died May 28th, 565) was feasted on July 28th, and the one great Feast day of the year in Barry and its surrounding area was the last Monday in July. His father Amon (Amwn) Ddu was from Brittany and his mother from Gwent, Anna ferch Meurig ap Tewdrig. The cousin of St Malo, St Samson was born in Glamorgan and trained under Illtud at Llaniltud Fawr. Samson's Well at Llanilltud seems to have been transmuted to 'Nancy's Well' over the centuries. He left to go to Ynys Byr, Barry Island, where he became abbot. However, he soon left, as he was disgusted by the drinking and poor behaviour of the monks who had not been controlled by Abbot Pyr (Peiro). After reforming an Irish monastery, Samson again retired as a hermit near the river Severn. In Cornwall he then led Austell, Mewan and Winnow in evangelising the area, and also visited the Scilly Isles and Channel Isles. He then founded the monastery at Dol in Brittany, becoming the most famous of the *Founder Saints of Brittany*, and another monastery at Pental in Normandy. Dol's great St Samson's Cathedral has 13th century stained glass windows and no less than eighty 14th century oak choir stalls. Barry has the saints Cadoc, Dyfan, Peiro, Samson, Doeninas, Baruc, Samson Gwalches and Illtud associated with it, of whom four were remembered in the 'houses' of the old grammar school (Cadoc, Dyfan, Baruc and Illtud). Nearby Llancarfan and

Merthyr Dyfan Church - Cathy Crompton

Llanilltud Fawr (Llantwit Major) have dozens of saints associated with them including the patron **St David**, and *the world's most famous Welshman*, **St Patrick**. How many other places can boast so many saints from 1500 years ago?

Unfortunately we ignore our past, preferring to be spoon-fed pap from the television and tabloids. Our Welsh cousins in Brittany celebrate their past, with feast days and 'pardons' with music, dancing, eating and drinking for each of their equivalent saints. Six of their seven *'founding saints'* were Welsh, and one was Cornish/Welsh, sharing the same British language with the Welsh and Bretons. There is an opportunity for the Vale to have a Celtic Festival to celebrate its saints, based upon the wonderful Festival Inter-Celtique held at L'Orient each year. It attracts around 700,000 visitors over 10 days, with over 600 groups performing in marquees, concert-halls, pubs, cafes and the streets. Culture and heritage need to be used, not just respected. We in Wales do not know our past, so do not use it, and so are inexorably losing it, becoming McDonaldised into a passive acceptance of the American way of life, eating and entertainment.

WALK 33 - JACKSON'S BAY TO PEBBLY BEACH/COLD KNAP
WALK H OF THE SEASCAPE TRAIL

About 3 miles (4.8 km) - suitable for wheelchairs and pushchairs from Nells Point to Barry Island, and Barry Island to Cold Knap, but Jacksons Bay and Friar's Point are sandy and grassy respectively.

To reach the sheltered Jackson's Bay there are three footpaths. One leads around Nell's Point from Barry Island, one is a sharp descent on a footpath from Redbrink Crescent, and one leads via Dock Road and past Barry Yacht Club. There has been a

new development involving Barry Yacht Club, which is in receipt of a lottery grant. Barry Yacht Club is based in the **old lifeboat station**, at the docks entrance inside the West Breakwater. (From the West breakwater one can take the boat to Flat Holm). The way to Jackson's Bay, from Powell Dyffryn Way or the Docks Road, used to pass by the Yacht Club, and past the public conveniences to the beach. Around 2000, a chain link fence was erected between the club and the beach

Roman Building, Cold Knap - Cathy Crompton

by ABP. Access was thus only down the steep walkway from Redbrink Crescent. As part of the lottery grant, a new footpath is being cut next to the cliffs. Skirting the yacht club, access will once again be made easy to the coast, linking the Docks Road with Jackson's Bay. The other piece of good news is that the WDA is to develop the site containing the fuel tanks on Charles Darwin Road, on the west side of No. 1 Dock. This may well mean that access from Barry Marina via Powell Dyffryn Way, or

St. Baruc's Chapel - Cathy Crompton

another road, will be made possible, linking up the coastal walk. If this happens, the only 'difficult' piece of the complete Seascape Path remaining will be between Bendricks Rock and Barry Marina. However, the WDA is also landscaping the old Atlantic Trading Estate at Bendricks, and this remaining problem can be overcome.

Jackson's Bay used to be even more sandy than it is, and was always the favourite beach for Barry people, who let visitors 'fill up' the far larger Whitmore Bay at Barry Island, on the other side of **Nell's Point**. Ewbank related that even before 1920, over 50,000 trippers used to visit Whitmore Bay on a single day. Nell's Point was leased to Butlins as a holiday camp in 1964, unfortunately sweeping away a wonderful resource and viewpoint for the people of Barry. Very little financial benefit came to the shops or people of Barry from Butlins. When the company left, another operator took it over, and the shabby buildings rapidly decayed in the salty atmosphere on the point. It has now been turned over to housing. The author has been informed that the documents recording the gift of Nell's Point by the Plymouth Estate *in perpetuity* to the people of Barry were shredded. This is an illegal act, as land deeds are legally binding documents, and have to be kept in a secure archive. **St Baruc's Chapel** on Nell's Point is early medieval. It seemed to have some materials of Roman origin in its building. You can see the chapel if you park in Redbrink Crescent or Friars Road. Cross Jackson's Bay sands and take the footpath around the headland, until you come to the Esplanade at **Barry Island.** Walk the length of the esplanade, diverting for a walk around the **fairground**, to see the steam trains at the **Railway Heritage Centre** or take a meal/drink. The promenade leads you to the covered shops overlooking the far western end of the beach. Take the road to the right of the public conveniences, past the back of the beach shops and cafes. Paget Road leads you onto **Friars Point,** with several tumuli, and Friars Point House (hopefully to soon be renovated after years of neglect). From Friars Point you have great views across the Channel, over Barry Island, and across the Old Harbour (inside the pier) and **Watchtower Bay** (outside the pier) across to Cold Knap.

Return to Barry island, and keep bearing left, with the fair on your right, and take the causeway (Harbour Road) west towards Barry. On your left is the **Old Harbour**, and on your right waste land where the sea used to be, before the causeway was built. (This was once the famous 'Steam Trains Graveyard' where the Woodhams collected hundreds of locomotives. Commendably, they did not scrap them, but kept them for preservation societies to restore and take away). At the roundabout, bear left along the Parade, taking in **Parade Gardens**. This leads to The Knap. **Cold Knap Farm** is Barry's oldest domestic building, dating from 1570. At the junction, turn left along Lakeside, with the **Knap Boating Lake** on your right. Follow the road alongside the old **Knap Lido** (unfortunately probably to be developed as flats - this used to be the largest open-air swimming pool in Britain), to **Watch House Bay**. Walk up along the headland of **Cold Knap Point** and you can see Friars Point to the east. Carry on walking west and you will come to the **Knap Promenade**, and Cold Knap Beach, known only as **Pebbly Beach** to locals. Walk along the ridged beach for the length of the promenade. Near the carpark entrance you will see the remains of **Glan-y-Mor Roman Villa**.

WALK 34 - BARRY CENTRE CIRCULAR

About 4.5 miles (7 km), suitable for wheelchairs and pushchairs, but a lot of crossing of pavements.

As has happened in Penarth, the Vale of Glamorgan Council will be placing a dozen interpretation panels around Barry, with one centrally on **King Square**. The walk starts from here, and parking is sometimes difficult near this centre for shopping, but never impossible. The **Town Hall and Library**, soon to be renovated, were built as a result of an open competition held in 1903, and have an imposing façade. The Library was built first, helped by a huge grant from the Carnegie Foundation. Along Holton Road here one can see many Victorian and Edwardian buildings, plus a really poor piece of modern architecture housing Woolworth's, Boots etc. (With your back to the Town Hall, turn right). Head down Holton road westerly, away from Woolworths, past Dan Evans department store, the main Post Office, and past the Theatre Royal cinema - Barry once had

Barry Island - Cathy Crompton

eight cinemas, and this is the only one remaining. Turn right to the roundabout, and one will see Gladstone Gardens and 'The Memo', used for public and private functions, and housing a small museum. The **Memorial Hall** was completed in 1932 with *'Portland Stone facing'*, and its recent re-naming as 'The Memo' has been opposed by those who understand their language. 'The Memo' was always the nickname for the Memorial Hall since at least the author's childhood, but it is short for *'memorandum'*, not memorial. (The Welsh in south-east Wales have always tended to shorten names, especially Christian names - David becomes Dai, Eric becomes Er, Terry becomes Ter, Derek is Der, Jason is Jace, Trevor is Trev, Carol is Car and so on.)

From the Memorial Hall, return to the roundabout, and one can head straight across to explore the new **Barry Marina**, or carry on along the continuation of Holton Road, now called Broad Street, past Barry Railway Station on the left, slightly up and then down a hill to **Romilly Park**. The park is surrounded by some of the finest housing in Barry, and there is a stone **Gorsedd Circle** commemorating the 1920 National Eisteddfod. If you turn right just before the park, skirt right of the park's east boundary, then fork left into Old Village Road, before turning left into Park Road. In the 'old village' of Barry, Rose Cottage was once Greenhouse Farm, built around 1600. Here is the only remaining thatched roof in Barry. On your right you will come to the remains of **Barry Castle**. Held by the de Barri family from the 12th to 14th centuries, it was partly ruined by 1530, possibly sacked by Glyndŵr's forces in the early 15th century. However, manorial courts were held in the gatehouse until 1720. The original castle on the site was an earthwork. One can still see the portcullis groove in the gatehouse, and it also had a drawbridge and double doors. Stone from the Roman port building at Cold Knap was used to build this Norman castle. *If you carry on along this road, it will bring you to the wonderful* **Porthkerry Park**, *described later in the book.* However, cut back into **Romilly Park** and head straight across down the hill towards the gates and public conveniences. *(Alternatively skirt the west side of the park, following the road to the same point).* Cross the road and head under the bridge into Lakeside, the area known as The Knap. Walk through **Cold Knap Gardens**, past the harp-shaped boating lake, and one can turn right along the promenade above **Pebbly Beach**. The 'terraces' on this beach are constantly changing, and sunbathers excavate 'craters' to protect themselves from the sea-breezes here. There is often reasonable surf here in winter.

Near the parking-attendant's kiosk there are the remains of a **Roman port-building**. It may have been a chandler's store or more likely a official guest-house or mansio with 19 rooms around a central courtyard, which formed part of the Roman port complex. The area was used up to around 300 AD. The present boating lake also had Roman remains, and it is the site of a silted-up sea inlet, which would have been used as the port. Walk as far west as you wish along the Promenade. Access to Porthkerry Park can be effected across the pebbles around Bullcliff Rocks point, if you wish, but it is not an easy walk for older people. Head back along the promenade towards **Cold Knap Point**, where you will see **Barry Open Air Swimming Pool** at present in a state of disrepair. Once the biggest pool in Britain, it has been closed for some years and is probably to be redeveloped for housing, destroying a unique opportunity for refurbishment. The Lido was built in 1926, and originally was tidal, with a sluice-gate allowing fresh sea-water in at high tides. There was a dummy fort built upon Cold Knap in the Second World War, to take attention away from the main defensive fort on Nell's Point. On Cold Knap Point there is a colony of cowslips, and one can carry on along Cold Knap Way, with **Watch House Bay** on one's right, to turn right along The Parade. Walk through Parade Gardens, past the old **Lime Kilns** and **Coastguard's Lookout** and **Rocket Store** (1864), and this bay is known as Barry's **Old Harbour**. You can now turn right along the Victorian causeway that joined Barry Island to the mainland, to explore the seaside resort, or head back to Barry, up Harbour Road, with the **Ship Hotel** on

Bendricks Rock - Terry Breverton

your left. When the island existed, one could only access it by boat, or by stepping stones at dead low water. One inhabitant of the island farm used to hang on to the tail of his horse as it swam the channel. Turn right at the top of the hill, back on Broad Street. Turn left at the Royal Hotel, and first right into York Place and then **High Street**. This runs parallel with Broad Street, and has some interesting shops and restaurants. You can cut back onto Broad Street at any time by turning right. Head back easterly to **King Square**.

WALK 35 - FLAT HOLM ISLAND

It is about a mile to circumnavigate the island and see the sights on the escorted tour, but embarking/disembarking and following the grassy footpaths make the trip unsuitable for wheelchairs and pushchairs. The boat is small and open, so wear wind-proof clothing to cross. Also, those affected by sea-sickness must remember that this is a small boat, and unless the sea is like a mill-pond, they will be affected by the swells of the Channel.

Flat Holm is three miles in a straight line out from Lavernock Point, the final extension of the Mendip Hills that pass through Somerset. It is 'owned' by Cardiff, but its near neighbour, Steep Holm, is English. Flat Holm is 500 yards in diameter, and you can reach it from Barry Pier (between the harbour and Jacksons Bay) in the motor vessel *Lewis Alexander. You have to reserve your crossing in advance.* The island is the breeding ground of thousands of herring gulls who feed off Glamorgan's rubbish tips. A guide will take you from the former inn and farmhouse to the refurbished **barracks**, the **lighthouse**, the **fog-horn**, the crumbling **cholera isolation hospital** and the small Flat Holm museum. There is a Neolithic axe head found during the excavation of two of the island's graves, said to be those of the murderers of Thomas a Becket. The island was farmed for over 700 years, but abandoned in 1946, and is now an official **nature reserve**.

Flat Holm's unique slow worm (which has a larger blue spot on its side that its mainland cousins) can be seen, usually under some corrugated iron sheets where the guide can find them. Flat Holm and Steep Holm also have a unique wild peony, and Flat Holm abounds with the huge (and rare) wild leek. The whole of Flat Holm is littered with military remains, protecting the Channel, from the **World War II Radar Station**, to **Palmerston's cannon**, earthwork emplace-ments and a defensive ditch which runs right across the island

Outside the ruins of the Grade II listed Cholera Hospital is the small **Guglielmo Marconi memorial**. The first radio signal arrived here in May 1897, transmitted by Marconi to his assistant from Lavernock Point - *"Are you Ready?"*

Cold Knap Rocks - Martin Green

In the late 6th century the island of Flat Holm was known as Echni, and its earliest known visitor was St. Cadoc, one of the founders of Llancarfan Monastery near Llantwit Major. He made frequent visits for periods of meditation, especially during Lent. His disciples St Gildas, St Baruc and St Gwalches are also known to have visited. The old priory here has long since vanished. In the year 914, Danish invaders took refuge on the islands of Steopanreolice (Steep Holm) and Bradanreolice (Flat Holm), following their defeat by the Saxons at Watchet. The name Holm or Holme derives from the Scandinavian for *river island* and the Danes certainly used both Flat Holm and Steep Holm as navigational aids during attacks along the Severn estuary. The *Anglo Saxon Chronicle* states *914 - In this year a great naval force came over here from the south of Brittany, and two earls, Ohter and Hroald with them. And they went west round the coast so that they arrived at the Severn estuary and ravaged in Wales everywhere along the coast, where it suited them... Yet they stole inland by night on two occasions - on the one occasion east of Watchet, on the other occasion at Porlock. Then on both occasions they were attacked, so that few of them got away - only those who could swim out to the ships. And then they remained out on the island of Flatholme until they became very short of food and many men had died of hunger because they could not obtain any food. Then they went from there to Dyfed, and from there to Ireland; and this was in the autumn.*

After the Norman conquest of 1066, Flat Holm became part of the hereditary property of the Norman Lords of Glamorgan. Another entry in the Anglo Saxon Chronicle reads: *1067 - And Gytha, Harold's mother, and many distinguished men's wives with her, went out to Bradanreolice* (the Broad Burial Ground of Flat Holm) *and stayed there for some time and so went from there overseas to St. Omer.* This was Gytha Godwinsson, the mother of Harold who was killed at Hastings.

A 12th century deed from William, Earl of Gloucester and Lord of Glamorgan, gave three acres of the Welsh mainland to the brothers at the religious house dedicated to 'Sancto Michael et Sancto Cadoco et Dolfino' in the island off Penarth. This has to be Flat Holm, but there was a St Michael's priory on Steep Holm also. It seems that Dolfino was the Latinised version of St Dyfan, as there are no alternative saints known. Another of Earl William's charters gave the Bristol Abbey of St Augustine 'Platam Holmam....with the chapels....on that island.' In yet another deed he gave the advowson of the church of Rumney, Cardiff, for the use and sustenance of the Augustinian canons of Flat Holm.

In the 1850's, wary of the strength of the French Navy, the British government decided to establish a number of fortresses along the coast. Flat Holm was to form part of a *strategic coastal defence system for the Bristol Channel* which was to include Brean Down, Steep Holm and Lavernock. Construction of the fortress on Flat Holm began in 1865 and was completed in 1869. However, these fortresses became known as 'Palmerston Follies' after the Prime Minister who instigated them, because the cannons on the island were only fired in tests. Although barracks were constructed for the 50 soldiers needed to man the four batteries, only a Master Gunner and 5 gunners were ever stationed on the island. In 1884 three cholera patients were taken to Flat Holm for isolation. The ward was in a tent and one of the patients died. The use of Flat Holm caused many complaints - from the Royal Artillery who had troops stationed there, from Trinity House who were worried about their lighthouse keepers, and from the tenants of the farm who suffered monetary losses from fewer visitors and could not sell their vegetables or rabbits, as no-one would buy 'diseased' gods from them. So, from 1886, Cardiff Corporation leased the island from its owner, the Marquess of Bute, to provide a permanent hospital on the site of the farm, away from the soldiers and lighthouse keepers. In 1896 a new, more substantial hospital was built and remained in use until 1935 when the building was condemned. During the Second World War it was decided to refortify the Bristol Channel and over 350 soldiers were stationed on Flat Holm. As an attack from the sea became less likely, anti-aircraft guns were installed, but modified to allow sufficient depression to engage sea-targets. Flat Holm became non-operational in 1944 and by 1946 was abandoned by the services.

Lorna Gibson lived on the island between 1987 and 1989, and recorded its flora and fauna. There is a problem with ragwort, which has to be managed, but as well as the wild peony and leek , you can see bluebells, sea campion, sea thrift, wallflowers, birds-foot trefoil, wild turnip, scurvygrass and sea lavender. The island has been an **SSSI** since 1972. Many of the plants indicate that there was a monastery here, for their healing properties are well-known, such as chickweed, yarrow, henbane, cleavers, common St John's wort, salad burnet, violet, great mullein, cowslip, mint and burdock. According to old maps there was a **friars' garden** here. There are many rabbits, but the population varies with waves of myxomatosis, and there is no longer a rat problem. Shelduck nest in rabbit-burrows here, and a few pairs of greater black-backed gulls nest on the east cliffs. There are lesser black-backed gulls, but the vast majority of nesting birds are herring gulls, many suffering from the deadly effects of botulism, having been affected by food-poisoning from ripping open black bin-bags on the mainland. You can see rock-pipits, meadow-pipits, goldfinch and wrens. Along the coast there are oystercatchers, dunlin, cormorants, turnstone and even purple sandpiper.

WALK 36 - THE LOST VILLAGES OF HIGHLIGHT AND MERTHYR DYFAN

Thanks to Cardiff Ramblers for the following description. *About 5 miles (8 km) - not suitable for wheel-chairs and pushchairs. This walk takes in two contrasting 'lost villages'. Highlight Village is now just a ruin on the edge of a golf course, and requires a lot of imagination to picture the once-bustling village that existed here. On the other hand, Merthyr Dyfan church is still standing, although surrounded by the estates of modern Barry. However, it lies in a little green valley and it is not so hard to imagine how it was once a small village out in the countryside.*

A convenient starting point is Colcot Road, in the area of the Colcot Arms pub, near the roundabout on the A4226 Port Road. The **Colcot Arms** is an old coaching inn, and the site was noted back in 1480. Oliver Cromwell (whose real name was Williams) is said to have stayed there in 1648. Start by returning towards the roundabout, and going left (westwards), to cross the main A4226 at the lights in front of the Comprehensive School. Go straight down Highlight Lane, and continue when it becomes a lane, crossing Hellas Drive and Lakin Drive past **Highlight Farm**. Behind the farm, although not visible, is the moat of the old manor house. Follow the lane into the countryside, downhill until a clearing allows views of the golf course and

St. Lythan's Burial Chamber - Cathy Crompton

beyond. To the left is an open space, and under a large old ash tree, are the foundations of the old **Highlight Church**.

After inspecting the remains of the church, continue down Highlight Lane until you cross Brynhill Brook on a small concrete footbridge. Keeping to the right hand side of the field, go over a stile that leads to another footbridge over a stream. Then go straight across the next field, toward a stile below a large oak tree. Go across the next field, bearing to the right towards the left-hand side of a large red barn. Behind the barn is a stile leading into the muddy farmyard of **Old Wallace**. Follow the track curving around the farm to the right. Then head out into a track alongside a field, going through a gate with a clever locking mechanism. The track follows the field edge, with southward views back to Barry, and the slope of Highlight Lane followed earlier. Then, after a gate, the track swings to the north side of the hedge, with views the opposite way to **Goldsland Wood**.

Soon you reach **New Wallace** Farm, with its old barn and stable block. After a metal barn on the right, go around behind the barn, where a stile leads into a field sloping down to a stile leading into a large field. Follow the left hand side of the field – before the end is a gate, which you go through, bearing right, to cut off the corner of the next small field towards a gated bridge. Go over the bridge and straight across the next field, until a gate leads through a small muddy field, heading left towards the farmhouse. At **Brynhill Farm** there is a good surface lane leading up the hill towards the A4226.

Cross at the pedestrian crossing, and continue down Meggit Road, in a housing estate. At the end carry straight on down a lane leading to Tennyson Road. Bear to the right, keeping an open space to your right, and the road with houses on your left, across an open patch of grass. Further down the hill go right down a road which soon becomes a track leading to the bottom of the slope. As the path starts to rise, watch for a fairly concealed track to the right, which leads to **Merthyr Dyfan Church.** This lovely little building, complete with churchyard cross, still has the atmosphere of a countryside church, although now surrounded by the town of Barry. It is early 13th century, with Roman remains being found nearby. **St Dyfan**, the saint sent by Pope Eleutherius with Fagan in 180 AD, is buried at Merthyr Dyfan Church, where many Roman remains have been found. Also known as Damianus, he died in 193, and was feasted on May 24th (with St Ffagan) and upon April 8th. There was a holy well at Merthyr Dyfan, later called Ffynnon Mynwen. It is believed that **St Teilo** founded this church in memoriam of Dyfan in the 6th century. The Grade II listed church dates from about 1250 and is dedicated to Dyfan and Teilo. Continue past the church, heading uphill across fields, until you reach Whitewell Road, which leads back to

Colcot Road, where you started. The name Whitewell indicated the presence of a 'holy' well, probably dating back at least to the 6th century.

WALK 37 - FROM HIGHLIGHT TO DYFFRYN HOUSE

(This route is also mentioned in reverse in the section upon Porthkerry Walks, in the walk from Dyffryn to Porthkerry). *About 5 miles (8 km), not suitable for wheelchairs or pushchairs. An ideal Autumn Walk across the valley of the Waycock (also spelt Weycock), incorporating a ruined medieval village, one of the finest Edwardian houses in Wales and a good example of a Stone Age Burial Chamber. It is a loop on the* **Highlight Trail**, *the first route cleared in 1996 by Valeways volunteers, the countryside charity dedicated to creating enjoyable walks within the Vale of Glamorgan. The Highlight Trail links the seaside town of Barry with the high downlands at the village of St Nicholas. Copies of the route map of the Highlight Trail can be obtained from: Valeways Unit 7 Barry Enterprise Centre Skomer Road Barry CF62 9DA Telephone: 01446 749000*

Start on Port Road West (A4226) by Barry Boys Comprehensive School. Using the Pelican Crossing, cross the road, turn right and then left into Highlight Lane, crossing Hellas Drive and Lakin Drive. Continue downhill into the country, passing the 18th century Highlight Farm, through the metal gate, continuing down through the golf course. Halfway down on the left can be seen the excavated remains of **Highlight Church**. Also uncovered were two medieval house-sites, a corn drying kiln and a **moated manor house**. The church was abandoned about 1563. Continue down the lane, cross the bridge over the stream and continue ahead along the right hand side of the fields, over three stiles. Continue over a further bridge and across the next field, to a stile to the left of a large single tree. Follow the track up to **Old Wallace Farm** keeping to the left past barns and the farmyard, and at the lane turn right and immediately left over stone stile. *(For an alternative shorter route, turn right at the lane, continue ahead over a stile and follow the track to New Wallace Farm, where you can rejoin the longer route).* From this stile walk ahead, and then downhill to cross a bridge on your left. Follow the path halfway around the pond, turn left at a waymarker, and cross over the stiles ahead, keeping to right-hand side of fields. The path now runs through **Dyffryn Mill** (Hen Felin). Please respect the privacy of the home owner and keep to the right hand perimeter. At the road turn right into the delightful village of Dyffryn with its thatched cottages and village pond. Continue through the village. *(At the left hand road junction by the pillar box is the way marker for continuation of the Highlight Trail).*

Walk out of the village and up the hill, and on the left is **Dyffryn House and Gardens**. The house was designed by Thomas Mawson for Reginald Cory, the coal owner, was built in the style of a French Chateau and the Edwardian Gardens are some of the finest in Wales, the formal gardens including a Mediterranean, Physic and Roman Garden. They are being restored to their former glory, thanks to National Heritage Funding. Continue up the hill to the notice of the **St Lythan's Monument**. Turn right into field and up the hill to the Stone Age Burial Chamber of the 4th to 3rd millennium BC. Six feet high, it stands in splendid isolation in the middle of the field, with several ancient track-ways leading from it. (Just to the south is an interesting circle of old oak trees on a raised wall, with a flat stone in its centre.) The massive capstone is 14 feet long, 10 feet wide and 2.5 feet thick. The insides of the two standing portal stones have been smoothed, and the back-stone has a port-hole in its top, to enable the spirits of the dead to leave the burial chamber. This Neolithic Burial Chamber is oriented East-West, and it was once covered by a mound of earth. The site was probably once similar to nearby Tinkinswood until the earth was cleared away.

Tinkinswood Burial Chamber - Cathy Crompton

One Welsh name of the Cromlech is Maes-y-Felin (The Mill in the Meadow), and the legend is that the capstone spins three times on Hallowe'en Eve, and all the stones go down to bathe in the River Waycock. The stones will also grant any wish whispered to them on Hallowe'en. Continue south downhill taking the right hand footpath at the stiles across the fields to New Wallace Farm. *(Here you meet up with the shorter walk).* At New Wallace Farm continue on the path southward to the bottom of the valley then start to climb towards the right, and the 17th-century **Lower Brynhill Farm**. Just above the farm, take the stile in the hedge on to your right and climb up to the lane, where you turn left up past the golf club, and emerge on the Port Road East (A4050) turning right to return to the starting point

Walk 38 - COLD KNAP TO PORTHKERRY (TO RHOOSE)

WALK I OF THE SEASCAPE TRAIL

About 5 miles (8 km) - not suitable for wheelchairs or pushchairs.

From the car-park at Cold Knap, take the path up the cliff from the **Roman port-building**. This is a fairly steep climb, and cross the fields with the cliffs on your left, until you come to the flight of steps taking you down into **Porthkerry Park**. One can alternatively walk to the end of Cold Knap promenade heading west, and cut around the Bullnose Point upon the pebbles, which is easier on the heart, but less comfortable on the feet.

*From here, one can detour on the way-marked path to see **Porthkerry Village, Church Farm** and the medieval **St Curig's** church. Turn right at the bottom of the **Golden Stairs**, cutting across the putting green to an entrance to a path in the woodlands. Head up to the church, and then carry on up the lane and take the Cardiff - Wales airport perimeter road left into Rhoose. Carry on into the village of Rhoose, straight on at the first roundabout. (Left here takes you down to Rhoose Point through some new houses). Take the left exit at the next roundabout, carrying on along the main road through the village. Turn second left down Station Road by a Spar shop, cross the railway line and keep ahead down a concrete path towards the sea. When you reach the beach, turn left across a wooden bridge and keep walking* *along the cliff path with the sea to your right. To your left a major reclamation project is taking place in the old quarry. You pass **Rhoose Point**, the most Southerly point in Wales. On your left you can explore the lakes and sculptures created in the old industrial area and limestone quarries. Eventually you reach a tarmac road by a caravan park. Turn left along it to go through the park, but as you get towards the end, turn right across the grass heading for the right-hand corner by the cliff. Here the path goes through trees, and you are walking through the earthworks of **The Bulwarks.** This Iron Age Hillfort was built between 700 BC and 100 AD, with an outer ditch and two massive closely set banks. It was also being used in Roman times, up to 400 AD. You emerge onto a field. Walk along the right of the field until you see a path dropping downhill to the right through trees. This meets the pebbles of Porthkerry beach. Follow the footpath signs back into Porthkerry Park and to the car park.*

The main trail however, leads you across the top of the beach to the far side of the golf course. At the end of the beach you will see a path leading up the hill. The cliffs here are a noted **SSSI**. This takes you to the remarkable Bulwarks and Porthkerry Caravan park. The Iron Age Promotory Fort must have been impressive when its ramparts had not been eroded and were surmounted by palisades. Inland from the Bulwarks was a site now on the airfield, noted as the site of **Rhoose Castle**. However, other reports say that its remains were obliterated when Castle Road was built, off Station Road. There once was an important port at Porthkerry before a huge landslip, and there **Castle Rock** can still be seen at extremely low tides. It was thought that this was also the site of **Porthkerry Castle**.

This next section describes Seascape Path J, the next walk:

Keep the cliff fence-line on the left, and pass through Porthkerry caravan park via a small wood. There are way-marks through the site to a road in its upper right-hand corner by the railway line. Follow the railway line and then road to the cliff, then find the path that leads you past the Rhoose redevelopment site. Quarrying took place from 1911 to 1980, and the site has been infilled with new housing, a nature reserve and a sculpture park. **Rhoose Point** is marked by a huge stone from the most northerly tip of Wales, with a piece of Rhoose limestone being erected in the north. The most southerly tip of Wales when the tide is out, however, is at Gileston, the end of the coastal walk. Carry on until you come to a small stream and a path up to Station Road in Rhoose. You can then return via St Curig's Church at Porthkerry, noted on the diversion above. Turn right at the top of Station Road, across two roundabouts heading to Barry, and take the first right, not the entrance to the Caravan Park and Bulwarks, but the lane to Porthkerry. An alternative is to walk another 200 yards on the verge, and turn down by the thatched cottages, where there are superb vies of Porthkerry Viaduct and the Channel. This leads past the superb Egerton Grey hotel and restaurant (once the Old Rectory) down to the viaduct, or you can turn right on a footpath to go to Porthkerry Village, and then left back down to Porthkerry Park.

The holiday camp on Nell's point, Barry Island (above)

The new buildings on Nell's point, Barry Island (below)

WALKS IN AND AROUND PORTHKERRY

Porthkerry Viaduct - Cathy Crompton

Ceri was a 1st-2nd century prince of Glamorgan, the son of Caid ab Arch, after whom Porthceri is probably named. He was said to be Caradog's nephew, and took over the Silure kingdom when Caradog (Caractacus) was taken to Rome in triumph by Emperor Claudius. In Norman times there was a Porthceri Castle, where **Castle Rock** can sometimes be seen at very low tides. The castle was swept away in the great storm of 1554. Porthceri was a port (now a 225 acre country park) and Ceri 'Longsword' was said to have constructed warships to defend the Glamorgan and Gwent coastlines. Edward Mansel mentions that the Normans invaded Glamorgan via this port. Two miles west of Porthceri is **Fontygari**, a village now joined to Rhoose, next to Cardiff-Wales airport. This seems to stem from, Ffynnon Ty Geri (the well of the house of Ceri), and there was an ancient well in East Aberthaw nearby. There is also a well marked on 1885 maps at the opening to Fontygary beach. William Thomas in 1788 calls the place Fondegary, which seems to confirm it as Ffynnon Ty Geri. There was also a Caer Ceri (Castell Ceri) in Llanilid, Glamorgan, mentioned by Nennius and in the Triads. Ffynnon Ceri holy well was near the field called Castell Ceri, and a paved causeway was found there three hundred years ago. Gwyl Geri celebrated St Curig and was held for several days in Midsummer between the churchyard and a tumulus called Y Gaer Gronn (circular fortress). It seems that Curig was later associated with Ceri's sites. Ceri's relatives Caractacus, Eurgain and Bran of the 1st century are also linked with Llanilid. 'The grave of Ceri' is supposed to be a large boat-shaped structure at Nash Point in Glamorgan. The ancient site here is still called 'Hen Eglwys' (Old Church). **St Curig** (d.c.550), however is the saint remembered at Porthkerry Church, next to the village green where John Wesley preached. It was built on an older site in 1327. Curig is remembered and feasted on June 16th, and was also known as Curig the Blessed and Curig the Knight. Curig was said to have been consecrated by St Paul Aurelian (Pol de Leon). He studied with St Tudwal at Llanilltud Fawr. Llanilid in Glamorgan is dedicated to Ilid and Curig. St Ilid was said to be a converted Jew, who accompanied Bran, Arwystli and Cyndaf from Rome. The Genealogy of Iestyn ap Gwrgan, the last native King of Glamorgan, tells us that Eurgain, the wife of Cadadog (Caractacus) sent for Ilid of Israel to help her convert the Welsh in 36 AD. This Ilid was sometimes identified with Joseph of Arimathea, who supposedly introduced order into Cor Eurgain at Llanilltud Fawr. Llanilid has always had local fame as the **first church in Britain**, being founded around 61AD. Possibly it was first called Cor Eurgain to honour Bran's grand-daughter.

WALK 39 - PORTHKERRY TO RHOOSE

WALK J OF THE SEASCAPE TRAIL

About 3 miles (5 km) - not suitable for wheelchairs of pushchairs - the path is described in the previous walk, as a continuation of Walk 39.

One can begin this walk at Cold Knap car park instead, to make it longer, as in the previous walk, and just follow the coastal pathway. If you walk across the pebbled beach instead, the headland is known as the Bull Nose, or Bullcliff Rocks, under Bull Cliffs. Park at Porthkerry. One can follow the path under the Viaduct up to the 13th century **St Curig's Church** with a 15th century cross, a 17th century **Old Church House** and other old buildings clustered around the old village green. Work began on the 18 arch, fifth-of-a-mile long **railway viaduct** in 1896, its was opened in 1897, closed because of subsidence in 1898, and reopened in 1900, a remarkable feat of engineering. Carry on along the lane, until it exits on the Barry-Rhoose main road, and turn sharp left into Porthkerry Caravan Park. (Alternatively, you can walk alongside the main road into Rhoose, and cut down towards Rhoose Point where signposted.) The caravan site borders on The Bulwarks - take the instructions to reach Rhoose along the coastal path from the previous walk.

Walk 40 - DUFFRYN TO PORTHKERRY (adapted from the Valeways Millennium Trail book, walk by Barbara Palmer) **-** 3.6 miles (5.8km). *Start at the carpark at Dyffryn House. Alternatively, one can reverse this route and park at Porthkerry carpark. Not suitable for pushchairs or wheelchairs.*

Walk up from Dyffryn carpark southerly (turn right out of the carpark) towards **St Lythans** and turn right at the junction, past some pretty cottages in the village and a stream that is often full of ducks. Carry on to **Dyffryn Mill**, and follow the path up the drive of the house. Follow the fence line, and turn behind the house, then come to a gate. (Please respect the owners of the property, and do not linger near their garden). Cross the field to a stile and you will see a lake. Take the path on the right of the lake, and to the left of the **River Waycock**. The path leads into woodland, then over a bridge and uphill to a stile, which leads into **Old Wallace Farmyard**. Carry on around the farm building in the centre of the farmyards, and you will then cross a stile on your right, next to a gate. The path carries on by the side of a barn, and across a field to a gate. Go through the gate, across the field to another stile, and cross another bridge. Turn left and follow the hedge to the next stile, over another bridge and into a sunken lane. This path leads uphill and is muddy in winter. At the top of the hill, near **Brynhill Golf Course**, the path widens.

Duffryn House- Cathy Crompton

Duffryn House- Cathy Crompton

Here is the site of the **medieval village of Highlight**, and on your right the remains of its 12th century church. This used Roman material, and is probably on a much earlier foundation. There was a priest's house at the edge of the churchyard, and the church had been abandoned by 1570. The deserted village was excavated in the 1960's. 'Highlight' seems to have come from **Uchelolau**, *uchel* meaning high, or lofty, and the soft mutation to *olau* of *golau*, meaning light. Being at the top of ridgeway which splits Barry on the coast from the lowlands of the River Waycock in the Vale, this may be the case. The Port Road from Cardiff to Aberthaw followed this ridgeway. The site of the original moated manor house is behind Highlight Farm, and **Lidmore Mill** is nearby, where villagers were forced by law to have their corn ground into flour.

Carry on to **Highlight Farm**, and through the new estate, to cross the Port Road. Across the road, you will see that the old path carries on in a straight line parallel to Barry Comprehensive School buildings on the right, with the playing fields on your left. You now join a main road near the new hospital. Turn right and after a short distance turn right again into Greenbanks Drive. At the end of the road, follow the path through an estate and then Severn Avenue. Turn right and go down steps and through a small 'Pocket Park', a remnant of the ancient **Cwm Talwg** woodland that has been adopted by the local residents' association for posterity. Continue on the path, which becomes a road, and then turn right at the main road traffic lights. Cross the road and turn left, taking the path leading off on the left to **Cwmcidi**.

Not many local people know that this is a corruption of *Cwm y Ci Du*, Valley of the Black Dog, which runs down to Porthkerry beach. William Thomas records on March 8th, 1763, the death of Ann Richmond *'of Cwm y ci du, of 100 years of age, some report 105. She was the mother of William Jenkin the extorter. She was buried since the 30th day of January last past and a Reported witch. All folks about dread her – and believe she could witch and the same belief is of her son, and tales of hurt she and her son made to cattle etc. And the report is that the devil before her death appeared to her with a Bull's head and offered a year longer on earth if at the end of the year she would deliver her body and all to he, which she denied and died. Vain belief of the Vulgar, who are as credible of tales as the Indians and Negroes are, for the devil have not a moment of time to give to any, not himself, much less than a year.'* There is a **deserted medieval village** at Cwm Cidi, alongside the path (Comkedye Street) up the hill past Cwm Ciddy House. There was also a medieval church here, noted in the 1254 *Taxatio*. The village dates from the 13th century, but only three cottages and the farmhouse were still in use by 1812, and now only the 1627 farmhouse remains. On the left, near the end of this path, there are the remains of an old **saw mill** dating from 1840. There is also a 4000 year-old tumulus above Bull

Cliff. The path after the gate, to the left, leads into **Porthkerry Park** and its beach. A deep anti-tank ditch reminds us of World War II defences.

Walk 41 - PORTKERRY PARK CIRCULAR

A 4/5 mile walk starting in Porthkerry Country Park, Barry, skirting the edge of the town and then back into the country. Park in the car park at the far end of Porthkerry Park (chargeable in season). Café and toilets are by the car park. Mostly easy walking but several steps and some short muddy stretches after rain. Part of this walk and the historical notes are taken from the leaflet 'Old Barry' produced by the Vale of Glamorgan Council but currently out of print. Not suitable for wheelchairs and pushchairs.

From the car park take the path towards the sea, with the excellent pitch and putt golf course on your right. Just before the path turns to the right, go straight ahead towards the trees, across the stream, and over a concrete bridge. Follow the path to the right, with the stream on your right. The path becomes concrete, and just as it

Porthkerry Park - Martin Green

emerges from the trees take the steps to your left leading up through the trees. There are quite a few of these steps (*known as the* **Golden Stairs** *from the once-abundant primroses and the setting sun which illuminates the steps in the evenings. There was also a tradition that a gold coin was buried under each stair*). At the top carry on with the cliff edge to your right, ignoring a path off to your left, before finally emerging onto a wide greensward. Keep ahead along the greensward, with the sea and tree-lined cliff to your right. After a while the greensward descends, with fine views ahead over Barry. Keep to the right-hand edge of the greensward as it descends, and at the bottom aim for a path with steps, and a white house to your left. Keep along this path with the houses on your left and the pebble beach (**The Knap**) to your right.

You pass the site of a **Roman villa** (*Glan y Mor*) on your left. Probably built in the early 290's, to protect against Irish pirates, it was stripped and demolished by the Romans after a short time, but reoccupied in the 4th, 7th and 10th centuries. At the bottom carry on along the sea front promenade passing **Marine Lake** (*shaped like a Welsh Harp*) on your left. At the end go up onto the grassy area, **Cold Knap Point**, where there are fine views. (*This was an island until the 17th Century and has Bronze Age burial mounds*). Retrace your steps to the promenade, but this time turn right past the old Lifeguard Station. Turn left on the edge of the bay heading towards some houses. To the right you will see the old **Watchtower** on the edge of the beach. The Watch Tower and **Rocket Shed** were built in the 1860's by the

Coastguard for storing and firing distress or warning rockets, when this was the entrance to Barry's original port. This is why the harbour inside the pier at Watch Tower (or Watch House) Bay is still known as the *Old* Harbour by locals. You reach a roundabout, but note the old white house ahead, **Cold Knap Farm**. Built in the 1570's and enlarged in the early 17th century, it is Barry's oldest inhabited house, and was used for smuggling by Richard Garby, the collector of taxes for shipping from the port. Head up the path with black lamp posts to the left of the Farm house.

The path emerges on to Cold Knap Way – keep straight ahead until you get to a T junction. Here, turn right on to The Parade and then right into **Parade Gardens,** but going ahead parallel with the road. At the bottom aim for the left-hand edge of the blue railings, to exit the Gardens. Cross the road and head uphill, following the road alongside the Porto Vista restaurant. Just before the railway bridge cross the road, so you are continuing on pavement. At the road junction cross the road carefully, heading up St Nicholas Road with St Nicholas Church on your left. Just before the Threshers Wine shop (*the building is Barry's oldest shop, 1860*) turn left (Old Village Road). On the right you pass a cottage and some terraced houses – all that remains of the **old village of Barry** (*this area has been inhabited since the 12th Century*). Keep ahead, ignoring a road to the left, until you get to a complex road junction where you keep in the same direction, aiming for some prominent ruins along Park Road.

The ruins are those of **Barry Castle**. Beyond the castle, where the road curves to the right, keep straight ahead down Porth Y Castell road. After 40 yards, turn right down Westward Rise. Go along this road until you meet footpaths crossing the road. This is just after a house called Crossways with blue metal gates. Take the footpath to the right through the hedge, down some concrete steps, and take the path to the left. After 40 yards the path branches – take the right-hand path, gently descending through the trees. At the bottom the path curves to the left. To your left the woodland is called Cliffwood. You pass the ruins of **Cliffwood Cottage** on your right. The original cottage was built in 1583. A later occupant, Ann Jenkin, was examined for 'Devil's Marks' by Cowbridge magistrates, and accused of being a witch. Cliffwood was first mentioned in 1578, and its wood was used in the 18th century for ship-building and oak bark used for tanning. The part of the wood still existing, known as Coed yr Odyn (Lime Kiln Wood), contains remains of lime kilns and quarries. **Cliffwood** was designated a Local Nature Reserve in 1970, the first in Wales.

On emerging into **Porthkerry Park** you can either turn left which takes you back to the car park or continue the walk by heading diagonally right, to the right of the white cottage, and aim for the road tunnel. Go under the bridge and immediately turn left following the yellow waymark

Porthkerry Church - Martin Green

The Bulwarks Camp - Cathy Crompton

('Circular Walk') alongside a metal gate, up an often muddy path. The railway line is to your left. The path goes up some wooden steps, and then after a wooden stile, emerges on to a field. Go diagonally left across the field, aiming for a house in the corner of the field where there is a wooden stile. 10 yards ahead is another wooden stile. Keep down the left-hand edge of field. At the end of the field follow the edge, as it curves to the right. Just by a metal gate on your left, cross the stile and hug the right-hand edge of the field to the next stile, a short distance ahead which you cross. Now descend down the left-hand edge of the field.

At the bottom of the field (which can be muddy), you will see a ruined building just to the right covered in ivy. Follow the direction of the waymark sign, heading slightly right as you pass the ruin to a bridge over a stream. Cross over the bridge and then turn left, keeping to the edge of the field. Aim for the wooden stile ahead. Cross this and another stile next to it. After 50 yards take the stone bridge, re-crossing the stream to your left following the waymark. Then turn right aiming for the bottom of the field, with the trees to your left. At the bottom left-hand corner is a wooden stile by a metal gate. Cross this stile and continue down the path to the right, with stone wall to the left. Cross a small stream and then emerge on to a metalled road, (*turning left here brings you directly back to the car park*). Head left down the road, but after 5 yards take the stile to your right heading across the field, towards the trees. Take the right-hand edge of the field and at the bottom you will see a waymark. Take the path which ascends steeply along the right-hand edge of the wood through the trees. *You will have been walking steadily for around two hours by this time.*

The path emerges on to a small greensward. Keep straight ahead towards the **medieval church** *(13th Century, dedicated to St. Curig, restored 1867).* The building was altered in 1867 when it was re-roofed, and contains a Tudor rood-screen. **Porthkerry House**, with its wonderful views over the sea, is below the church, and only visible from the park below. It dates from 1787 in the ownership of the Lord Romilly family. Just before the church turn left following the footpath sign, and where the road splits take the left-hand fork. Just before the house at the end of the drive, turn left down a clearly-marked red footpath sign which drops down through the trees. Keep ahead following the waymark sign when it crosses another path, and at the bottom emerge on to the pitch and putt area. Head back to the car park and café, which you can see from here.

WALKS IN AND AROUND RHOOSE

Rhoose Point, on the site of the old Rhoose Limestone workings and cement and asbestos factories, has been one of the largest regeneration schemes in Wales. On the 240 acres, there are new walks to the coast, plans for a 9-hole pitch and putt golf course, and 500 new houses. New habitats for displaced reptiles and amphibians are being formed, and although the 'wildness' of the lakes has been lost, this has been one of the more thoughtful regeneration projects in Wales.

WALK 42 - RHOOSE (TO FONMON) TO PENMARK TO LLANCARFAN TO LLANBETHERY (TO LLANCADLE) (from the Valeways Millennium Heritage Trail) by Graham Woosnam - *5 miles (8.1 km), plus diversion to Fonmon (1 mile, 1.6 km). Double the distance to return, or take the walk in stages, e.g. Rhoose to Penmark and return, and Penmark to Llanbethery and return). Much of this area is designated by CADW as being a* **'landscape of outstanding historic interest'**. *The Thaw, Carfan and Waycock rivers have cut not only small floodplains, but their tributaries have cut steep wooded valleys, which are host to a variety of rare flora and fauna.*

From where Station Road meets the main road through Rhoose (the Spar shop is on the corner), turn right (east towards Barry) then after a few yards first left into Brendon View Close, leading into a lane, which takes you to the Cardiff-Wales Airport perimeter fence. Follow the fence until you come to a road and walk past the **Highwayman Inn** (formerly the Whitehall), which sells real Irish (not English-brewed) Guinness. (Alternatively one could park here on a circular tour). Head west along this road to the hamlet of Nurston, and head right at the next road junction, then as this road bends left, take a stile on your right. From this stile the path leads to Penmark.

However, if you wish to visit **Fonmon Castle** *instead, or first , do not cross the stile but head along the road to a junction where you can turn left into the lovely Fonmon Village (Ffwl-y-Mwn) and* **Fonmon Pool**. *The hamlet contains a 16th century house which was the local forge, a thatched long house, and remains of a medieval village scattered all round the village pond and its wooded walks. In the village turn right past the pool, up a hill, to come to the castle entrance. The 12th and 13th century castle has a 16th century lodge, and was owned by the Parliamentarian and great friend and advisor of Cromwell, Colonel Philip Jones. The castle was remodelled in 1762, but the drawing room, library, hall, kitchen and gardens are open to the public at specific times. Fonmon is one of the few*

Ffontygari Beach - Cathy Crompton

93

Penmark Church - Cathy Crompton

medieval castles still lived in as a home, and has changed hands only once. The Watchtower in the grounds is only 18th century, and thought to be a copy of that of St Donat's Castle. Fonmon Castle now stages August's **Vale of Glamorgan Agricultural Show**, since its departure from Penllyn. There are alternative footpaths around here, to keep you off the road, all fairly well marked.

Carrying on with the walk to Penmark, from the stile cut across the field to the corner boundary of Cardiff-Wales Airport. Keep the airport fence on your right and its landing lights on your left, then swing slightly to the left, heading for the gap in the field boundary ahead of you. Head across the next field, bearing slightly left, until you reach a stile which leads to the road underpass. After passing under, climb the right-hand road bank to a stile. Keep the right hand road bank on your right for about a third of the distance of the field and then cross the field diagonally left to come to a stepped stile onto a road. Turn right, downhill, until you come to a stone stile on the left. Cross this and walk up the field to a way-maker and carry on towards the top left-hand corner of the long field. Remains of the **medieval village** of Penmark can be seen around here. Cross the stile into a narrow path which leads into Croft John. Follow this street to the main road. On your right are the medieval **St Mary's Church**, the 16th century **Six Bells** and the remains of Penmark Castle, all worth exploring. The church seems big for the village, but it used to lie within the curtain wall of the Castle, and be the garrison church. Its list of vicars goes back to 1242, and the church dates from the 12th century. **Penmark Castle** is on the Waycock's deep river-bank, not far from the church, and seems to have witnessed a Civil War battle, because cannon balls and musket shot have been found here. There is a 13th century wall, surrounding a court of 70 yards by 50 yards, plus an outer court. The moat has been filled in but you can see the remains of a tower, 24 feet in diameter. The original 12th century castle was timber, built by the de Umfravilles.

From where Croft John meets the main street, turn left for a short while, and then take the short lane on your right leading to a stile. Cross the stile and head diagonally to the left to the wood's edge. Head downhill, still bearing left, to cross the footbridge over the **River**

Llancarfan Church - Cathy Crompton

Waycock. Walk uphill, bearing slightly left to a house named Ross Kear, where there are the humps of a **medieval farmstead** on your left. Take the concrete path to **Pen-Onn**, where Edward Williams, the great **Iolo Morganwg**, was born. Turn left on the road and head downhill to the stone bridge over Ford Brook.

As well as Barry, St Baruc was also credited with the founding of Penmark, but it is is now dedicated to St Mary. Penmark was formerly known as

St. Mary Church - Cathy Crompton

Penmarch Hywel. Roman coins and signs of occupation were found at Penmark, and at nearby East Aberthaw, Nurston, Fonmon, Llanbethery and Llanilltud Fawr. Penmark is one of the largest churches in the Vale, and a November 1881 article by John Rowland in *'Yr Haul'* records: *'Englishmen have held the living of Penmark as far back as the history of the parish can be traced. Dr Casberd was one of the most fortunate Englishmen. He received thousands of pounds of Church money every year for nothing. He did not understand any Welsh; he could not administer the sacraments or pray at a sick bed in the language the people understood. His parishioners did not know him. This was scandalous and disgraceful. The appointments were nothing but a fiction. It wasn't the care of souls but emoluments which were in view. There is room to fear that the bishops, patrons and others will have much to answer for their negligence in the great day which will come. The present vicar is the Rev. Charles Fred Bryan Wood, precentor of the Cathedral Church of Cardiff. An Englishman.'*

*If you make a diversion on the next right to Ford Farm, there is a footpath on its right leading up the slop to the massive **Iron Age Ditches and Hill-Fort** and encampment of Llancarfan, with views over the Channel and Vale. It may be that Cromwell used cannon to bombard Penmark Castle from here.* If you do not divert to the Hill-Fort, carry on down the hill into **Llancarfan**, *'the village of 1000 saints'*. It is surrounded by history dating back to the Age of Saints. It was a ford across the river and important even in Roman times, said to be the crossing of two Roman roads. Like all llannau associated with the early Welsh saints, it is hidden away from pagan attacks from the sea. There are many walks around this lovely village, and there is not enough scope in this book to cover them. There is an 18th century pub and shop, the **Fox and Hounds**, (belonging to the villagers) an old corn mill with a water wheel, and a 12th - 14th century medieval church to explore. The church is devoted to the 6th century St Cadoc, and *'St Dyfrig's most famous well is near the ancient monastery site of Garnllwyd at Llancarfan, where Cadog was presiding at this time. Ffynnon Dyfrig can still be found in the woods known as Coed Ffynnon Dyfrig, and nearby at Llanfeithyn he had another healing well. These survivals certainly seem to authenticate his stay, possibly with Teilo, at Llancarfan. There is a case to be made that Dyfrig founded the colleges of Llancarfan, Caerworgan (Llanilltud Fawr) and*

Caerleon, and that he should have been made the patron saint of Wales for the effects that these monasteries had upon Celtic Christianity'. The **Church of St Cadoc Llancarfan** is a Grade A listed building. St Cadoc's was given by Robert Fitzhamon to St Peter's Abbey, Gloucester, in 1107. It is mainly a 14th-15th century church of a decorated and perpendicular style. There is some evidence of 12th century origins. Unlike most Vale churches the windows are of unstained glass. There is a wall painting of the apostles' creed on the south wall of the nave, probably 17th century. The church was built on or near the site of the monastery set up by Cadoc in the Dark Ages. No convincing physical evidence of this monastery now exists. It was ravaged by the Danes in 988. It was possibly located in Culvery field, just south of the present church.

Carry on along the main road heading north and almost out of the village, and cross a stone stile on the left. Head up a short hill to another stile, then carry on uphill,

bearing left, past a wood on your left. Then swing right, keep the field boundary on your right, through two fields and their stiles, to the main road. Cross the road, turn right and there is a stile not far away on your left, near **Aberogwrn Farm**. Over the stile, walk diagonally south-westwards across a large field to its opposite corner.

Turn right at the stile into the village of **Llanbethery (Llanbydderi)**, with the **Wild Goose** pub (which opens erratically, so do not rely on

Ring and Bailey at Pancross - Cathy Crompton

refreshment). **The Manse** is a thatched medieval house and was rebuilt in 1650, and **The Vines** is also medieval, with an 18th century kitchen. North of the village, but inaccessible, is a **Roman villa** site, where a Constantinian hoard of 857 coins dating from 330-335 AD were found in 1957. This strongly suggests that the occupants had to flee quickly. About the same time the great Roman villa at Llanilltud Fawr was attacked. Some cottages in Llanbethery are called Castle Cottages, so there may have been a castle here, associated with the original 'llan' or church, which has long since disappeared. From Llanbethery, past the pub, one can descend into the Thaw Valley take a walk to Flemingstone or Old Beaupre, crossing the Thaw Valley. If you wish, you can walk to **Llancadle** from Llanbethery.

Footnote on Llancarfan

The villagers have bought the pub to prevent its closure, and there is an active local history society. Llancarfan was one of the earliest Christian monasteries in the world, and sent missionaries to France and Ireland. Stan Awbery's small book gives a flavour of this important village, which nestles under the embankments of a huge hill-fort. The church was founded by Cadog or Garmon in the 6th century, but Dyfrig is also associated with it, especially with Garnllwyd, and Ffynnon Dyfrig is one of the many holy 'healing wells' in the vicinity. Llancarfan needs a new study on its ancient history, some of which is recorded in the author's 'Book of Welsh Saints', but we shall stay with Tathan's association with the village here. There was a flour mill here, and also a woollen mill, now converted into Llanveithyn Cottage. (Llanfeithyn means 'the holy place of Tathan, 'Meuthi' being the same name as Tathan). Llancarfan was famous for its breeches, and men used to try them on in the nearby 'Coed-y-Beeches'. Llancarfan's 'Mabsant', or holy week festivals, were held in a building at the rear of Llanfeithyn. It was held in January, so it probably celebrated Tathan rather than Cadog. The Mari Llywd was still seen in the area at Hallowe'en until the early 20th century.

The legend linking Tathan with Cadog and Llancarfan is as follows. Gwynlliw, Lord of Glamorgan and Gwent, took Brychan's daughter Gwladys from Talgarth, and was chased by Brychan into Glamorgan. Gwynlliw appealed to Arthur's army to fend off his pursuers. Arthur asked who owned the territory, and backed Gwynlliw. The child of Gwynlliw and Gwladys, both noted as Welsh saints, was Cadog. The night before Cadog's birth, Gwynlliw's soldiers broke in and plundered Tathan's monastery at Caerwent. Tathan went to Gwynlliw the next morning to claim restitution, baptised the infant Cadog, and taught the boy at Caerwent from the age of eight. At 20, Cadog refused to take up life as a warrior-prince, and set up a monastery at Llancarfan. Its boundary stretched from the sea to Penmark, St Tathan and Llanbethery. Llanveithyn was its centre in this earliest time, named after Tathan, Cadog's mentor. Cadog converted the knight Illtud at this time, to monasticism.

Nearby Garnllwyd is another ancient foundation, supposedly the home of Dyfrig (St Dubricius). The main hall is 30 foot long, and skeletons have also been found here. Llancarfan, Garnllwyd, Llanfeithyn and Llanilltud Fawr were attacked by Danish pirates in 987. Near Llanfeithyn is a field called 'Traitor's Close'. This is supposed to be where a monk was hung at this time. He had shown the Vikings how to approach the hidden Nant-Carfan valley from Aberthaw. There are many stories of battles in the area. One mystery is that many standing stones seem to have disappeared over the years. Some were noted by Malkin, and others may have been inscribed Celtic Crosses. A non-intrusive survey around the burial sites of Lancarfan may reveal more early Welsh history. The superb Pillar of Samson, now in Llanilltud Church, was only found because Iolo Morgannwg remembered a story about its existence, and managed to dig it from six feet underground. Cadog's monastery grew to rival that at Llanilltud Fawr (Llantwit Major), said to be the oldest university in Europe, but was ravaged by the Danes in 987-988 and never really recovered. Around 1900, there were four chapels as well as the church in this small village. The castle associated with Llancarfan is probably the site at Pancross.

Llancarfan Hill-fort ditches - Cathy Crompton

St Cadog (497– 577) was also known as Cattwg, Cadoc, Cathmael and Cadfael, and was feasted on September 25th and February 24th. He was an important Welsh saint and missionary, who like Dyfrig, Teilo, Beuno, Gwenfrewi and Padarn could have been Wales' patron saint. Venerated in South Wales, he probably visited and was influential in Ireland because he instructed Finnian at Llancarfan. He seems to have been a contemporary of the saints Gildas, David and Samson. According to Cressy he was taught by Tathan at Caerwent. He was associated with Arthur, and was said to have attended his court with the warrior-saint Illtud. His parents, King Gwynlliw (Gunleus) and Gwladys, lived at Stow Hill in Newport, where St Woolos Cathedral (a corruption of Gwynlliw) now stands on the remains of a Celtic fort. Cadog was first named Cadfael (Battle Prince) and has been associated with Galahad. He took his father's crown when Gwynlliw was converted. There are two versions of his death. One is that he was killed fighting the Saxons at Weedon in Northants, where there is now a huge church. A more plausible story is that the Welsh hid his relics during the Norman invasion of Glamorgan, and used this story as a smokescreen when the great monastery of Llancarfan was placed under St Peter's of Gloucester. Gwynlliw is said to have left his kingdom to Meurig, the son of King Tewdrig. Meurig had married into Gwynlliw's family, and was the father of Arthur. According to Lifris, Cadog's successors as abbot at Llancarfan were Elli, Pawl, Concen, Iascob, Sulien, Dagan, Gnauon, Elisael, and Cadifor, who died in 883. Lifris was probably the last abbot, and also archdeacon of Glamorgan. Cadoc's *Vita*, by Lifris, is the most complete of all the Lives written in Wales. Lifris's father was Bishop Herwald (1056-1104) and it is probable that Lifris was the last abbot of the great Llancarfan foundation, before the Normans stripped it. Gildas is said to have copied this '*Life*' when he stayed with Cadoc, and Caradoc of Llancarfan, who wrote Gildas' *Vita*, states that it was still in the great church of Cadoc in 1150, covered with silver and gold. This original was probably destroyed to hide land ownership details by the Normans. Cadoc is linked to Arthur by giving sanctuary to a man who killed some of Arthur's men.

A Further Note on Cadog's Foundation

Seven small streams meet under Llancarfan's great hillfort, the Whitewell, Greendown, Gowlog, Coed-Abernant, Whitton Bush, Walterston and Moulton, forming the small river Carman with its (often-flooded) ford. One tradition states that the stream and settlement were named after a saint 'Garman', the 'Apostle of Britain'. Both Germanus and Dyfrig are associated with the foundation, which appears to have been called Bangor Garman. Another legend is that the river was called Nant-Carw, the stream of the stag, because Cadog was assisted by two stags dragging timber from the forest to build his church. Dubricius was said to have lived at Garnllwyd monastery, a mile north of Llancarfan, specifically so he could be near Cadog, and Ffynnon Dyfrig holy well is still in the woodlands here. Llancarfan Well in the Culvery (Calvary?) Field cured many illnesses, and several other local wells cured King's Evil, the skin disease. Stan Awbery wrote a lovely little book on Llancarfan in 1959, in which he records: *'The chief festival of the year was called the "Mabsant" or the "Gwyl Mab-Sant". It was held in January each year. Marie Trevelyan tells us that it was held in a large building on the hill at the rear of Llanveithin.* (Llanfeithyn, just a mile from Llancarfan, is dedicated to Tathan, whose feast date was December 26th and 30th until the 12-day date change, so this must have originated from Tathan rather than Cadog, whose feast day is in September and February). The Reverend Louis Nedelec visited Llancarfan in 1870, and retold a Breton tradition about the *'seven wise men of Llancarfan'*, the saints Talhaiarn, Teilo, Gildas, Cynan, Eidden (Aidan), Estayfan (Ysteffan) and Taliesin *'the chief of bards.'*

WALK 43 - LLANBETHERY (LLANBYDDERI) TO FLEMINGSTONE TO ST MARY CHURCH TO OLD BEAUPRE (Valeways Millennium Heitage trail booklet) - *about 4 miles (6 km)*

Starting at the Wild Goose Inn in Llanbethery, walk downhill westwards on the lane/path into the Thaw Valley. The Thaw valley was created during the Ice Age, with its sides rising up to 135 feet from the flood plain, and is often flooded far north past Flemingstone at high tides or in spells of wet weather. Thus there are no buildings in the valley. Cross the old railway bridge and go through a gate, heading across the **Thaw** under three lines of pylons. Walk up the slope across the other side of the Valley where you will see a path with a stile on the left. Turn right and head north along the side of the valley, aiming for the village of **Flemingston** (known locally as **Flimston**, its original name may have been **Llanelwan**).

Penmark Castle - Cathy Crompton

You will pass through a field with uneven humps, the remains of Flemingston's **medieval village** dating from the 12th-13th centuries. You may be able to make out 5 house platforms and enclosure boundaries. Pass through a gate, bearing left uphill to another gate and stile. Keep going in the same direction until you come to a well-marked track and head right. Go through the gate towards buildings in front of you, and turn right on the road, with Greenfield House on your right. Fork left into Flemingstone, past Flemingstone Court Farm, Court House, and the Church. **St Michael's Church** is on 11th century foundations, with a 15th century roof and contains an early 14th century effigy to Joan le Fleming. Iolo Morganwg believed that the original church was dedicated to the 6th century Welsh **St Elwan**, and that Flemingston was originally Llanelwan. **Flemingston Court** is a 16th century farmhouse with detached kitchen, built next to the 12th century **Flemingston Castle**, of which a curtain wall separates the farm and the churchyard. Turn right past Gregory Farm and left again at the T-junction. There are lovely views of the Thaw here, despite the pylons.

Carry on left for around 3/4 of a mile and you will see a gate and stile on the left. Head across the field to a metal gate and barns. Keep the barns on your right and the pond in front of you, and turn right between the houses, with **Fishweir** on your left. The **Tithe Barn** here is late 16th-century and said to be the tallest in Wales. Fishweir was a home for the Bassett family, a 16th century farmhouse with Tudor arched mullion windows. Next bear right towards a stile and cross the next field to the far right-hand corner. Take the stile onto the road, turn left, heading uphill for 300 yards, then right into a smaller country road.

Rhoose Point lakes - Terry Breverton

After 600 yards this leads to **St Mary Church** village, on a ridge of Liassic limestone. It is a nucleated village, centred around the church. Celtic stone crosses have been found in the area, and just to the west of the church is an ancient **holy well**, so it was probably a pre-Norman foundation, like most of the Vale's other churches. The circular graveyard again proves an ancient origin for the site. There are terrific views from the village. Turn right at the next junction, past the Old Rectory on your left, to a waymarked lane that leads you to the right. In the village, the **Old Rectory** (Church House) was built in 1623 on an older building and is claimed to be the oldest inhabited rectory in Wales. In the church, only the medieval roof of the nave and chancel survived its restoration in 1862. Turn left at the stile in front of the barn, and proceed downhill to the stile in the bottom right-hand corner of the field. Carry on downhill through woodland and cross two more stiles into a large field. Cross this, heading to the left of a paddock (with views of Old Beaupre Castle on your right) to a house drive.

Turn left for a short distance and then via a stile, downhill, with the house garden on the right, go through a small metal gate and steps to the main St Athan-Cowbridge Road. *(Turning left will take you down to The Herberts, a village near an Iron Age enclosure).* Turn right and after 300 yards, you will come to the grand building called **Howe Mill Farm** with a gatehouse on the left, and a stile on the right. There are traces of a castle at Howe Mill. Cross the stile and follow the River Thaw to **Old Beaupre Castle**. This belonged to the Bassett family, whose motto was *'Gwell angau na chywilydd.'* There is a tradition that the Welsh and English barons met here first to sketch out the **Magna Carta**. Sir Philip Bassett, Lord of St Hilary, was Lord Chief Justice of England in the reign of King John, and it is said that he drew up the first draft for the lords to discuss at the castle. Alan and Thomas Bassett were among the charter's signatories, as well as Prince Llywellyn. It was originally medieval, dating from 1300, then became a Tudor manor house, and is built around two courtyards. In the 16th century the Mansels and the Bassetts extensively remodelled the house on the banks of the Thaw. If you access the castle via the footpath from Howe Mill, you will pass a series of **medieval fishponds** on the Thaw on your right. On the wonderful storeyed porch dated 1600, the inner wall is lined with brick, the earliest known use of brick in Glamorgan. The **Gwrach-y-Ribyn**, the Welsh equivalent of the Irish Banshee, was said to frequent the castle in the 17th to 19th centuries, and also New Beaupre, which was built in the 18th century to replace the castle.

WALK 44 - LLANCARFAN NORTHERN CIRCULAR - *3 miles (5 km), plus a mile for the Amelia Trust Farm diversion. Waterproof footwear is advisable when walking this route, as parts can get wet and muddy, and there is a ford to cross. However, you can avoid the ford by taking the road on the other side of the river from the Fox and Hounds..*

As over most of the Vale of Glamorgan the landscape is made up of Liassic limestones and shales, but here they have been cut into by small rivers such as the Nant Carfan and Ford Brook creating pleasant valleys, the sides of which are steep and wooded. *As with all circular walks you may start it at any convenient point. In the following route description the walk is begun in Llancarfan itself. However, there is an extension to this walk, linking it to **Amelia Trust Farm**. This is still marked on O.S. maps as Whitton Rosser farm. It underwent a name change when it was taken over by a Methodist charitable foundation. It can now be described as a very diversified working farm open to visitors, and is involved in rearing unusual animals, woodland*

conservation and various crafts. It also contains a hostel, children's play area, café and toilets. Thus it is a good starting/finishing point for this, or the longer Llancarfan circular walk. If so, the start of the walk is at the point where the Farm drive swings right into the activity area. You walk across a short stretch of field to a stile and gate. Once past these you walk directly across the second field, and at a stile you turn sharply left. Reaching the stile on the far side of this third field you have, on a decent day, very good views

Rhoose Point land sculptures - Terry Breverton

*across the Channel to the Quantocks and Exmoor. It is then downhill to a footbridge at the bottom right-hand corner of the field. You then cross a long field to a stile situated between two trees. This leads you on to a quiet country road. Turn right and follow it for the short distance into **Walterston**. A feature of this hamlet is the historic house, **Trewalter Fawr**. At this point you join onto the Northern Circular walk from Llancarfan.*

From the 18th century **Fox and Hounds Inn**, Llancarfan, walk along the road northwards, parallel to the stream for 50 yards, until you reach the ford. Cross the stream and walk on past the 'Try your Brakes' sign. At the crossroads turn left and then almost immediately right at the footpath sign. Here follow a tree-lined path to a stile where you bear left for a very short distance. Now proceed across the field to a crossing point over a muddy ditch. Head across the next field towards the far right hand corner. Cross double stiles, then continue through a long field diagonally upwards towards the far right hand corner, where there is a ladder stile. *(There is the probability of a path diversion in this field so look out for any relevant signs).*

Once over the ladder stile you are in a **Nature Reserve**. Take heed of any notices.

Coed Garnllwyd ancient woodland, growing from a limestone derived soil, contains oak, ash, hazel, field maple, holly, crab-apple, spindle, hawthorn and wayfaring-tree. The ground flora contains some unusual plants, typical of lime-rich ancient woodlands, such as herb-paris, broad-leaved helleborine, early-purple orchid, as well as the more common bluebell, goldilocks buttercup and wood anemone. It is part of the **Nant Whitton SSSI** site half a mile north-east of Llancarfan. If you just want to visit this site, park the car in Llancarfan, and access by the public footpath just south of Garnllwyd Farm on the Llancarfan-Bonvilston Road, or through the livery stables on the Walterston to Llancarfan road. **Garn-llwyd** itself is a Grade 2 listed building. It is situated about a mile north of Llancarfan. It is a late medieval house possessing a first floor hall with a 'minstrel gallery'. A 17th century wing was added to the house. Close by there is an interesting barn that has now undergone residential redevelopment. A 100 yards to the south west there is an old mill (on the route of a Public Right of Way) which is also now a private residence. Coed Garnllwyd covers both Nant Whitton and Llancarfan Valleys, and there is a spring-line forming wet flushes and wells throughout the woodland. Buzzards abound in these valleys, along with the shy treecreeper and nuthatch. Bullfinches and whitethroats are also fairly common, and at dusk you may spot a tawny owl.

Follow the path to the right and then uphill along the steps. At the top, turn left at the waymark. 30 yards further on, just past a very large beech tree, turn right and follow the path up a slope to a stile. Immediately after this there is a second stile, that leads into a field to your left. Turn immediately right, hugging the right-hand field boundary, until you reach a stile that leads you back into the field, the corner of which you crossed earlier. Cross this field to a stile beside a gate. *This area can be very muddy in winter.* Now walk down a drive beside a garage and over a stile to a road. Turn left for 500 yards, passing a Walterston sign, until you reach a house, **Flaxland Fach**, on your left. *Opposite this there is a track to Flaxland Farm, which you may follow if you wish to shorten the walk.* Otherwise, continue along the road to the hamlet of Walterston.

Turn right in front of the historic **Trewallter Fawr** then through a gate at a footpath sign. **Walterston Fawr farmhouse** (Trewalter Fawr] is a Grade 2 listed building, a typical 16th century farmhouse. However the left-hand section of the house and the doorway were built in 1725. The house has been rendered and colour-washed. Go straight across the field and down to a footbridge. Once over the footbridge, bear left uphill to a stile between the trees. Cross two fields following the line of trees on your left, until you arrive at a farm track. Turn left through the gate and then immediately right, with the hedge on your right, to the stile in the far corner. **Flaxland Farm** is to your left. Continue in the same direction, but with the hedge now on your left. At the next stile cross the field, diagonally, to the far right corner. Continue with the field boundary now to your right to the next stile, then in the same direction, but with the boundary on your left, downhill to a cottage.

Along this stretch of the walk you can see to your left **Llancarfan Iron Age hillfort**. Continue down the track which swings right. Go over a bridge. Here you have a choice of routes. *You may continue along the quiet country lane, uphill at first and then down, past the primary school back into Llancarfan.* Or you can, almost immediately, turn left at a stile into a long field. Cross this field walking parallel to the small stream on the left, possibly over an electric fence, and then via a gate and stile to the road near **Ford Farm**. To the right of Ford farm is the easiest access to the hill-fort, with its splendid views of the coast. Turn right along this road. Soon you will reach a road junction. Turn right if you wish to return to Llancarfan. However, you can turn left if you wish to continue on the full Llancarfan circular walk (available from Valeways).

Footnote on Llancarfan Wells

Francis Jones's *Holy Wells of Wales* lists at least four holy or healing wells in Llancarfan. Firstly, Coed Ffynnon Dyfrig near Garnllwyd at the far end of the wood and above Abernant. The 6th century St. Dyfrig is one of the dedicatory saints of Llandaff Cathedral and he ordained the great St Samson, one of the founding saints of Brittany. Dyfrig's authority extended over the monasteries of Llantwit Major and Barry Island. Secondly, to the south, is Ffynnon y Clwyf (the Well of Sickness) on the north bank of the Ford stream, and just below Llancarfan Castle Ditches hill fort. It was known as 'King's Evil Well' and used to heal the King's Evil, scrofula. *Clwyf y Brenin* is the old Welsh name for the King's Evil, so Ffynnon y Clwyf possibly comes from *Ffynnon Clwyf y Brenin*. Llancarfan's wells are rich in iron and sulphur, and dietary deficiencies meant that iron was needed by peasants. Sulphur-based ointments were recommended for skin diseases, so it is possible that bathing in the water would have helped people suffering from mild skin complaints. Scrofula is a type of tuberculosis, and regular bathing in the well's water could have eased the skin eruptions which were its most obvious symptom. According to Francis Jones, this well was also called the Rag Well. Traditionally, the rags hung at wells are suppose to be left untouched and never removed or taken away. Anyone who touched them would risk contamination with the original disease or problem. The third well, Ffynnon y Fflamwydden, was also used as a rag well. It is the well on the south side of the Moulton brook in the Breach Wood, and known locally now as Breach Well. This was used for the healing of skin complaints, used at least until 1935. *Fflamwydden* is the Welsh word for erysipelas, which was still quite common in the area in the early years of the 20th century, and local people resorted to the well when conventional medical treatment failed. Ffynnon Llancarfan was described as being *'about two fields from the village'*. It is possible that this is the sulphur well in the grounds of the Old Bakehouse, described by Francis Jones as a rag well with a reputation for curing the King's Evil. One well not mentioned in *Holy Wells of Wales* is the chalybeate well in the grounds of Garnllwyd House. Like the other wells in the area, this would have been rich in iron and might therefore have had therapeutic properties. There are many more wells - healing and holy - throughout the Vale, which were

Rhoose Point southerly point standing stone -
Terry Breverton

detailed in the author's 'The Book of Welsh Saints'. The estimable and flourishing Llancarfan Society has an excellent website with more information on local wells.

Footnote on Caradog of Llancarfan

This monk flourished around 1135. It seems that Caradog and Geoffrey of Monmouth knew each other, for Geoffrey said that he would leave the history of the Kings of the Welsh to Caradog of Llancarfan, and the history of the Kings of the English to William of Malmesbury and Henry of Huntingdon. Whether Caradog completed his history is difficult to tell, as so much early material has been destroyed. He is known in history, however, for his Life of Cadog, the founder of Llancarfan. It seems that Caradog moved to Glastonbury because of the Norman despoiling of Llancarfan, and it is said that he died there in 1156.

WALK 45 - RHOOSE POINT TO FONTYGARY BAY

WALK K OF THE SEASCAPE TRAIL

About 2 miles, unsuitable for pushchairs and wheelchairs. Park at Rhoose Point (sigposted from the Barry-Rhoose Road. Alternatively, park in Rhoose, or at Fontygary (Ffon-ty-gari) Leisure Centre and walk the other way.

Simply follow the cliff path until you reach the caravan park, through which the walk continues to Aberthaw and Gileston. There are land sculptures around the lakes at Rhoose Point. If you follow the main path between the lakes, from the stone pillar noting the southern-most point in Wales, you will see on your right, in the dip of the

The Coast near Fontygari - Terry Breverton

old quarry, the foundations of a church. This is a modern sculpture. After exploring the landscaping around Rhoose Point, take the cliff path west. You will follow a ridge of limestone, with on one side the sea, and some fine views of the beach and its tessellated pavements, and on your right the huge quarries, no longer worked. This quarry would make a fabulous boating lake, if allowed to fill with water. The path is quite good and wide here, until you come to some stone steps down into a small valley. The footpath to your right leads to Station Road in the centre of Rhoose. The path now, up some wooden steps, becomes very muddy in winter, and still follows the clifftop. You eventually reach a football field, and in its corner a **Millennium Beacon**. Just past the beacon are steps leading down to Fontygary Bay. You can turn right and head up to the Leisure Park, or carry on along the coastal walk up the steps opposite you. If you turn right, there is an excellent Fish and Chip shop based in the old Fontygary/Rhoose station, just before the railway bridge, and it is open from around Easter until October. If you go under the railway bridge, you will see opposite the Fontygary Inn, a Brains pub, and the road past it leads to Fonmon Pool and Castle.

You can use the excellent facilities at the leisure park's **leisure centre**, including its indoor swimming pool (for a small charge) and café and bar. The beach can be accessed down steep steps from the caravan park, which is on **Watch House Point**. Rhose Lifeguard Club is just next to the steps, and there are some superb viewpoints from the cliffs. **Fontygary Cave** is just west of the beach access at Fontygary, but inaccessible at high tide. If you access the beach, please be aware that the tide comes in very quickly, and you can be cut off, and that there is **always** the danger of falling rocks at every cliff face from Penarth to Gileston. The steps to the beach and rocks at Fontygary are very slippery in winter.

Never walk too close to the cliffs, nor rest/sunbathe under them. The author has personally witnessed several rock-falls in the last five years, ranging from a few stones to tons of rubble. Even a small stone can break a skull. There is sand when the tide is out. Generally, it is much safer to swim when the tide is coming in on this coastline. There are strong currents and undertows along the whole coastline, which are far more difficult to counteract when the tide is receding. There are many newcomers in the Vale, who have not grown up here. Locals are more aware of the dangers of the sea here, and should be consulted about swimming. If in doubt, or by yourself, never go into the sea above your waist, and keep very near to your children. I will not let my children, who are reasonable swimmers, go out of their depth in certain conditions, and always go into the water when they go in. The sea here is a wonderful asset that many of us do not appreciate, much warmer than off Cornwall, but has to be respected. It can be a great spectacle in winter storms, with crashing waves, but keep a very safe distance - people get swept out to sea every winter along the Welsh coast.

WALKS IN AND AROUND ABERTHAW, GILESTON, ST TATHAN AND FLEMINGSTON

St. Hilary Church - Cathy Crompton

Aberthaw (Aber Ddawen) used to be an important port, but the river was straightened and the medieval port was covered by the Coal-Fired Power Station. The cement works opposite the Blue Anchor now belongs to the French company, Lafarge. The villages of St Tathan (Llandathan), Gileston (Llanfabon-y-Fro), Aberthaw (Aberddawen), Flemingston (Llanelwan) and Eglwys Brewys, in the present parish of St Tathan, are all covered in far more detail in the author's 'The Secret Vale of Glamorgan'. There are books on most of the Vale villages, such as St Hilary. Your knowledgeable local bookshop, such as Cowbridge Bookshop, Nickleby's at Llanilltud Fawr and Dolphin Books in Barry, will be only too pleased to help you find whatever you want. The large chains hold a very poor selection of books of local interest.

WALK 46 - EAST ABERTHAW (BLUE ANCHOR) TO PLEASANT HARBOUR TO GILESTON

About 4.5 miles (7 km) - not suitable for pushchairs and wheelchairs.

Park in the large carpark opposite the thatched **Blue Anchor** inn. Turn left out of the carpark, and left again down the hill to start the walk. *(Alternatively, make a small detour not turning down Well Road, but carry on on past **Aberthaw Bethel Baptist Church**, which was founded before 1800. The hill leads down to the junction of the Thaw and Kenson Rivers, and on your left just past the chapel is a small pottery, the only one in Wales making copper 'lustre' jugs. This type of pottery can be traced back to the 1700's, when tin was brought from Cornwall for smelting in Swansea. Retrace your footsteps past Marsh House and turn right down Well Road.)* The integral village of East Aberthaw is a **Conservation Area**, with **Marsh House** (formerly the Maltster's Arms) being Grade II and the thatched Blue Anchor being Grade II*. Next to Marsh House, the Old Granary is also early 17th century. Part of this group of buildings, Marsh Cottage is around the same date, and is now two houses. The former Marsh House, down the Leys, was also noted by the Commissioners, but has been destroyed by the dumping of fly-ash. It was the last castle built in Wales. There was Roman occupation at Penmark, Fonmon, Nurston and East Aberthaw. In 1957 a pipeline was laid through East Aberthaw when 2nd - 3rd century pottery, shells, tiles and animal bones were found. 1959 excavations in **Well Road** found dry stone wall foundations of a Roman settlement, and an oven with charcoal marks. There were

Llantrithyd - Cathy Crompton

thousands of limpet shells, pieces of cooking pots and dishes, a bangle, a T-shaped brooch with a spring, a Valentinian I coin dating from 364-375, tiles and Samian ware pottery. Turning down Well Road, Tyle House is opposite the 18th century Well Cottage. The Haven is an early 17th century hearth passage house, and next to it is Cape Horn Cottage, reminding us of the former importance of the port. *Coming back up Well Road to the main road, Lower Farm House on the right is possibly as old as the Blue Anchor, predating Marsh House and Marsh Cottage which were built in 1602. Rose Cottage is mediaeval with 17th century additions, until recently thatched, with joist-beam ceilings and a clay bake-oven. The thatched* **Blue Anchor** *Inn is a fine example of a well-built yeoman farmhouse, like Breach farm at Llanblethian. It has the only two-centred mediaeval doorway in timber in Glamorgan, leading to an inner room. There is also a 16th century timber doorway with a three-centred head there. Mid 16th-century, there is rumoured to have been an inn on the site since the 13th century, and an old tale that there was a smugglers' tunnel to the beach. The view over the Channel, when seated outside, has been obscured by the ash tips of Innogy, now German-owned.*

Pass under the railway bridge at the bottom of Well Road, and in front of you is the site of an ancient **holy well**, marked on OS maps but seemingly covered over. Perhaps it can be uncovered and restored. Cross the stile and head left. *(You can take a right turn along the path, which leads to an old quarry through mixed woodland, and either cut back up to the village over an old and ornate railway bridge, or take a parallel trail returning alongside the small pond and tips to the stile).* One of the great tragedies of the siting of the Power Station is that '*...there is always the unique and unexpected in South Glamorgan. There is no finer example than Marsh House at East Aberthaw. Here, in 1636, a local entrepreneur named Thomas Spencer built what amounted to almost the last castle in Wales. He constructed for himself a fortified compound used for the storage of illegally imported tobacco and probably other valuable cargoes. These were released onto the market when prices were highest'.* There was a fortified house, store-rooms and a

Ruin, Gileston Beach - Cathy Crompton

107

Aberthaw Beach looking to Fontygari - Cathy Crompton

large compound enclosed by walls pierced by musket loops. Unfortunately and illegally, the CEGB and then National Power, Innogy's precursors at Aberthaw, tipped tonnes of waste ash upon it, just before a conservation order could be processed. Also the remarkable old 16th century Customs House, the Booth, was destroyed. Along the path through the woods, you can cut off right onto a parallel path, or return that way. You will come to a small cottage on your right. It is known as Pleasant Harbour, and although much altered, was originally was an end-entry hearth passage house. Before the sea-wall was built, ships used to lie at anchor in the shelter of **Pleasant Harbour**, tying up to buoys off Lime Kiln Wharf. A quay was built next to the great kiln building and trams were used to take the burned limestone to the railway and the boats. The lime factory was erected in 1888 and should be preserved as a reminder of the past heritage of this port. Unfortunately, there is a dispute about its ownership, with both relevant parties claiming that it is not their responsibility. *(You can shorten the walk by taking the stile on your right at the end of the lane, and skirting to the right hand side of the pool. A path can take you back to Aberthaw, or you can cut between the waste tips and the lake to the sea wall, and follow it all the way to Gileston).*

You cross the lane in front of you, and carry on, past signs telling you to beware of snakes, to the back of the Lime Factory. Carry on down to the sea wall. From here you can cross the SSSI and take the steps up to Fontygary Caravan park and continue the coastal walk. The area known as Pleasant Harbour used to be an expanse of tidal sandy pools, heated by the sun and extremely popular with holiday-makers. Hundreds of people from the valleys used to walk from Aberthaw Halt and Gileston Halt down to the seaside on weekends. A couple of pools survive, of which Andrew's Pant is the tidal SSSI, and the lake behind the sea wall is now freshwater. This larger pool is home to swans, moorhens, coots and recently the ubiquitous Canada Geese. The rushes and reeds contain warblers, and at least four types of orchid can be seen here, as well as Evening Primrose. The orchids are the impressively tall Southern Marsh Orchid, the Pyramidal Orchid, the

Old Limeworks, Aberthaw - Cathy Crompton

St. Michael's, Flemingston - Cathy Crompton

Lady's Tresses Orchid and the Marsh Helleborine. Take the sea wall walk to **Limpert Bay**, heading west. As with many of the walks in this book, if you want to spend some time, take two cars - leave one on the carpark on Gileston Beach/Limpert Bay and one at Aberthaw. There are parking spots on the road above Pleasant Harbour, but one cannot rule out the danger of vandalism as there are no properties overlooking them.

WALK 47 - FONTYGARY TO ABERTHAW TO LIMPERT BAY

WALK L OF THE SEASCAPE TRAIL

About 4 miles (7km) not suitable for pushchairs or wheelchairs

Fontygary was originally a separate village, but is now joined to Rhoose. From Fontygary you can walk up inland to Fonmon Pool and Castle, passing medieval house platforms on your left. Access the coastal walk at Rhoose Point, and follow the coast to Fontygary Caravan Park. There is an excellent fish and chip shop open here, except in the winter months, on the premises of the old railway station. The Leisure Park itself has a bar, café, swimming pool, sauna and leisure facilities open to the public. From Fontygary Bay, you can go up the steep (and muddy steps) heading west. If you park in the car park, it is easier to walk down towards the cliffs, and take the public footpath which follows the line of the cliffs, forming the southern boundary of the caravan park. Please do not 'explore' the caravan park - it is private.

The coastal path passes along the top of the cliffs inside the caravan park, and access can be made to the beach by steps, at the end of the park, to **Aberthaw Saltmarsh** (marked as Andrew's Pant on the OS map). From the top here is a lovely view onto the lagoons, and you can imagine what the whole area was like before the power station was erected. Take care walking down the steps. *There is a right-hand path, but ignore it - it leads over the railway line to the main Aberthaw-Rhoose Road.* These cliffs, saltmarsh, sand dune and pebble beach form part of the East Aberthaw **SSSI** of 90 acres, just east of the power station soil tips. It is not the lake near the disused cement mill, but the lagoons over the sea-wall, protected by the storm beach of pebbles and shingle. At its eastern limit, where it converges with the pebble beach, a small salt-marsh can be seen, with salt-tolerant plants and coastal grasses. The Yellow Horned Poppy can be seen here. There is also the remains of the huge sand dune system that once extended across much of south Wales, with Sea Holly. Teasels are common, and Stinking Iris, Marsh Helleborine and Autumn Ladies Tresses can be seen, while the cliffs support Maidenhair Fern and Water Figwort. The reserve is one of Glamorgan's premier bird sites, and Whimbrel, Little Ringed Plover, Little Grebe and Turtle Dove have been recorded. Redshank, Turnstone and

Ringed Plover are usually present on the beach the year through, and regular wintering birds include Little Grebe, Grey Plover, Merlin and Peregrine Falcon. Over 80 different species were spotted over 6 months in 2002, among them being egret, wryneck, grey phalarope and warblers. The saline lagoon is on land owned by Innogy -Aberthaw Power Station, and is one of only four such sites in Wales. The constant salinity allows the lagoon cockle to breed there. The lake inside the seawall is home to several species of birdlife, and the grassed waste-tips are covered with Southern Marsh, Bee and Pyramidal Orchids. On the SSSI, the convoluta flatworm is only found here and upon Jersey. The True Service Tree, Britain's rarest tree, grows near here. Not so long ago, there were dozens of these saline lagoons and sand dunes (the Twts) along the coast here, now covered by waste heaps from the power station.

From the salt marsh you come to the **sea wall** protecting the power station. You can walk inside it, but most walkers prefer to walk upon it. On your left you will see groynes which form small sandy beaches which you can explore. At low tide the inlet and outlets for the power station can be seen. On your right you will see a lake and

the old **limestone works**. *(Alternatively you can cut up the path on the right hand side of the large* **freshwater lagoon** *towards Aberthaw and the thatched Blue Anchor pub.)* In front of you are the waste tips of Aberthaw Power Station. These are scheduled to be moved, but it will take decades. The whole site of the power station in front of you used to be part common land and part golf club. Legislation is in place that the land must be returned to its natural state when the power station closes, but

Llantrithyd Place - Cathy Crompton

there have since been two changes of owner with privatisation. Whether the people will once again have access to what was a site frequented by holiday-makers is a moot point. The fate of the ancient port of Aberthaw, and the beaches here, have been covered comprehensively in the author's *'The Secret Vale of Glamorgan'*. The sea wall allows the exit of the Thaw, and after crossing the river, to walk inside it usually means that you have no view of the sea whatsoever. There is also a persistent problem with dogs being allowed to foul it, so most local people walk on the wall. There are excellent views, including an upturned concrete WWII emplacement. The sea can be awesome here in winter.

Follow the sea wall around the power station, to come to the eastern end of the **Glamorgan Heritage Coast**, at **Limpert Bay**, where the road leads north to Gileston and St Athan. The house next to the beach used to be the sail-loft south of the Limpert Inn. Just opposite, where the Power Station is now, was Mustow's Café for day-trippers. Looking at the sea, the land on one's right is called **'The Walls'**, and the small lake that fills with fresh water every winter is known as Walls Pool. The bay in

West Orchard Castle remains - Cathy Crompton

front is Limpert Bay, with the coastline just a few hundred yards west called Penry Bay, which had its own pier. You can see the line of massive concrete blocks to prevent landings during the war. The power station now occupies the site of Ocean House, about halfway between the Limpert Inn and Breaksea Point, and there was also a lime-kiln and a boat-house in this area. At the point where the sea wall now is a right-angle and disappears from your sight, was a series of sand dunes and pools known as The Twats on old maps, but to the locals as the 'twts'. Carrying on past this place along the sea wall, just fifty yards, was the site of the Ship Inn, with a flagstaff and rocket station (for firing flares). Between Ocean House and the Ship Inn were several footbridges, public footpaths and the mediaeval Limpert Well, north of which was the freshwater Leys Pool, a noted place for anglers.

Looking directly south from the Limpert, at low tide **Gallant Acre** and Table Rock are exposed. Just to the west of these, the outcrop is called Little Breaksea. Breaksea Point is the most southerly part of Wales, and a lightship used to be based on the offshore Breaksea Sands. Gallant (or Galliant) Acre, just south of Breaksea Point, is supposedly named for the mariners who lost their lives here as ships foundered in past storms. Earlier this century, no less than 20 ships are supposed to have come ashore in the fog on one bad night here. It must also be remembered that forty foot tides are common along this coastline, second only in magnitude to the Bay of Fundy. However, rumours of a settlement and old walls at Gallant Acre were so strong that the author discovered that there was a castle here, destroyed in the same great storm that obliterated Porthkerry Castle in the time of the Normans, which stood where Castle Rock can still be seen at low tides. From 'Siluriana' we read *'In the reign of Richard II, a very high tide in the month of March, drove on by a great south-west wind, destroyed the castles of Aberthaw and Porth Cirick (Porth Curig, i.e. Porthkcrry), and also utterly destroyed the harbour of Porth Cirick. The **Castle of Aberthaw** stood on the place now called the Garland Acre, where were games kept yearly on May-Day, and where those who excelled in them set up garlands decked with the favours of their sweethearts on a May pole. This spot of ground was the castle green. The beach and sand were driven up so high that the wide plain called the Lays (sic) was almost entirely ruined and torn away by the sea. The town of Cynfick and Cantelupeston were also destroyed by this tide, which together with the winde, threw the sand up in such large heaps, as to overwhelm the houses, and destroy all before it. The church of Towin was so damaged, that it fell down, and was never after repaired or rebuilt. Here was the principal place of burial for the Lords of*

Glamorgan.' There were great recriminations from the villages of St Tathan and Gileston when the golf club was built, as it illegally took over common ground and public footpaths. The imposition of the first Power Station was equally fought against, with three older villagers petitioning the House of Lords, but, as always in these cases, 'might equals right'.

Blue Anchor, East Aberthaw - Cathy Crompton

WALK 48

GILESTON TO ST ATHAN TO EAST ORCHARD CASTLE

About 3 miles (5km)

Park on the beach car park at Gileston. There are toilets and public conveniences on the car park just inland, but it is better to have the car less hidden, and parked in the open. Walk up to Gileston Village, and bear left past Gileston Manor and Gileston Church.

According to Iolo Morganwg, **St Mabon** ab Usyllt (Enlleu) was the brother of Teilo, also called Mabon Wyn, and he was feasted on September 21st. In Llandeilo Fawr. Gileston Parish Church was originally dedicated to St Mabon, and the Welsh name for the parish was **Llanfabon-y-Fro**, not Silstwn as the local road sign states. The name of Gileston came from the Norman family that held the lands around 1350. Gileston itself is a **Conservation Area**, and the Church of St Giles is a listed building, with Gileston Manor being Grade II* listed. The old red telephone kiosk is listed Grade II. Gileston Barn is also listed. During the laying of a lawn at Gileston Manor,

The Bush, St. Hilary - Cathy Crompton

many bones were found, some badly damaged. It appears that they were buried here after a skirmish, possibly when the Danes fired Gileston and Llantwit in the 11th century. They may be linked with the helmet, sword and bones found near Gileston Cross (the crossroads where we see the War Memorial on the outskirts of St Tathan) in the 19th century. The bones were re-interred, forming a small hillock which can be seen in Gileston churchyard.

Fonmon Castle - Cathy Crompton

Gileston Cottage (c.1600) used to be thatched, Ivy Cottage is medieval (although much 'modernised') and **Rose Cottage** in Gileston has been dated to 1600, and is the village's last thatched cottage. The village well is still in existence in a garden on the left, heading eastwards out of Gileston. The **15th century Church** lies on the site of the earlier church, and is romantically situated, next to Gileston Manor in the grounds of which it lies. There is a chancel, nave, south porch and tower with battlements with one bell. The large four-step **churchyard cross** was destroyed by Cromwell's soldiers as being idolatrous (somehow only that at St Donat's escaped vandalism across the Southern Vale), but was restored in 1900. There is a tomb to the Giles family dated 1618, with the arms of Matthew Giles and his wife.

Gileston Manor is a fine Grade II* Queen Anne house enclosing an earlier 16th century first-floor hall-type residence. Gileston Farm lies just south of Gileston Manor, and seems to be early 19th century. Past the farm, following the lane past the cemetery, is another part of the farm known as 'The Cott.' In the fields down from the Cott are the remains of a barn, limekiln and smallholding. Near the Walls, 'Dunne's Pool' fills up every winter, and there appear to have been buildings on the beach here. 100 yards up from Dunne's Pool there used to be a big stone in the hedge bank, which may have been a Celtic or Romano-Celtic burial marker still in existence. Curlew, Lapwing (less frequently) and Skylarks can still be seen on the fields leading down to the Walls. Most winters a pair of shelduck appears, but there has been no breeding recorded recently. There is probably not enough cover from foxes and dogs.

You can divert from Gileston to West Aberthaw (East Aberthaw is the other side of the river) - take the road, or there is a path on the lane between Gileston and the sea. The port of Aberthaw was East of the power station, and at very low tides a few piles mark where the harbour was. The Thaw has been channelled through the power station, and its outlet is about 300 yards West of the original one. From the port, carts went through Gileston and St Tathan to Cowbridge. There was a causeway at low tides for traffic approaching the harbour from

Old Beaupré Castle - Cathy Crompton

113

Barri and Cardiff. Just below Booth House was a chain used to pull boats up onto the riverside for caulking, tarring, repairing and sealing.

The 17th century **West Aberthaw Farm** is a Grade II listed end-entry hearth passage house, with lateral-entry stone stairs and a bake-oven. The 'terracing' of the fields here suggest that the Romans grew vines on these fields. **West Aberthaw Chapel** is a mediaeval building west of the farmhouse,

Castell y Moel - Cathy Crompton

dedicated to St Nicholas, now a cattle shed and part of West Aberthaw Farm. Iolo Morgannwg noted it, along with the other ruined chapels at Castleton, West Orchard and East Orchard, but it was 'lost' for many years. It measures 21 feet in length and has an inserted upper floor, cutting across a large blocked window which used to illuminate the altar. The nearby well could make it a Celtic Christian foundation, but the name of the founding saint may never be known. Perhaps, however, this is where Tathana lived. West Aberthaw, with its farm buildings, earthworks and chapel, was once one of the most romantic places in Wales, prior to the building of the power station. Surface traces of two platform houses are visible of the deserted **mediaeval village** in West Aberthaw, and ancient stone wall foundations are still below the earth there. **West Hall** was owned by the Morgan family, but financial problems led to the abandonment of the conversion of the Georgian Hall into a retirement home. Thus the building is in limbo, half-converted, with its Georgian fireplaces and mouldings stripped out. There was a magnificent spiral staircase, and the view from the first floor balcony, over the Channel before the power station blighted the view, was superb. The **'Boys Camp'** with many buildings including a chapel, has been closed for many years. This was formerly a Miners' Welfare Home, then taken over by the YMCA. At present no-one seems to know who owns it, or its future.

Gileston Beach - Cathy Crompton

Heading up the lane to St Tathan, cross over the road at the crossroads, past the **War Memorial**, and head down into St Athan Village. Visit the **medieval church of St Tathan**. In the Church of Sain Tathan are two beautiful painted tombs of the Berkerolles. Sir Roger Berkerolles died in 1351, and lies with the effigy of his wife, Katherine Turberville of Coity Castle. At the

Fontygari beach - Cathy Crompton

end of his tomb is the coat of arms of Iestyn ap Gwrgant, the last native Welsh Prince of Glamorgan (Morgannwg). Sir William Berkerolles, who died in 1327, is nearby with his wife Phelice de Vere.

*From the churchyard, you can divert and take the west exit and head straight across on the old Llantwit Road leading to Higher End. You will pass the thatched Myrtle Cottage and the remarkable 15th century **West Orchard Farm**, with 5 in-line* chimneys. **West Orchard Castle** *is a series of humps, next to some springs, through a gateway, where there is a lane turning left towards Llanilltud Fawr. West Orchard Castle was first destroyed by 'Ifor Bach', Ifor ap Meurig, Lord of Senghenydd, probably around the time he captured the great Earl William of Gloucester from Cardiff Castle in 1158. It seems to have been rebuilt by the Norman Berkerolles family in the thirteenth century, and was destroyed again in the Llywelyn Bren revolt of 1318. It was probably slighted yet again in the great Owain Glyndŵr rebellion between 1401 and 1410. It then passed to the Stradlings of St Donat's Castle when one married the heiress of Sir Lawrence Berkerolles in 1411. The Stradlings then again rebuilt the castle there to rival that at East Orchard. Iron shot from the Second Civil War has been found on the site, plus a cannon ball, and it appears that the castle was almost destroyed after the Battle of St. Fagans in 1648. Experts can still detect the remains of a chapel there, but much of the masonry has been used for local building since the seventeenth century. Some arches can still be seen in the old West Orchard Farm, and its converted barn, Porth Glyndŵr, opposite. People have tried to dump rubbish and gain planning permission on this site, which has been defended against Ifor Bach, Llywelyn Bren, Owain Glyndŵr and Cromwell! There is* even the ghost of The White Lady near the castle, buried to her neck by one of the Berkerolles and left to die. The lane in front of you was the old village road to Llanilltud and Eglwys Brewys, and passes near the medieval, listed **Batslays Farm**, but is a dead-end now. This detour up Higher End adds about a mile-and-a-half to your walk.

If you do not wish to walk up Higher End, west to West Orchard Castle, come out of

Fontygari Bay at low tide - Martin Green

the church by its main entrance, and turn left, and then turn left into the old village of St Tathan, **'The Lanes'**, past the old village school (now a nursery) and corrugated iron library. Follow the little lane to a kissing gate, and down to cross a lane. (*To your left up a small hill is one of the Vale's finest pubs, with superb food, the* **Four Bells**. *If you divert this way, you head down into another old part of the village, Beggars Pound, and can take the lane right into the hamlet of Castleton*). To reach the castle, cross the lane, and take the stile and footpath

Sain Tathan Church - Cathy Crompton

just to the right of the two houses in front of you. Keep the Rills Valley on your left, and skirt Castleton Wood, keeping to the edge of the fields above the valley.

East Orchard Castle is on the site of an older castle, recorded before 1314. Half-hidden by woodland, it overlooks the marshy valley of the Thaw, and has its own chapel, barn and dovecote. The columbarium, or dovecote, is twenty feet square, with two hundred recesses. The hall was forty feet by twenty-five, the outside kitchen twenty-eight feet by twenty-five, and the chapel forty-four feet by nineteen. In 1350, an octagonal bellcote was added, and it was taken to Fonmon Castle's stable block around 1850. The thatched Castle Mill is in ruins on the main road nearby, but was working until the early twentieth century. The orchards around here, protected by the village's castles, flourished for centuries. It is said that Henry II (1154 – 1189) passed by in 1171 and was so impressed

Gileston Church - Cathy Crompton

that he ordered all further fruit for his table to come from them. The orchards were probably managed by Flemish cultivators (from nearby Flemingston) who were settled in the Vale of Glamorgan by the Normans. An ancient fig tree was reported to be still bearing fruit back in 1823. King John, whose divorced wife Hadwisa is said to have haunted Boverton Castle, is said to have favoured apples from St. Tathan. Owain Glyndŵr was supposed to have been a 'guest' at East Orchard Castle.

WALK 49 - ST ATHAN TO CASTLETON TO LLANBETHERY TO LLANCADLE

About 6 miles one way, not suitable for wheelchairs or pushchairs.

From St Tathan Church, either take the lane past the nursery and library noted in the walk above, or head east along Rock Road, keeping the fields on your right, past the Four Bells pub, and you will come to the stream and cross-roads in **Beggars Pound**. Turn right along the lane to Castleton. The converted barns on your left are listed buildings, and Castleton Farmhouse on your right contains part of the **medieval castle** of Castleton, guarded on its south side by the steep drop into the Rills Valley. The sea used to come up the Thaw Valley, so the castle could be provisioned against any Welsh sieges. The castle is hidden under the existing farmhouse, on the brow of a steep hill about 100 feet above the confluence of two marshy valleys. There was once a mill in the valley. A few hundred yards further south the two streams join the Thaw near East Orchard Castle. It seems that a simple Norman castle was added to, around the 13th century, and a courtyard enclosed. The defensive walls were removed in Tudor times, and the castle was converted to a manor/farmhouse.

East Orchard Castle - Cathy Crompton

Follow the farm road, around the barns and take the footpath through a gate. Head diagonally to the far corner of a long field, and take the left of the two fields in front of you. Keep to the hedge on your right, and at the end of the field go through a gate. Carry on in a straight line until you reach the woods, and turn left, and towards the end of the field, you will find that the path goes through woodland. It meets the path from Flemingstone to Llanbethery. Turn right on this path, cross the Thaw, and you will come to a small lane heading right. Follow this to **Llanbethery**, past Redholme. Unfortunately mink have over-run much of the beautiful Thaw Valley, wiping out moorhen, coots and other wildlife. There are kingfishers on the Thaw, and towards Cowbridge, breeding otters have returned, however. Hopefully the pylons which disfigure the valley, leading out from Aberthaw Power Station, will one day disappear.

Not far from the **Wild Goose**, after two houses on your right, you will see a footpath on the right. After one field, this forks left to Middlecross and Llancarfan, but fork right, as per the OS map, and following the footpath over seven more fields brings you to Llancadle, on the banks of the Kenson. In the early 7th century, **St Cadell** ab Urien Foeddog ap Rhun Rhion ap Llywarch Hen possibly founded **Llangadell** in Glamorgan. This is now called Llancadle (Llancatal), and his little church is now a farm outhouse. It may well be however, that Llancatal was dedicated to Cadog (Cathmael). The hamlet is just upriver from Aberthaw. This village, with 'The Green Dragon' pub and about fifteen houses, was variously known as Talcatlon and Llandili. St Catlon (a witness to the Landaff Charters) and St Cadell have been associated with it, but

Fonmon Pool - Cathy Crompton

possibly it was once known as Llan Gadfael. Catlon was a witness to the Llandaf Charters, and he is another contender for the founder of the church. Again, Vortigern (Gwrtheyrn) has also been called Catel, which is another possibility for the founder. There is also a legend of the Romans or Normans fighting on the bank of the nearby river Kenson. *Cad-lle* means place of battle. Some of Cromwell's soldiers are also said to be buried in the field leading down to the river, and there is a tradition that he worshipped in the church. The ancient Lancadle chapel was visited by the vicar of Llancarfan until about 1925, and is now a barn.

There are several footpaths leading from Llancadle, and its **Green Dragon** pub, which usually has draft scrumpy on tap. The most direct route back to St Tathan is to follow the lane south, and turn right on the busy, twisty road past the remains of Castle Mill. Just opposite the petrol station, a lane leads to St Tathan, being the former main road across the Vale between Barry and Llanilltud Fawr.

WALK 50 - ABERTHIN TO ST HILARY

About 5 miles (8km) circular, not suitable for wheelchairs or pushchairs.

While Aberthin, just north of Cowbridge, is outside the original remit of this book, this walk links up with the St Hilary to Flemingston pathway (Walk 51) and then from Flemingston to the Heritage Coast. It is one of the links on the continuous path from Bryngarw Country Park via Heol-y-Cyw, Penllyn and Llansannor to the coast. This *'Walk Through the Vale'* leaflet is available from the Bridgend Countryside Access Project (01656 722315). A future book by this author will include some wonderful walks around Cowbridge and in the Northern Vale towards Bridgend.

The coast between Aberthaw and Fontygari
- Terry Breverton

There are *'Cowbridge Circular Walks'* leaflets available from the Information Office at Cowbridge, a hundred yards east of the Town Hall. From the Roman town of Bovium (Cowbridge), you can take the eastern Cowbridge Circular Walk into Aberthin, or park in Aberthin. Walk up Llanquian Road, and turn right onto a waymarked path up a steep hill. This area is **Stalling Down**, from which there are superb views, and where Owain Glyndŵr fought a battle in 1401 in the great war of independence of 1400-1415 (see G.J. Brough's *'Glyn Dwr's War - the Campaigns of the Last Prince of Wales'*). You will reach the access road to **Hollybush Farm**, when you turn right, and follow the main road past the garage and over the dual

The SSSI at Aberthaw - Terry Breverton

carriageway. (Near Hollybush Farm are the remains of the medieval **Llanquian Castle**, with a hall over a vaulted cellar, and also the great **Iron Age hillfort** in Llanquian Wood.) Head for the restaurant, and shortly after the restaurant turn right and follow the path, making for the top of the hill, near a radio mast. **The Clump** or **Hanging Wood** was planted by John Montgomery Traherne in the 19th century. Prisoners were marched from Cowbridge Gaol for public hanging at this spot. Carry on the track, now going downhill, to St Hilary. **St Hilary** is a pretty village with a 15th century church, and a 17th century thatched pub/restaurant, **The Bush**, which sells excellent draught scrumpy. There is a circular stone pigsty at Church Cottage, similar to that near Llantrithyd and the one at the Museum of Welsh Life.

WALK 51 ST HILARY TO FLEMINGSTON TO ST TATHAN

About 7 miles (12 km) - not suitable for pushchairs or wheelchairs

The medieval church at St Hilary was founded in 1090, and the village was one of those where the Mari Llwyd was celebrated every Christmas. In nearby Beaupre Woods are old silver and lead mines. The 6th century Welsh **St Hilary** was also known as Eilian or Elian Geimiad (The Pilgrim), and was feasted on January 13th and 14th, as well as the first three Fridays in August. He was a contemporary of the noted saints Cybi and Seiriol on Anglesey, where he founded Llanelian. He was the son of Gallgu Rieddog and Canna, the daughter of Tewdwr Mawr of Llydaw. He may have founded a cell here, which was taken over by the Normans. The church, built in the late 12th century, is now dedicated to the 4th century saint, Bishop Hilarius of Poitiers. Nearly every Welsh church was rededicated by the Normans.

Leave St Hilary and the Eastern Cowbridge Circular Walk and take the lane to Flemingston. Keep the Manor House on your right as you leave. Turn right just after the Old Vicarage and follow a rough road south-west and downhill. Turn right and the junction, and then left. *(You can make a detour if you wish to visit **St Mary Church**, a medieval church high on the ridge overlooking the Channel).* You will soon reach **Flemingston**. If you take the other lane out of St Hilary, south-east, you come to a cross-roads where the old barn used to be the Cross Inn. Go straight across, past

Treguff, and you come to Aberogwrn Farm. Merrick in 1578 noted the fish-ponds at *'Lanrithyd, Lancarvan, Est Orchard, Bewper, St Hillary, Tregoof, St Donnett's'* etc. Their remains can still be easily seen at East Orchard and Old Beaupre. The incidence of a fish-pond may denote a monastic settlement at **Treguff**. The old house is mediaeval, with plaster Tudor roses and ER monograms found in several rooms. A mediaeval chapel has been found here, and there used to be twenty-six houses at Treguff in the 18th century, but all that remains is the great house and a couple of barn conversions. The nearby Nant Treguff has brown trout in it.

Aberthaw - Terry Breverton

Either head straight on to Pancross (near Pancross is a ring and bailey **castle**) and then left down into Llancarfan, or take the next left to **Llanbethery**. Ken Wall, in a 1994 Llancarfan Society newsletter, records an open field across the deep valley of Pant-y-Coed. *'Sixteen hundred years ago the area would have probably been all forest except for a small clearing in which there was a Roman building. Excavation has revealed a layer of occupation soil with coarse pottery of the 2nd to 4th centuries AD. Animal bones, iron nails, slag, roof- and box-tiles were also found (O.S. 0355 7023). About 58 metres from the building was found, in 1957, the lower part of a vessel of grey ware containing the remains of a Roman hoard. This consisted of 814 coins, many of them Constantinian issues of 330-335 AD.*

From Llanbethery you can cross the Thaw to get to **Flemingston**. **St Michael's Church** dates from the early 13th century and the attractive village was the home of Iolo Morganwg. (There are many legends of the Ceffyl-Dwr along the moors between Flemingston and the Old Mill at Aberthaw, an evil spirit in the form of a water-horse). From Flemingston, as you leave the village, take the footpath on the left across fields and down to a bridge over the River Thaw, if you wish to follow the paths to Llanbethery, Penmarc and Porthceri. However, to reach St Tathan, do not cross the bridge, but head uphill towards **Oxmoor Woods** and continue on the waymarked route. You will reach Castleton Farm, and follow the waymarks along the Rills Valley to cross the stream at **Rills Well**. At Castleton, the **castle** is the oldest in the area, and is hidden under the existing farmhouse. Its cattle-sheds and fine 3-bay barn (now all converted to luxury homes) are also Grade II listed, and there is a spiral staircase, Tudor windows and a fine carved fire bressumer. The rubble-built barn (now a home) is mediaeval, with a large opposing arched doorway in dressed stone. From Rills Well, head to the left of the houses, and when you cross the stile to the road, there is a little path between the houses in front of you, which will take you through 'The Lanes' of the old village towards **St Tathan's Church**.

Legends place **St Tathan** as a warrior saint, the son of Amwn Ddu and Anna, the daughter of Meurig, the king of Glamorgan and Gwent. This would make him King

Arthur's brother-in-law, the brother of Samson and nephew of Illtud. He was trained at Llanilltud Fawr (Llantwit Major) and founded a church at nearby Llandathan (Sain Tathan) in the 6th century, then went to Caerwent to found a monastic school, Cor Tathan, where he became known as the *'Father of Gwent'* and was renowned for miracles. His great influence almost certainly indicates that he was from royal stock. He was feasted on December 26th and 30th. He was said to have taught Abbot Catwg (Cadog), who founded Llancarfan. **St Tathan the Younger** (6th century) was possibly Tathan's son, noted on a panel in St Tathan church. **St Tathana** or **St Braust** is an intriguing story attached to the village. In some local histories, Tathana is posited by some as the founder of St Tathan, not Tathan, and an intriguing part of the legend places the court of Meurig ap Tewdrig at 'Treberfaidd' (Boverton, wrongly named Trebeferad in recent years. The meaning seems be 'sparkling', 'perfect' or 'beaver' town). As local legends constantly place Boverton as the birthplace of Arthur, and Athrwys ap Meurig ap Tewdrig was the real Arthur of history, perhaps the ruins of Boverton Castle should attract tourism into the area. The author recently found a rectangular shape in the Thaw Valley. Made up of a mixture of dressed stone with traces of mortar, and rubble, the ground-level walls were aligned approximately 25 feet East to West, and 15 feet North to South. The Thaw then meandered through the valley, and this would have been close to the high tide level - could this have been the site of Tathana's 6th century church? She was recorded as living in a cell in a valley just above the high-water mark. The site has now been recorded by the Glamorgan-Gwent Archaeological Trust.

WALK 52 BONVILSTON (TRESIMWN) CIRCULAR - SOUTHERN LOOP (A Valeways Walk)

About 4 miles (6 km) - not suitable for pushchairs and wheelchairs. The northern loop of this walk carries on above the A48 and will be included in a future book on walks in the Northern Vale. Cutting down to Llantrhyd and returning will add about another 2 miles to the route. Walking down to Llancarfan and returning will add about another 4 miles). In Bonvilston (Simwnstwn), **St Mary Church** *was built in 1150, has a 15th century tower, and rebuilt in 1863. There are two old pubs which are now more like restaurants, the* **Old Post** *and the* **Aubrey Arms** *(a Beefeater). Further along towards Cardiff in Bonvilston Village on the A48 is the* **Red Lion**, *a more traditional pub, with the added benefits of selling Brains beer (as does the Old Post). The walk starts at the Aubrey Arms, the pub just west of Bonvilston after the Old Post, on the main A48 Cardiff-Bridgend road. Walk south, down the minor road by the side of the pub with Pant-y-Ffynnon quarry to your right. Cross the minor road junction, still heading south, and continue along the lane until you reach the next junction. Carefully cross the road and go through a gap in the hedgerow opposite where waymarks give clear direction. (Instead, if you wish, you can divert, following the signs to* **Llantrithyd**, *where there is an enclosure. This ancient site is dedicated to the 6th century St Illtud, but may have been founded by his wife* **St Trinihid**. *The evocative ruin of Llantrithyd House, next to the church, was once the home of the family of the famous essayist and diarist John Aubrey (1626-1697). Aubrey was also a great antiquarian, recognising the significance of Avebury before anyone else, and he named the 'Heel Stone' at Stonehenge.*

Fontygari Cave - Terry Breverton

Head diagonally up the hill to a stile. To the right of you is the site of a 10th century moated earthwork, one of four in the Bonvilston/St.Nicholas area. It is known as **Castell-y-Moel**, and sometimes as Liege Castle (Leach Castle Farm is next to it), and was an important site guarding this main road (the Via Julia) through South Wales. From its summit there are splendid views across the Vale and Channel. Cross this stile and then another by the side of a gate. *The stile on the left leads to one of the short cut loops that are all clearly waymarked.* For the main trail continue over the brow of the hill past the riding stables (**Liege Castle**) on your left. Walk down the field to a stile at the bottom that can be seen clearly as you approach. The area around the stile can be very wet and muddy.

Walk straight ahead to the waymarked gap in the hedgerow and on across the next field where you have another choice of routes. *You are at White Well, marked on maps. The paths beyond the gate in front of you lead to the village of Llancarfan along the Nant Llancarfan valley, via Garnllwyd, and you can also get to Llanfeithyn.* (A corncrake was shot in Garnllwyd Fields in 1953). To continue on the Bonvilston circular walk turn left to the gate in the corner of the field. Go through the gate then turn right and then left through **Whitewell** farmyard and onto the road. Please ensure that all gates are securely closed behind you.

Once on the minor road turn left and walk northwards for about 200 yards. The hedgerows alongside this road can be very colourful during the summer months with masses of wildflowers. Pass the main entrance of **Ty'n-y-Coed Farm** on your right, and continue onto the next field gate on your right. Enter the field and cross a small bridge, leading to the gate at the top of the hill. *Here another short cut leads back to the village of Bonvilston and is clearly waymarked.* To continue the main walk go straight across the field to a gap in the hedgerow by a wall. Continue to the next stile which is in the left hand hedge approximately half way down the field. Cross the stile and then a second stile that has a sleeper bridge on the far side.

Walk across a large field towards trees and a waymarker post that can be clearly seen from the sleeper bridge. Directly in front of you is a delightful copse which in summer is full of wild garlic and flowers. *Another short cut also leads back to the village through this copse.* To continue on the main route turn right at the waymarker post and walk to a stile in the left hand corner of the field.

Continue straight ahead with the hedge line on your left. Go through a metal gate on the left and cross a field to a stile which is visible from the gate. Cross this stile and follow the path that runs through a private garden to a stone stile leading onto the road. In front of you is a lovely thatched cottage. At this point of the walk it is possible to return to the Aubrey Arms and the start of the walk. Turn left and walk alongside the busy A48 until you reach the public house. A visit to the church could be made en route. The church is always locked but the area around is interesting. Note the arched steps to the churchyard from the road. Bonvilston (formerly named **Tresimwn**) used to belong to Margam Abbey. A little further along the road to Cardiff, the great mansion of **Cottrell** was dismantled (like Dunraven Castle) because of government taxation policies. Rice Merrick lived there, as did the Arctic explorer Thomas Button, and the grounds are now a golf-club. Button Gwinnett, the brother of a later owner, was one of the Welsh signatories to the American Declaration of Independence, along with Francis Lewis of Llandaff, John Adams and Thomas Jefferson.

PLACES TO VISIT

Apart from the Vale's medieval churches, and the castles where entry is free, the following tourist attractions are within the region described in this book.

Barry
Barry Island Pleasure Park 01446-732844
On the seafront. Over 50 funfair rides, on level ground. Disabled access and toilets. You purchase a 'book' of tickets for the rides. Free parking.
Barry Island Railway Heritage Centre 01446 748816
All weather attraction with 'steam days' when one can learn to drive a steam locomotive. Next to Barry Island Station. New rides available to Barry Waterfront.
Barry Island Triassic Towers 01446-733344
Children's adventure playground above the Esplanade Building. Over-5's £2.90; Under-5's £2.10.
Barry Pierhead - Flat Holm Project 01446-747661
The Lewis Alexander sails most days to Flat Holm Island, but pre-booking is absolutely essential. Unsuitable for children under 5 years old. The crossing takes about 45 minutes, and there are no toilet facilities on the boat. There is a café/gift shop on the island. Adverse weather conditions may mean that crossings can be cancelled. Age 5-15 £5; Adults £10. While the Steep Holm visit (from Penarth) is not suitable for the infirm or elderly, my parents and mother-in-law enjoyed this trip recently, and all are aged over 75. The guided walk is at a gentle pace, and apart from the steps from the beach, is relatively flat.
Welsh Hawking Centre 01446-734687
On the 'Five-Mile Lane' heading north away from Barry, there are over 200 birds of prey, with regular displays, and also children's favourites such as ponies, ducks and rabbits. Phone for details. Free Parking. The Amelia Trust Farm Park is also on this road.

Cardiff
To find out what is happening in Cardiff and the Bay area, contact Cardiff Marketing on 02920 347800, or visit the information office, at present in Wood Street.
Cardiff Castle and Grounds 02920 372737
The Norman tower on its central motte is an excellent place to gaze over Cardiff. The main castle was reconstructed by Jasper Tudor and the Marquis of Bute, and is a fabulous guided tour. Roman walls can also be seen on this ancient site which used to be fully moated. There are also the regimental museums of the 1st Queen's Dragoon Guards and the Royal Regiment of Wales. Park in City Centre.
Cardiff City Hall 02920 872000
Between the Law Courts and the Museum in Cardiff's magnificent Cathays Park Civic Centre, it is open to the public.
Cathays Park Cemetery Trail
A marked path through one of Britain's biggest Victorian cemeteries.
Millennium Stadium 02920 232661 [Stadium Tours 08705 582582]
Next to Cardiff Rugby Club's Arms Park, this futuristic venue on the banks of the

Taff held the 1999 Rugby World Cup and recent FA Cup Finals, and there are guided tours.

Museum of Welsh Life and St Ffagans Castle 02920 573500

A wonderful full-day experience walking the castle grounds and seeing the recreation of Welsh life over the past 2000 years, all set in 100 acres of woodland and park.

National Museum and Gallery 02920 397951

In the Civic Centre, an imposing museum which is one of Europe's finest, with a superb collection of Impressionist art, and an excellent section upon evolution.

New Theatre 02920 878889

A refurbished Edwardian 'gem' of a theatre in Park Place, with 900 seats.

Parc Cefn Onn

A lovely natural woodland valley in the north of Cardiff, with wonderful camellias, azaleas and rhododendrons. Free and open all the year round.

Roath Park 02920 755964

With greenhouses, long strolls and a boating lake with a monument recalling Captain Scott's departure to the Antarctic from Cardiff. Free entry, small charge for greenhouse.

St John the Baptist Church 02920 395231

Rebuilt in the city centre in 1404, with the tower added in 1473, there are wonderful views from the 132-foot 10-bell tower. Free entry, small charge for tower. Café.

Cardiff Bay

Telephone 02920 873690 for events at the Bay, or email: events@cardiff.gov.uk. There are many events in July and August at the Cardiff Festival (02920 872087).

Atlantic Wharf Leisure Village is just north of the Bay, with a UCI cinema and restaurants. Mermaid Quay is the heart of the bay, with restaurants and bars.

Atlantic Wharf Leisure Village

Just north of the Bay, one of Wales' largest entertainment complexes.

Butetown History and Arts Centre 02920 256757 (opposite The Baltimore Arms in Bute Street). The history of the Bay over the last 200 years, with Britain's oldest black community. Open Tues-Fri 10-5, weekends 11-4.30. Check the website bhac.org for exhibition details.

Cardiff Bay Visitor Centre - The Tube 02920 463833

Meant to be a temporary installation, this is a remarkable piece of engineering that should be preserved or replicated. Free entry, disabled access.

Cardiff Cats 02920 712693

Regular trips in covered catamarans to see the Barrage, to take the Taff up to the Millennium Stadium, sail to Penarth Marina, or head up the River Ely.

The Coal Exchange

This dominates Mount Stuart Square, built in 1896, where millionaire coal dealers gathered at the turn of the 20th century.

Craft in the Bay 02920 484611

A new purpose-built venue near the tall water sculpture, showing all the best in Welsh craft. Free entry.

Lightship (Goleulong) 2000 02920 487609
The Helwick lightship has been developed as a Christian Centre. Free access, and a café.
Norwegian Church Arts Centre 02920 454899
A traditional white-painted wooden church built in 1867, which now houses art exhibitions and concerts and has a café. Free entry, except for some concerts.
Pierhead Building
This wonderful turreted and castellated redbrick building was the headquarters of the old Bute Dock Company, and dominates the waterline.
Techniquest 02920 475475
A unique science discovery centre with 160 interactive exhibits and a small planetarium, the largest 'hands-on' science centre in Britain.

Cosmeston
Cosmeston Medieval Village - Pentref Canoloesol 02920 701678
A Heritage project unique in Britain, with a reconstructed 14th century village. Tours with costumed villagers. Special historical and culinary events throughout the year, which are well worth attending. In 2002 there was a Manorial Court and Welsh Uprising, a Wars of the Roses reconstruction; a Medieval Fayre, a Heritage Weekend, and Halloween (Nos Calan), etc. Adults £3; Children and OAP's £2; Family Ticket (2+2) £7.50. Accessible for wheelchairs with assistance available. Free Parking and Toilets in the adjoining Cosmeston Country Park
Cosmeston Lakes Country Park - Parc Gwledig Llynnoedd 02920 701678
Over 200 acres of lakes, woodland and walkways with a massive variety of flora and fauna. Disabled toilets and ramp access to visitor centre. Free parking and access.

Dyffryn Gardens
Near St Nicholas, 55 acres of Grade 1 Listed Edwardian Gardens. The finest surviving Thomas Mawson garden in Britain. The Pompeian Garden has been reopened. A lovely day out, with flat walks through a variety of gardens, Italianate terraces, lakes, cloister garden, physick garden, rose garden, vine walk and arboretum. Free in December-March. Telephone 02920-593328 for events and walks. From April to November £3 Adults; OAP's £2; Family Ticket (2+2) £7.50. 'Wheelchair Friendly', with courtesy wheelchair available at Visitor Centre (only open Apr-Nov). Disabled Toilets. Free Parking.

Fonmon
Fonmon Castle 01446 710206
Walled and kitchen gardens surround a medieval castle with 17th and 18th century additions. There are guided tours, and the castle and gardens are open April-September on Tuesday and Wednesday afternoon.

Fontygari
Holiday and Leisure Park - Rhoose 01446-711074. Overlooking Fontygari Bay, to which there is a footpath, there are bars, play areas and a health club/swimming pool complex at this holiday village. Disabled access and toilets. Free Parking.

Llandaff

Llandaff Cathedral 02920 564554
Restored after bombing in 1941, its focal point is Jacob Epstein's immense sculpture, Christ in Majesty, dominating the aisle.
The Bishop's Palace
Fragrant herbs and herbaceous borders within the medieval walls of the building that was sacked by Owain Glyndwr in the early 15th century.

Penarth

Penarth Pier 02920-708212
Built in 1894, the famous 658-feet long pier has been recently refurbished. Parking is limited and difficult in summer months on Penarth Esplanade. There are refreshments and toilets on the pier.
Penarth Pier - Waverley and Balmoral Pleasure Steamers 02920-704520
Day-trips, evening and excursion cruises. The Waverley is the last sea-going paddle-steamer in the world. Sailing from Penarth Pier. Note that Steep Holm Island is an infrequent tour. The details of all trips can be posted to you. Both ships contain cafÈ/bars. Disabled toilet facility on the Waverley.
Penarth Water Bus 02920-488842
Regular trips from Penarth Marina to Cardiff Bay and all its attractions.
Turner House Gallery 02920-708870
Near Penarth Station, home of the South Wales Arts Society, and host to exhibitions from the National Museum and Gallery of Wales. Free Entry.
The Washington Gallery 02920-708047
Set in the Art Deco surroundings of an old cinema, it houses new artistic talent and a café. Free Entry.

Porthkerry

Country Park 01446 733589. 220 acres of woods and meadowland, nature trails, barbecue areas, café, toilets, mini-golf, cliffs and pebbly beach. Toilets, Free parking.

Sully

Sully Island - free to visit, but beware the tides. The causeway crossing is slippery and not suitable for the aged or infirm. There are no facilities on the island. Swimming back to the mainland, if cut off by the tide, is not an option. The rip-tides and currents here are terrible, and the sea comes in extremely quickly. If you want an extended visit, go across as the tide is ebbing. Once the tide starts to turn, walk off the island. You might see some people staying and think you have time, but they will generally be anglers, who are staying over on the island. Park in The Captain's Wife car park. In summer, because of the density of demand, there is a charge collected by a parking attendant, but this facility used to be free.
Avalon Beauty Spa 02920 531245
On Swanbridge Road from Sully village to Swanbridge/Sully island, there is a swimming pool, sauna, Turkish bath, beauty treatments and wine bar. Call in advance for details. Free parking.

Postcript

My wife and I, in a few Sundays in February and March 2003, went on the following walks:

8th February – Aberthaw to Rhoose, across the cliffs, sat outside Ffontigari Cave in the sunshine. Ended with a pint of Old Peculiar in the Blue Anchor, West Aberthaw. Bright sunshine.

l5th February – in Carmarthen for the weekend. Had Dryslwyn Castle completely to ourselves, and watched the Red Kites displaying. Drifts of snowdrops in the local woods. On way home, stopped off at Carreg Cennen Castle and watched the buzzards displaying. The day before we had been to Aberglasney (*The Garden Lost in Time*) and the wonderful National Botanic Gardens. A sunny weekend.

22nd February – Coed-y-Bwl nature reserve, near Castle-upon-Alun - the wild daffodils were just beginning to show, and just two wood anemones were seen. Beautiful weather.

2nd March – Dyffryn Gardens - some snowdrops were out, as were some daffodils and the camellias. On the way, at Walterston, we saw a nearby sparrow-hawk, and Dyffryn was full of buzzards and jays. We also heard, approached and then saw a green woodpecker in the Arboretum. Primroses, crocuses, iris and auricula were in full bloom, and we disturbed a hare at the far end of the grounds. We were the only people in the gardens from 9-10, and watched a buzzard being mobbed by crows. Excellent weather. By 11 there were three cars in the carpark.

9th March – Tinkinswood Burial Chamber, watching buzzards and a nuthatch, then Dyffryn Gardens and then St Lythan's Burial Chamber. Again, wonderful weather with no other walkers about. At Coed-y-Bwl all the daffodils are now out, with a huge show of delicate wood anemones. Walked through local woods and saw a huge yellow brimstone butterfly, which obviously thought that summer had come. Went down to Nash Point to explore the Iron Age Camp, and then across the other side of the Valley to the lighthouses. Ended up at 'Pugsleys' - The Plough and Harrow at Monknash, drinking scrumpy.

APPENDICES

APPENDIX A

THE 45 MEDIEVAL CHURCHES OF THE VALE OF GLAMORGAN

Geoffrey Orrin's marvellous book gives us the following churches which are still in use, and are all worth visiting. Which other small area has so many medieval gems? Bonvilston; Cadoxton-juxta-Barry; Colwinston; Cowbridge; Eglwys Brewis; Ewenny Priory; Flemingstone; Gileston; Llanblethian; Llancarfan; Llandough-by-Cowbridge; Llandow; Llanfrynach; Llangan; Llanmaes; Llanmihangel; Llansannor; Llantrithyd; Llantwit Major; Llysworney; Marcross; Merthyr Dyfan; Michaelston-le-Pit; Michaelstone-super-Ely; Monknash; Pendoylan; Penmark; Peterston-super-Ely; Porthkerry; St Andrews Major; St Tathan's; St Brides's Major; St Bride's-super-Ely; St Donat's; St Fagan's; St George-super-Ely; St Hilary's; St Lythan's; St Mary Church; St Mary Hill; St Nicholas; Sully; Welsh St Donat's; Wenvoe; and Wick. To add to this knowledge, Glyndŵr Publishing will be releasing 'Castles of Glamorgan' in 2003, for the first time noting all our 'lost' and minor castles, as well as the castles we see around us in the county.

APENDIX B

APPENDIX on VALE RIVERS

The lengths of the 'statutory main rivers' in the local environment agency plan are: Ely 102km; Thaw 77km; Cadoxton 36km; Kenson 28km and Clun 23km.

Unfortunately, the depredations of wild mink, which can often be seen near and in the **THAW (Ddawen)**, have led to the near extinction of water-voles and moorhens on the river, but a few kingfishers can still be seen. Perhaps we need a programme of mink eradication put into place. The swans who summer on the 'safe' pool at Pleasant Harbour, to nest and bring up their cygnets, spend the winter months further up the Thaw. In 1769 Leland describes the Thaw thus: *'From the Mouth of Thawan Ryver up half a mile by the West Ripe* (bank) *standith a Pile or Manor Place caullid Gilestoun and Village of the same Name: but it (is) distant from the very Ripe a Quareter of a Mile by West. One Giles a Gentilman of an auncient House yet having a Hundred Markes of Lande by the Yere, is Lorde of it. A very little more upward is a stone Bridg called Pontnewith* (this was 'new bridge' on the Aberthaw to St Athan road, shortly after the Burton Bridge over the Kenson, replaced by the modern road bridge/bypass). *There is a Quarter of a Mile above this bridge a Manor Place hard on the Ripe caullid Norchete* (East Orchard Castle). *Mr Stradeling sumtime lyith in it; and it is of his Enheritaunce.*

And a Quarter of Mile above Norchet is a litle from the Ripe Castelton on a Hille ascending from the Ripe. And a late it longgid to one Hugh Adam a man of mene Landes, whose Doughter is now Heir of it. Half a Mile above Castelltoun is Trefleming alias Flemingeston and shortely Flemeston. And Fleming is Lord of it. This Fleming is taken as one by Descent of the 13 Peeres of Glamorganshir. From Trefleming to Pontgigman (Gigman Bridge) *a Stone Bridge half a Mile. From Pontgigman to Pont Ile a Bridge of Stone 3 Quarters of a mile (audax Ponthe). Thens half a mile to Llandouche where is a Village and a Castelle much in Ruine on a Hille. Syr Edwarde Carne brought this Lordship of the Erle of Wicester that now is.*

Againe this Village is a Bridge of stone Caullid Pont Landouhe. Sum say that Douhe came with Fagan and Divian from Rome into Britain. (Douhe was probably the 6th century St Cyngar, also known as Dochwy, who also founded Llandough near Penarth. Ffagan and Dyfan were 2nd century Christians, remembered at Merthyr Dyfan and St Fagans. Llanmaes was formerly called Llanffagan Fach, 'little St Fagan's', to distinguish it from Llanffagan Fawr where the National Museum of Welsh Life now is situated.) *From Landouhe to Lanlithan Village* (Llanblethian) *half a mile and heere is a stone bridge. Moste of the Village is on the West Ripe. The other Parte and the Castel is on the Est Ripe. This Castel longging to the King is yet partly standing and is in Terstuard Lordship and kept as the Prison for it.*

From the Mouth of the Thawan to Cowbridge a longe by the Ripe self and more from by West from the Ripe is very good Corne and Gresse. As much of Cowbridge as is enclosid within the waull stondith on the Est Ripe and the Bridge of ston there. The great Suburbe of Cowbridge is cis pontem. The waulle of Cowbridge is 3 Quarters of a mile aboute. There be 3 Gates on the waulle, the Est, the West and Porte Meline by South. There is a Chirch in the Town. But the saying is, that Lanlithen is the Hed Paroch Chirch to Cowbridge. The Towne self of Cowbridge standith in a Valle.

Penlline Castele and Village is almost a mile by West North West from Cowbridge. This Castelle yet stondith and longith to Turbeville. There were a while ago 2 Brethren of the Turbevilles whereof the Elder left a Doughter and Heyr; the youngger left a Sunne. The Doughter was maried to a Loughor. After great strife the 2 Turbevilles Children partid the Landes. A little above Cowbridge on the Est Ripe cummith yn Terstuard.

.... Bridges notable on Thawan

Ponte Vain alias Cowbridge, of Stone. Ponte Lanlithan of Stone a Quarter of a Mile lower. Pont Landoughe of Stone 3. Quarters of a Mile lower. Ponte Melinehe of Stone half a Mile lower. Pont Kigman of Stone a Mile lower. Pont Newith of Stone a Mile lower and a half. And half a Mile lower is Severn.'

Thus the Thaw flows down the wide flood plain of the Thaw valley, perhaps seen to its best extent from Flemingston, starting with a chain of streams near Ton Breigam and passing in a wide valley between Craig Penllyn, past Llansannor and across Penllyn Moor into Cowbridge. From Cowbridge it flows between the sites of two castles in Llanblethian, where it is joined by Factory Brook, which comes from Wilton farm, not far from Nash manor. This brook passes the ancient wells of Ffynnon y Breach and Ffynnon y Grotto. A small stream runs into it from the east at New Beaupre, and then it runs parallel with St Athan Road past Llandough Castle. At the Castle Precinct a stream enters which has come from Sigingston via Llanmihangel Place and Ffynon Math Llwdd. Another brook enters at Howe Mill Farm from The Herberts, past the ancient Parwg Well, perhaps a holy well of the 6th century St Baruc. Then the Thaw passes the mediaeval fishponds of Old Beaupre Castle, passing under Gigman Bridge before flowing over the wide Tre-gof Moors into Llanbydderi Moors. Dozens of springs and streams lead into Tre-gof Moors, from Cross Inn Well, Coed-y-Ffynnon, Kingsland, Treguff (Nant Tre-guf) and Coed y Colwn. From the Flemingston side a stream runs from Gregory's Well and 'the' Good Well, and Nant y Stepsau runs from Eglwys Brewis and through Flemingston to join the river. The springs in St John's Valley near West Orchard Castle form a stream which pass St John's mediaeval well at Beggars Pound (in St Tathan) and runs between Rills Well and Howell's Well to form a steep-sided valley, north of East Orchard castle, where the stream meets the Thaw before it joins the Kenson at Burton. At this junction, before the artificial new exit to the sea through the power station, two American Wood Ducks were recently spotted, and there are plenty of buzzards and herons in the area.

The **KENSON** River joins the Thaw at Burton Bridge, and has two sources, at St Lythans ('Lluen Lithan') and Bonvilston ('Bolston' to Rice Merrick, but in Welsh Tresimwn). Leland describes it thus: *'Half a Mile from the Moth of the Thawan there cummith in by the Est Ripe* (East bank) *of it a Brooke caullid Kensan. The Castelle of Fonmone standith on a little Hille in Penmark Paroche, a Quarter of a mile by Est from the mouth of Kensan. This Castelle yet stondith and longith to Sir John S. John. This Kensan hath 2. Heddes, whereof the North Est is caullid Nantbrane, the Hedde wherof is in the Paroch of Lluen Lithan. This Hedde is 3 Miles from the Confluence and more. There is good Pasture and Corne about it'.* The old road from Rhoose/Aberthaw, before the Airport was built, came over Burton Bridge on the Kenson, and is still intact to Llancadle crossroad. Here the Kenson meets the Thaw, after travelling through Castle Wood, where Ffwl-y-Mwn Brook meets it from Fonmon Pool, then alongside Kenson Wood. Near the springs at Kenson and Penmark Place, the River Weycock joins it. The **Weycock** (Waycock) originates in a series of springs and streams near St Nicholas, near two standing stones and an Iron Age earthwork, before joining the Nant Bran at Duffryn Gardens. Nant Bran rises near St Lythan's (Llwynelidon) north of Nant-Bran (Crow-Stream) in Coed Nant-Bran, and passes between Duffryn House and St Lythan's, past Duffryn Mill to Old Wallace where it is joined by Goldsland Brook from Wenvoe. The river then runs past Lidmore Mill and parallel with the A48 across the Vale, where the river is known as the Waycock. The Waycock passes Mill Wood and Cuckoo Mill before it runs under the North side of Penmark Castle, the bank forming a natural defence.

The other Hedde risith at Bolston Village. Gal: Tresimon, North Est more upward in Wales by West, a 3 Miles from the Confluence. First it cummith by Carnellued (Garnllwyd outside Llancarfan, the farm that is the site of a 6th century monastery) *ii. Miles douneward to Mr. Ragelandes House on the Est side of it. Then thorough Llancarouan Village* (Llancarvan village, past the pub) *3 Quarters of a Mile. Then a Quarter of a Mile to the Confluens wher the hole stream is caullid Kensan. On both sides of this Arme is good Corn and Gresse. To cross over from Llancarouan to the next part of the Thawan is a Mile.*

The Bonvilston source of the Kenson from Burton passes Pennon, the birthplace of Iolo. Just North of here it is fed by the Moulton Brook via Ffynnon y Waun, and passes Ffynnon y Briwlon and Ffynnon y Fflamwyddan in Breach Wood. The Moulton has carved out a valley here, and to the North of Ffynnon y Fflamwyddan is the huge Iron Age fort known as Castle Ditches at Llancarfan. Ffynnon y Fflamwyddan (Flamebearer's Well) was one of many healing wells in the holy area of Llancarfan, used until the 19th century to cure eripsylas. There is a famous chalybeate spring near the monastery site of Garnllwyd here. Ford Brook comes from Ffynnon Whitton Mawr near Whitton Lodge, and Walterston, through Ford Farm to join the Moulton

Brook just before it joins the Kenson. More streams join the river at the 6th century foundation of Cadog at Llancarfan. Incidentally, there is a castle earthwork near Pancross, between St Athan and Llancarfan. Streams come in from the ancient monastery site at Llanvithyn and from the equally old site of Gowlog. Another joins from Flaxland Fach. North of here, from the east comes Nant Whitton past the 6th century holy well of Ffynnon Dyfrig. The river it joins flowing into Llancarfan in Nant Llancarfan, fed by many springs and with sources at Leach Castle, White Well and Bonvilston. There are many earthworks in this district, and an ancient chapel was recorded between White Well and Cae Maen Farm.

We can now see how the Thaw and Kenson acted as a natural conduit for water across a huge part of the southern Vale of Glamorgan, from past Llansannor in the North to Wenvoe in the East and Sigingstone in the West. This explains the width of the valley from Treguff to the sea, and the sheltered estuary of the Thaw between the cliffs of Summerhouses and those of Fontygari. The Thaw has sea trout (sewin), occasional salmon and eels. Flounder and mullet are found in its lower reaches, and the Thaw Estuary is designated as a bass nursery area. There are otters and kingfishers in the northern stretch near Cowbridge.

Ewbank's book on Barry tells us that the **COLDBROOK** River was known as the **Gwrimi**, or Gwy-Rymy (Lesser Rhymey) in the past: *'It rises in a small spring (pond) in Colcot called Colcot Uchaf (High Colcot), just opposite the Colcot Inn, at a height of about 280 feet. Crossing under the road at Colcot Fawr Farm it flows down a deep dingle or ravine until it reaches the old Merthyr Dovan Church. During this short course it has dropped to 190 feet. From there it flows down an easterly direction past Gibbonsdown Farm, and then right through the centre of Cadoxton Village. In its course it has passed three noted wells - Ffynnon Wen (near old cottage), Ffynnon Mynwent (near the church) and Ffynnon John Lewis (near Ty Du Farm), the last being noted for curing all diseases of the eyes. Passing under the road near Cadoxton Church, it makes two sharp curves before it reaches Coldbrook Fach Farm. Near Gwaen-y-Nant (brook meadow) it receives its most important tributary, '"The Channel's Brook", which rises near Wellfield House. Another noted well, "Channel's Well", stood on the banks of this brook, which was supposed to cure skin diseases. A little below Coldbrook Fawr it makes a wide sweep to the south, and is joined by the Dinas Powys River (now known as the Cadoxton River). Its course is now through a long stretch of low land ... an old mill used to stand on its banks. Previous to the construction of No. 1 Dock it passed through the channel between the (Barry) Island and the mainland, but, as it interfered with the scheme, a new channel was made for it to discharge its waters near the Bendricks. Near the sea it is joined by Sully Brook.'* This flat land reclaimed from the sea, which comprises Biglis Moors, Sully Moors and Cog Moors, used to be the haunt of otters, and in his youth the author saw kingfishers here on the Cadoxton River.

The **CADOXTON (Tregatwg)** River flows south-west through Dinas Powys and the industrial and docks area of Barry, before reaching the Severn Estuary via an artificial cut onto Bendricks Beach. There are small species such as bullheads and stone loach, as well as eels and a small population of brown trout.

The River **ELY (Elai)** flows 26 miles south-easterly to its confluence with the Taff Estuary, in what is now Cardiff Bay. Its northern catchment consists of uplands of around 1200 feet, cut by narrow valleys, and it opens out into meandering lowland as it heads south. Salmon spawn in the Ely, but along with sewin (sea-going brown trout), their run is constrained by the Ely Paper Mill Weir. There will also be problems with the Cardiff Bay water quality for such fish, until it is properly colonised by oxygenating plants. There are plenty of coarse fish, such as roach, chub, dace and gudgeon. Eels abound, and mullet and flounder can be seen near the Ely Weir. There are several SSSI's associated with the Ely (and Thaw), but invasive plants such as Himalayan Balsam and Japanese Knotweed need to be controlled. However, the Ely is the best site in South Wales for the rare Monkshood (Aconitum Napellus).

The **TAFF (Taf)** is an important river on the eastern boundary of most of these walks, and rises at about 975 feet in two headstreams in the Brecon Beacons, flowing about 40 miles south into Cardiff Bay. It passes through Merthyr Tydfil, Abercynon, and Ponytpridd. There have been major improvements to this once heavily-polluted river, with sewin and salmon again becoming prolific in its lower reaches, being found as far up as Pontypridd. There are brown trout also, a well as chub, roach, gudgeon, grayling, dace and barbel. The Ely joins the Taff at Penarth, both waters now being impounded by the Cardiff Barrage. The **RHYMNEY** is the third river flowing into Cardiff, but is not impounded by the Bay, with its outlet in the Severn. It passes through Rhymney Reservoir to New Tredegar, Bargoed, Ystrad Mynach and Caerffili before it veers east to East Cardiff, and holds trout, grayling and the occasional sewin.

APPENDIX ON LLANCARFAN

The Llancarfan area has been identified as a *Landscape of Outstanding Historic Interest*, as one of the best surviving and most complete typical historic parts of the Vale of Glamorgan. *Llancarfan - Extracts from "A Topographical Dictionary of Wales" 1833 - In this parish was established the first choir of saints before the institution of monasteries by St. Germanus, who came to England to suppress the doctrines of Pelagius. Here he placed certain religious men for the instruction of the people in the Christian religion. The first principal was St. Dubrig, or Dubricius, who was afterwards raised to the see of Llandaf of which he was the first bishop. He was succeeded at Llancarvan by St. Cadoc, or Cattwg, in honour of whom several churches were subsequently erected throughout the principality. To this saint Hungy, a British chief, gave lands for the benefit of the institution, which rose on the ruins of the old British choirs: it flourished under the ancient Latinized name of Carbani Vallis, and the abbot, who was considered to be one of the principal ecclesiastics in the diocese, assisted at a council held at Llandaf, in 560, which passed sentence of excommunication upon Meurig, King of Morganwg, or Glamorgan ... Within the parish are several farms, forming an extra-parochial district, called Llanfoethin, where were formerly some vestiges of an ancient chapel : this district comprises the farms of Caer-Maen, Llanbithon, and Velin Vach; and those of Carn Llwyd, Llanbythery, Llancadle, and Treguf, which are each subject to a modus. A fair is held on the Wednesday before Easter ... The church, dedicated to St. Cattwg, an ancient and spacious structure, now in a dilapidated condition, is said to have been built in the twelfth century by Walter de Mapes, chaplain to Henry I. The altar-piece, which is elaborately embellished, and a portion of the ancient stone screen still remaining, convey some idea of its former grandeur. At present it consists of two aisles: in the north chancel is a remarkably fine window, measuring eleven feet by twelve, the mullions and tracery of which were destroyed during the civil commotions of the seventeenth century, by a fanatic named Bush. There are places of worship for Baptists and Wesleyan Methodists ... In the parish are some remains of an ancient intrenchment, called the Castle Ditches; also a mineral spring, called Llancarvan Well, the water of which is said to be efficacious in the cure of scorbutic and cutaneous diseases. Caradoc of Llancarvan, the historian of Wales from the abdication of Cadwaladr to his own times, and cotemporary with Geoffrey of Monmouth, was a native of this parish : he wrote his work in Latin, and it was afterwards translated into English by Humphrey Llwyd, who accounts for the different periods to which the history is continued in different copies (in some of which it is brought down to within two years of the death of the last Llewelyn), by attributing to the monks of the abbey, in which they were deposited, an annual addition to the original, by way of continuation. The English version, with a continuation to the reign of Elizabeth, was published in 1585, by Dr. David Powel, and is considered as the standard history of Cambria. Walter de Mapes, son of Blondel de Mapes, who accompanied Fitz-Hamon into Glamorganshire, and obtained for his services the lands of Gweinydd ab Seisylt, lord of Llancarvan, a writer of some celebrity in the twelfth century, was born in this parish : he built the church and a mansion for himself, and also the village of Walterston, a hamlet in this parish : he married the only daughter of Gweinydd, and, with unusual liberality, restored to their original native proprietors part of the estates which he inherited from his father.*

REVIEWS OF OTHER PUBLICATIONS FROM WALES BOOKS (GLYNDŴR PUBLISHING)

THE WELSH ALMANAC - **T.D. Breverton** ISBN 1903529107 320 pages illustrated £16.99

WELSH BOOKS COUNCIL BOOK OF THE MONTH (July 2002)

Dean Powell, Wstern Mail Books Review, July 27th, 2002

Terry Breverton's ongoing series of Welsh history books continue to enthuse as my library steadily increases with his work. And the latest, The Welsh Almanac (Glyndŵr Publishing, £16.99) is one of the most enjoyable to date. In fact, I'll go so far as to **say it's a must for anyone with a drop of Welsh blood in them.** *Continuing his solo mission to make Wales' proud history more accessible or for that matter readable, in comparison to the huge dusty tomes hidden in darkened libraries,* **The Welsh Almanac is yet another success**. *Filled with fascinating facts and figures, Breverton explains that the rationale behind the publication is two-fold. On the surface it is for welsh people to remember their loved ones' birthdays, anniversaries, important dates and events.*

There is also an A-Z section annexed, so that addresses and telephone numbers can be entered. But on the other hand it is to record information about famous Welsh people and events upon each of these days. For each day there is also a quotation, usually from a Welsh source, tying in with people and events of the day. Hoping that readers will be enthused to find out more about Wales from these entries, the genesis of the book was the author's The Book of Welsh Saints, when Breverton revealed the 900 saints from the Dark Ages that are universally neglected.

As Breverton explained, "We have records of our saints' days, only because their feasts were kept until the 19th century in the places still named after them. Their 'llannau' were sparks of Christianity and learning in a pagan world, but the Welsh contribution to the survival of Christianity has never been properly addressed." But the saints are just a fraction of his latest publication, with references to colliery explosions and Petula Clark, Freddie Welsh and Kitchener Davies, the Battle of Crecy and rugby triumphs. **A tremendous undertaking and a very worthwhile and absolutely fascinating addition to the library of Welsh history.**

Review by Meic Stephens, The Western Mail magazine 28th September 2002

'Although most of the books I read are works of fiction or of the creative imagination, I also enjoy ones that deal with facts and the more ordinary world in which we all live. Terry Breverton's 'The Welsh Almanac' (Wales Books, £16.99) takes the form of a hefty desk diary in which for each day he gives the events that took place on it. Some days are pretty much without incident, but on September 28th, for example, quite a bit happened that merits a note.

On this day in 1400, Henry IV led his army of 13,000 into Wales, slaughtering and pillaging as he went. On this day in 1842 was born W. J. Parry, leader of the North Wales Quarrymen's Union during the Penrhyn Strike and, as it happens, the great-

great-great-grandfather of one of my grand-daughters. On the same day in 1898 Thomas Gee, publisher, died ... and so on.

Every day has space for the reader's own notes and a few apt quotations to add interest to the page. So this is a Book of Days in which people can record important dates in their personal histories and see them in the context of Welsh history. It's useful for jotting down birthdays and anniversaries, especially those one tends to forget, **and will take its place on the shelf with other works of reference.**

Review by Dr Peter Williams, Ninnau (US) December 2002

According to the American Heritage Dictionary of the English Language, one of the definitions of an almanac is that it is composed of useful information in various unrelated fields. A new Welsh Almanac by prolific Cardiff-based author Terry Breverton contains a host of useful information. It is not only **an ideal book** in which to record family birthdays, anniversaries, important dates for each day of the year, but it also contains an alphabetical section in which to write addresses, telephone numbers, email addresses and other records. What makes this almanac so very special to people proud of their heritage, is that not only each day's entry commemorates the Welsh saint feasted on that day, but also let's us know about famous Welsh people and events connected with the same day. All in all, it is **a prodigious work, chock full of facts and figures from every age of Welsh history**.

One example will hint at the wealth of information contained within this fascinating book. On the 1st of January, Welsh people can celebrate not only Dydd Calan (New Year's Day), no fewer than six saints, the birth of the first Welsh language newspaper, a Welsh defeat of a Norman army, and Welsh team victories in rugby football and so on. The entries for each day are accompanied by a quotation that ties in with the people and events of the day. This wonderful book, attractively priced at £16.99, was be ordered directly from Wales at website walesbooks.com or www.gwales .com.

100 GREAT WELSHMEN - T.D. Breverton ISBN 1-903529-034 £18.99, 376 pages illustrated (April 2001) **Welsh Books Council Book of the Month**

Part of a double-page Review from the Western Mail Magazine, June 1st 2001

'... 100 Great Welshmen is a revealing volume illustrating the great and the good with Welsh connection, either by birth or family ancestry. Admittedly all the usual suspects are included - Richard Burton, Tom Jones, Sir Geraint Evans, Gareth Edwards, Gwynfor Evans, Idris Davies, Aneurin Bevan, Jimmy Wilde and Saunders Lewis. But probably the most fascinating are the ones we either tend to forget are Welsh, or had no prior knowledge of their Celtic connection in the first place. John Adams, the first occupant of the White House; father of the American Revolution Samuel Adams; revolutionary Oliver Cromwell; cinematic pioneer D.W. Griffith; comedian Tommy Cooper, the list goes on and on. From heroes of Waterloo and computer engineers to lethal pirates and gold champions, Breverton has attempted to include them all, and that's no mean feat given our colourful heritage. Hats off to him for the **painstaking research** involved in every single one, a trademark which is typical of his previous work in "An A-Z of Wales and the Welsh", followed by "The Book of Welsh Saints" and "The Secret Vale of Glamorgan", all printed and published in Wales...'

Review from Ninnau (US) by Dr Peter Willams

'Now and again a book comes along that answers most, if not all your questions about your Welsh heritage. Who are the Welsh, who are their military heroes, political leaders, writers, poets, kings, princes, saints, historians, explorers, men of industry, famous actors, athletes, and religious leaders? T.D. Breverton, who gave us *The Book of Welsh Saints and An A-Z of Wales and the Welsh*, has provided the answers in his latest body of knowledge: a single volume with the informative title l00 Great Welshmen. The author includes not only those who have contributed so much to the making of Wales, but also many personalities who made their mark on American history. The single volume reference book gives biographical information on those persons of Welsh descent whom became influential in the political and industrial life of the United States, such as Presidents John Adams, John Quincy Adams, James Monroe, and Thomas Jefferson; the father of the American Revolution Samuel Adams; business tycoon J.P. Morgan, film pioneer D.W.Griffith, explorers John Evans and Meriwether Lewis and so on. The author even includes those terrors of the high seas, Black Bart, the infamous pirate, and Captain Henry Morgan. The amount of research that went into the making of this book is astounding; it seems that the author left no stone unturned in order to ferret out information concerning his subjects. He has produced a veritable gold mine of a book that you can dip into again and again. **100 Great Welshmen will make you proud of your Welsh heritage** by reminding you that the little country of Wales has contributed so much to the modern world in so many different areas...'

100 GREAT WELSH WOMEN - **T.D. Breverton** ISBN 1 903529 042 £16.99 304pp illustrated

Review from Ninnau (USA), January 2002, by Dr Peter Williams

'perhaps the most prolific Welsh author today is T.D. Breverton, of Glyndŵr Publishing, in the Vale of Glamorgan, South Wales. This astonishing worker has recently produced such practical reference books as An A-Z of Wales and the Welsh, The Book of Welsh Saints, The Secret Vale of Glamorgan, and 100 Great Welshmen (Vol. I of Eminent Britons). Now Terry has done it again. His latest book has finally arrived to fulfil the massive gap in our knowledge of our enormously important, but sadly unheralded contribution of our women, not only to Welsh society and Welsh history, but to Western civilisation itself ... This book is an **absolute must** for all those who value their Welsh heritage, and for all those who wish to see women accorded their rightful place in history...'

Review from South Wales Echo, November 17, 2001 by Mark Stead

It's not often you see Charlotte Church and Catrin Glyndŵr - daughter of one of Wales' favourite sons, Owain - in the same list. Or Shirley Bassey and Tanni Grey-Thompson rubbing shoulders with Elizabeth Tudor, who ranks among England's greatest monarchs, and Gwenllian. But that's exactly where you'll find them in a new book celebrating Wales' most fascinating females. Author and publisher Terry Breverton, who estimates he has written over a million words in two years - launches his latest work, 100 Great Welsh Women, next week. The result of another extensive trawl through time, it celebrates the achievements of Welsh women through the ages ... The journey through time starts with Wales' greatest saints, many of whom were women, and continues through the stories of Elizabeth Tudor, Gwenllian, Boadicea, Petula Clark, Laura Ashley, Shirley Bassey, Mary Quant, Sian Phillips, George Eliot, Elizabeth David, Delia Smith and modern-day icons such as Tanni Grey-Thompson and Catherine Zeta-Jones. 'Tanni is such an interesting character, but she kept telling me she wasn't good enough to be included,' laughs Terry. The book also lifts the lid on some hidden stories - such as the Welsh woman who was the mother of the first Bishop of Rome, and the Pembrokeshire lady who was the unacknowledged Queen of England.

THE BOOK OF WELSH SAINTS - **T.D. Breverton** ISBN 1-903529-018 £24.99
hardback, 606 pages, illustrated (September 2000)

e-mail from Dr Rowan Williams, Archbishop of Canterbury:

...the book is a **really extraordinary achievement**: a compilation of tradition, topography and literary detective work that can have few rivals. I have enjoyed browsing it enormously, and have picked up all sorts of new lines to follow up...'

Review from 'Cambria', January 2001:

'Another work from the prolific pen of Terry Breverton who is blazing a trail in producing bodies of knowledge about Welsh heritage and history. The Book of Welsh Saints is **an enormous work of research and will provide a welcome and ready book of reference** to the men and women who in Tad Deiniol's words "created Wales". The much bandied term "The Dark Ages" may well have meant just that east of the Severn, but to us this period is the Age of Saints. And there are hundreds of them - over 900 in fact - monks, scholars, warriors, missionaries. Breverton places Arthur firmly in the context of Welsh history and shows how the seminal folk legends of European romance and literature originate in Wales. We see Wales at the very heart and very root of Western Christian civilisation, a pre-eminent position...

Meic Stephens, in 'The Western Mail Magazine', April 7th, 2001

An even more **impressive** work is Terry Breverton's Book of Welsh Saints, which lists over 900 saints - those holy men who lived as ascetics and hermits in the first centuries after Christ and to whom, so often, miracles were attributed ... The book was written with one eye on the potential tourist market, because it argues in favour of celebrating the saints' days in villages the length of Wales....'

Review from Ninnau (US) by Dr Peter Williams

'Did you know that Wales had a St Elvis?...According to local tradition, St David was baptised by his cousin St Elvis at a church near Solva, in Pembrokeshire, where St Elvis Parish is now the smallest in Britain. Within the parish is also St Elvis farm, St Elvis Holy Well, St Elvis Cromlech (prehistoric tomb). Off the coast at Solva are St Elvis Rocks. St Elvis is only one of the hundred of Welsh saints of the 5th and 6th century, a time when the light of Christianity shone brightly in Wales when it had *been extinguished over all of Europe, a time when England was still pagan. It was a time when Christianity itself was in danger of disappearing, the survival of the Church in Wales creating a bastion from which Ireland was first converted, and from the Irish missionaries, the rest of Britain and Europe.*

Over 100 Welsh saints are associated with the leader Arthur, long before the legends had taken hold in France. It was a time when the stories of Arthur and Guinevere, of the Holy Grail, Tristan and Isolde, The Fisher King, the Black Knight, the Green Knight and all of the great and famous knights associated with Camelot and Avalon came into being, and all originated in Wales. Wales certainly seems to have not only the oldest surviving language in Europe, but also the oldest Christian heritage; for the first millennium, it was accepted by Rome as "the cradle of the Western Church".

*The unique historical importance of Wales has for too long been neglected until now...the book lists over 900 saints, gives not only their history but the historical background of each saint, their feast-days and feast Weeks, and the religious events associated with them. The book is a veritable goldmine of information. Its appendices give the derivation of Welsh place-names, the location of Roman sites in Wales, a discussion of the language problem, and even an essay on the state of parliamentary representation in Wales. **The book is a must** for anyone interested in the history of the Church in Wales, indeed for anyone interested in learning the glorious heritage bequeathed to them from the time when Wales was the only Christian country in the world.'*

THE DRAGON ENTERTAINS - 100 Welsh Stars - Alan Roderick ISBN 1-903529-026 £12.99 paperback, illustrated 230 pages (May 2000)

Review by Meic Stephens, The Western Mail Magazine, January 2001

Lastly, another book published by Wales books, The Dragon Entertains (£12.99) by Alan Roderick, a highly-readable reference work listing 100 of the most famous Welsh stars of stage, screen and radio, from The Alarm to the TV comedian, Ronnie Williams.The list is a roll-call of the theatrical talent that Wales has produced over the last century: Ivor Novello, Tommy Cooper, Donald Houston, Donald Peers, Emlyn Williams from among the dead. And Tom Jones, Anthony Hopkins, Bryn Terfel, the Super Furry Animals, Harry Secombe, Kenneth Griffiths, Victor Spinetti and Max Boyce among the gloriously alive and still performing. It also includes fascinating information about the Welsh connections of stars like Glen Ford, Bob Hope, Rolf Harris, Griff Rhys Jones and Petula Clarki.

This is the book to reach for the next time someone tells you that Wales has not nurtured any great talent in the world of entertainment and showbiz.

THE SECRET VALE OF GLAMORGAN - T.D. Breverton ISBN 1-903529-00X £13.99 paperback, illustrated 230 pages (June 2000)

Review by Meic Stephens, in 'The Western Mail Magazine', April 7th, 2001

Terry Breverton belongs to that rare breed of Welshmen who stake their livelihood on trying to publish books in which they passionately believe. His imprint Glyndŵr

Publishing/Wales Books has already made its mark on the Welsh publishing scene by bringing out substantial and handsomely produced books on Welsh subjects, particularly local history. He was born in the Vale of Glamorgan, to which he has returned after many years as a management consultant in Britain and overseas. He is the author of several useful books such as An A-Z of Wales and the Welsh and One Hundred Great Welshmen. What drives him as a publisher is the belief that the Welsh people have been deprived of their own history. He aims to provide the information that will make them proud of their country. If that means he has to lose some money, he thinks it's well worth it. Among his most recent books is The Secret Vale of Glamorgan (Glyndŵr, £13.99) which shows a local man's pride in the history and culture of his native patch, combined with a historian's delight in tracing the past and relating it to the present. For anyone born or living in the Vale, this book should be essential reading. There are chapters on Cowbridge, St Athan, Gileston, Aberthaw, Flemingston, and all the places in between, together with a wealth of information about the area's most famous son, the wayward genius Iolo Morganwg.

A RHONDDA BOY - Ivor Howells - ISBN 1-903529 050 £6.99 paperback 144 pages, 33 illustrations (November 2001) A charming evocation of his childhood in Porth, Rhondda, and summer holidays in Ferryside, by the 93 year-old former headmaster of Porth and Tonypandy Secondary Schools, edited and researched by his former colleague Owen Vernon Jones.

GLYN DWR'S WARr - The Campaigns of the Last Prince of Wales - G.J. Brough
ISBN 1903529069 illustrated 240 pages £13.99 (May 2002)

Western Mail Books Review July 20th, 2002

Dean Powell finds the legacy of Owain Glyndŵr lives on in a new history charting the seven years of the patriot's glorious war of independence. *Six centuries have failed to diminish the incredibly powerful emotions encountered by so many Welsh people when confronted with the name of Owain Glyndŵr. There is something almost hopelessly romantic about the national hero in his attempt to achieve full and lasting independence for the homeland. We remain fascinated by his fiercely sustained rebellion, achieved with no standing army, and few resources against possibly the greatest military force in the world at that time.*

*For more than any other he was the greatest leader in the history of Wales, who succeeded in eliciting spontaneous and passionate loyalty by uniting and leading the Welsh to break the English shackles. In a **fascinating new publication**, Cardiff-born Gideon Brough courageously attempts to piece together Owain's outstanding military triumphs. A massive undertaking indeed for a 30-year-old, first-time author, but one which Brough, who himself boasts an impressive military background, has tackled with immense confidence and success.*

"Glyn Dwr's War - the Campaigns of the Last Prince of Wales" (Wales Books, £13.99) tells the enthralling story of a rebellion ignited by greed and injustice, and the emergence of the bards' "mab darogan", the son of prophecy, who would reclaim Welsh independence lost in 1282 with the murder of Llywelyn ap Gruffudd. It is the

latest in a series of books published by Terry Breverton, whose ongoing mission is to enhance the image of Wales by ensuring that its inhabitants are aware of its immensely rich historical background - his passion for Wales and Welshness cannot be doubted....

Cambria Magazine Review - Summer 2002

I don't think we can ever have enough books about the Great Liberation War and our greatest hero. When every schoolchild knows the story backwards, the dates of the battles, and the main events and personalities, then, perhaps, I would suggest that it was time to move on to Llywelyn Fawr or Gruffudd ap Cynan or the story of Rebecca, but the Great War is a very good starting-point for gaining a necessary appreciation of our history.

This book will be a welcome adjunct to the study of the great Owain, set out as it is in chronological detail with boxes, footnotes and maps complementary to the text. Mr Brough sets out to do what many historians fail to do, and that is to place the struggle of 1400-1416 within the context of the broader panoply of Welsh history, rather than seeing it as a sort of sideshow of the English imperial pageant or, worse still, as some have attempted to do, a mere element of the feuding squabbles between Anglo-Norman barons.

The Great Liberation War is THE defining moment of our nation's history. Had it not been for Owain Glyndŵr and the men and women who stood at his side against over-whelming odds, there would be no Welsh nation today. **You will find all the details here**.

THE PATH TO INEXPERIENCE - T. D. Breverton ISBN 1903529077 160pp 2002 illustrated £10.99 (March 2002)

Terry Breverton is known as a tireless recorder of Welsh achievements in many fields. In this poetry collection, he allows us a glimpse of the tumultuous feelings that drive him. A tortured energy rushes through this book. There is bitter anger, a keen sense of injustice, national pride, compassion, fear of loss. The images whirl. He jokes and parodies, he gets drunk on words, and there are quieter moments too. Sometimes he gives us a long "found poem' like his 'inventory' of statistics about the sufferings of the miners of South Wales, where the plainly stated facts are the agonised poem; or his 'final list of endangered species' with their evocative and often musical names. It is good to know that out of this turmoil have come - and are still coming - books so positive in their celebration of Wales, its people, history, religion and arts.' (Ruth Bidgood, the leading Welsh poet)

'Magnificent, compassionate and moving'. 'Chalice' will surely help Aberfan to always stay in our memories.(Derek Smith, *Mabon*)

DAVID THOMAS - FROM WALES TO PENNSYLVANIA - Dr Peter N. Williams ISBN 1903529085 104 pages illustrated £8.99 (March 2002)

In this completely revised and updated version of his *David Thomas: Man of Iron*, Dr Peter Williams takes us back to the days of mass emigration to the United states.

The terrible conditions at home, which sparked the Chartist riots, are described, to put into context the reasons for this difficult transatlantic flight. Through Dr Thomas's correspondence with Wales, Dr Williams shows the Welshman's immense contribution to the industrialisation and economic growth of America.

THE BOOK OF WELSH PIRATES AND BUCCANEERS by T.D. Breverton ISBN 1903529093 - *over 400 pages*, illustrated, published in Spring 2003 contemporaneously with Glamorgan Seascape Pathways, so there are no reviews yet available. ***WELSH BOOKS COUNCIL BOOK OF THE MONTH*** April 2003

The world's most famous buccaneer, Admiral Sir Henry Morgan, the most famous pirate of the 16th century, John Callice of Tintern, and dozens of other Welsh pirates and buccaneers are described, complete with a fascinating glossary of pirate terms. Of particular interest are Howel Davis, the *'Cavalier Prince of Pirates'*. Davis captured John Robert off a slaver on the Guinea Coast. Turning pirate, *'Black Bart'* Roberts became the most successful pirate in history, taking over 400 recorded ships between Africa, the Americas and the West Indies. He was noted by Time-Life magazines as *'the last and greatest pirate of them all.'*

ALSO BY Terry Breverton: AN A-Z OF WALES AND THE WELSH ISBN 0- 715407-341 £14.99 paperback 296 pages April 2000 (available from Christopher Davies Publishing, Amazon, gwales.com, blookshops and the Welsh Books Council)

Review from 'Ninnau' (US)

'This A-Z has many surprising as well as predictable entries and is clearly the result of a passionate interest in post-devolution Wales combined with impeccable research... an important addition to the Welsh reference bookshelf'

Review from 'Cambria', January 2001

'Hwyl and Hiraeth, heritage and history, people and places, myths and imagination all come together in Terry Breverton's comprehensive anthology and compendium of Welshness. He starts by asking the question "What is Wales?" and then goes on to show us. The book is, as Breverton says, a sort of "Hitchhiker's Guide to the Galaxy" that is Wales and declares modestly that his background is more modest than academic. We have just what's needed in this unashamedly proud-to-be-Welsh work. Everythin from "Assassination" (Owain Llawgoch) to "Zulu Wars" (Rorke's Drift) is covered with few stones unturned (sadly Tom Ellis, one of the greatest of our political heroes, fails to get a mention). **A massive treasure chest of facts and figures covering thousands of years of history, which no collector of books on Wales can overlook.'**

Review from the 'South Wales Echo'

'The author wants the world to know what Wales has to offer... alongside the Cool Cymru actors and pop stars, there is a wealth of information on more traditional Welsh culture, history, legend, art, literature and so on...'

Review from New Welsh Revie

'This book is great fun....'

Partial List of Books Referenced

Ordnance Survey Explorer 151 - Map of Cardiff & Bridgend. This double-sided map is an absolute necessity for exploring the Vale, costing only £6.99 and showing the footpaths outlined in this book.

Valeways Millennium Heritage Trail (no ISBN, but available from Vale of Glamorgan bookshops or from Unit 7, BCEC, Skomer Road, Barry. Valeways' email address, in case of difficulties, is . The booklet and maps come in a small plastic folder, and cost around £9.

The Book of Welsh Saints by Terry Breverton ISBN 1903529018

The Secret Vale of Glamorgan by Terry Breverton ISBN 190352900X

Annals of South Glamorgan by Marianne Robertson Spencer, 1913, republished by Stewart Williams in 1970

Let Us Talk of Barry by Stan Awbery, 1954

The Geography and History of Barry by Thomas Ewbank and A.W. Storey, 1921

Barry - the Centenary Book ISBN 0950973815 edited by Donald Moore 1984

Penarth - The Garden by the Sea ISBN 0953219704 by Barry A. Thomas 1997

Circular Walks in the Vale of Glamorgan ISBN 0863816037 by Dorothy Hamilton 2000

The Glamorgan Village Book ISBN 1853062545 Glamorgan Federation of Women's Institutes 2003

Flat Holm - Bristol Channel Island ISBN 0948699507 Bob Jory 1995

FORTHCOMING TITLES FROM GLYNDŴR PUBLISHING

WALES BOOKS AND GLYNDŴR PUBLISHING ARE NON-PROFIT-MAKING ENTERPRISES DEDICATED TO PUBLISHING BOOKS UPON WALES, ITS HERITAGE, CULTURE AND HISTORY. Our (non-subsidised) books are all produced in Wales, and are available via the Welsh Books Council, direct from the publisher, from walesbooks.com or from 'good' book shops. Although it is difficult to get shelf-space for books on Wales and the Welsh, any of our books can be ordered at your

local bookshop. Our publications all have a two-fold purpose - to tell the world about Wales and encourage tourism, and to tell the Welsh people what they have never been taught in schools, colleges and universities. The Welsh legacy has been deliberately suppressed for hundreds of years, and publication policy is to open up the truth about their past to the Welsh people. Without culture, a nation cannot exist. Without a knowledge of its culture, a nation will quickly die - there is nothing to hold it together.